Retire and C

Retire and Go!

*Two Seniors and a Year
of Slow Travel on a Budget*

RUSS FIRLIK

Foreword by Katrina S. Firlik

Toplight

Jefferson, North Carolina

LIBRARY OF CONGRESS CATALOGUING-IN-PUBLICATION DATA

Names: Firlik, Russ, 1942– author.
Title: Retire and go! : two seniors and a year of slow travel on a budget /
Russ Firlik ; foreword by Katrina S. Firlik.
Description: Jefferson, North Carolina : Toplight, 2022 | Includes bibliographical references and index.
Identifiers: LCCN 2022000702 | ISBN 9781476687803 (paperback : acid free paper) ∞
ISBN 9781476645384 (ebook)
Subjects: LCSH: Retirement—Planning. | Retirees—Finance, Personal. |
Retirees—Travel. | BISAC: TRAVEL / Special Interest / Senior
Classification: LCC HQ1062 .F5637 2022 | DDC 332.024/014—dc23/eng/20220228
LC record available at https://lccn.loc.gov/2022000702

BRITISH LIBRARY CATALOGUING DATA ARE AVAILABLE

ISBN (print) 978-1-4766-8780-3
ISBN (ebook) 978-1-4766-4538-4

Front cover photograph: the author and his wife;
background photograph: view of Florence city and
the Cathedral at sunrise (Shutterstock/Rasto SK)

Printed in the United States of America

Toplight is an imprint of McFarland & Company, Inc., Publishers

*Box 611, Jefferson, North Carolina 28640
www.toplightbooks.com*

Table of Contents

Acknowledgments

All my gratitude to Adam Prince for his invaluable advice and continual encouragement for this book.

A very warm thank-you to Katrina Firlik, my daughter-in-law and fellow writer, for her endless support, insights and imagination.

To our children: Hattie, Dava and Andrew for their love and affection. I thank them for always giving me reasons to be hopeful and joyful and to complete this book.

To our three grandchildren: Annika, Ty and Cole, who bring another extraordinary level of excitement and enjoyment into our lives.

Thank you to everyone on the McFarland publishing team who helped bring this book to fruition. A very special thanks to Susan Kilby, who demonstrated suburb patience and guidance during the entire project.

You have this book because of my wife, Emily—my indispensable, intuitive and brilliant traveling partner. She is my joyful life-advisor, inspirational mentor, and I love her dearly. In my mind, I'm hearing the melody and lyrics of "More than Yesterday," the inspirational words from the American pop band Spiral Starecase.

Finally, in memory of, I am grateful to two influential leaders in early childhood education. Francis Backhouse taught me the value of and appreciation for the child-centered education in the British primary schools. I also thank Loris Malaguzzi, known for his central role in the creation and development of the child-centered philosophy and pedagogy of the Reggio Emilia approach to early childhood education.

From both my British primary and the Reggio Emilia experiences, as a teacher, parent and a slow traveler, I learned directly how creativity emerged in children (and in me) from multiple experiences, strengthened by well-supported and appropriate resources and the sense of freedom to roam, explore and discover beyond the known.

"Nothing without Joy"—Loris Malaguzzi.

Foreword
by Katrina S. Firlik

There are many ways to travel abroad. In our current fast-paced, social-media fueled era, the version of travel that involves squeezing multiple destinations into a whirlwind tour is popular. Travelers seek to tick famous monuments, vistas, and museums off their bucket list. "Must-see" sites serve as required backdrops to selfies. Photos and postings are the prizes. But this version of travel, particularly if experienced passively, risks providing a hollow experience.

Russ Firlik, in this book, gives us inspiration for the polar opposite form of travel. This form of travel can be described as "slow travel," which accurately conveys a key element. But it could just as easily be called "deep," "passionate," or "thoughtful" travel because these descriptors reflect equally important facets. Russ's version of travel is one that promises a richer, more memorable, and more transformative experience. Lifelong learning is the prize.

I have known Russ and Emily Firlik for over 30 years. They are my in-laws. I married their son, Andrew, 27 years ago, and we delighted them with a granddaughter, Annika, 14 years ago. I've always thought of them as travelers and adventurers in addition to their professional roles as educators. Travel is a central element of who they are as a couple. In fact, they raised their three children, Hattie, Andrew, and Dava, in four different countries: England, Spain, Germany, and the United States.

This book will allow readers to gain insights into how to do slow travel well. Russ and Emily picked their locations thoughtfully, created central themes that guided their itineraries and research, and followed a sensible budget that encouraged living like locals rather than tourists. They then enjoyed recording their experiences.

I and other family members receive daily emails from Russ and Emily during their travels. Their photos and descriptions are often centered around interesting themes: beautiful doorways, architectural details of historic churches, paintings of a certain era or style, simple lunches made from local market provisions. Now, with this book, the details of their travels are able to reach a broader audience.

Readers will not only learn something new about the arts and architecture in France and Italy—central themes of Russ and Emily's lifelong learning—they will also gain insights into how to plan their own adventures. If readers were under the mistaken impression that only the very wealthy can afford to spend months abroad or that language barriers prevent one from living like a local or that seniors should only travel as part of a sensible group with a professional tour guide, Russ's book will dispel these myths.

As their daughter-in-law, I have been inspired by Russ and Emily's approach to retirement, travel, and lifelong learning. Now, with this book, I am delighted to know that readers far and wide will be able to benefit from their insights as well. Enjoy!

Katrina S. Firlik, MD, started her career as a practicing neurosurgeon and on the clinical faculty at Yale. She then co-founded a digital health company, HealthPrize Technologies, and serves as chief medical officer. Katrina is also the author of Another Day in the Frontal Lobe: A Brain Surgeon Exposes Life on the Inside, *published by Random House. Her author website is* www.katrinafirlik.com.

Preface

We rekindled the joys of travel and rediscovered the excitement of learning new and different things after retirement. Through traveling we also learned something about the purpose and value of education as a whole. *Retire and Go!* is a memoir and travelogue: Rome, Florence and Paris.

When we decided to spend a year abroad, as seniors, we were looking for the promise of what the next stage in our lives would be. Having a keen sense of purpose in life is what motivated us. It shaped our goals, guided our direction and decisions, influenced our actions and strengthened our relationship.

We embraced our fixed income, a deficiency in foreign language skills and leaving family not as difficulties but as delightful opportunities to expand our confidence and open our minds, bodies and hearts by living a year abroad. Our purpose, developed from a sense of wonder and dispositions to discover, was to increase our limited knowledge of the fine arts and art history: painting, sculpture and architecture. While art history continues to afford multiple opportunities for understanding about humanity, it also fosters the critical study of art from different and not necessarily compatible perspectives.

Never having the opportunity to spend a year abroad ourselves, we did have, many years ago, the good fortune to live and work in Europe with the Department of Defense Dependent Schools. Since retirement, we have been diligently searching for the origins of those initial travels' joys that at times seemed as if they could never happen in retirement.

Emily said, "If not now, when?!" We decided on three months in Rome, two months in Florence and four months in Paris. Although Florence was the major center of the Renaissance, where the Renaissance and new architecture were born, it was in Rome that it reached its climax. Rome was selected first as we were perceptually seduced by Donatello, Leonardo da Vinci, Michelangelo, and Raphael and later on by Artemisia Gentileschi and Gian Lorenzo Bernini. With some rich background formulated from our Rome experiences came Florence and Giotto, Dante, Petrarch, Botticelli, Ghiberti, and Pisano. The final four months living in Paris, the birthplace of Gothic architecture, the paintings and sculptures of the Realists, Impressionists and Post-Impressionists were waiting for our continuing quest for new learnings, knowledge and connections.

Retire and Go! examines the value of diligent planning and extensive researching; highlights various attractions; discusses ways and means to reach destinations; addresses some dos and don'ts of travel; explores a number of non-touristy destinations; and offers some photographic descriptions. The nine months of slow travel experiences portrayed reveal the delights and benefits, along with the difficulties and conflicts, that are everyday occurrences in overseas travel. The various benefits of travel are explicit throughout the book, and I have tried to show how those benefits from our junior year abroad enriched our relationship and gave us solace in our lives.

Recent studies have demonstrated that travel relieves stress, enhances creativity, and boosts happiness. One study in particular strongly indicated that boomers get at least one health benefit following travel.

Although we are retirees, one with ornery knees and the other with asthma, we never felt hindered in our quest. Anyone who has time and a desire to expand their knowledge and follow their passion, is unafraid to feel daft due to language deficiencies and is on a fixed income will find comfort, and I hope this book gives you the confidence to slow travel.

It certainly helps to pay attention to what Ernest Hemingway said, "Always travel with someone you love." Thank you, Emily, my love.

PART ONE

Introduction

Retirement for us was only a suspension of our past, but the question arose of how do we rediscover the joys of travel and learning after retirement, and how have those joys emerged from our slow traveling experiences and learning along the way? And how, in turn, did what we learn through traveling teach us something about the purpose and value of education as a whole? How do we make traveling enjoyable and maintain our quest to learn new aspects of our lives that will foster a real purpose after retirement? Will slow travel change us, or will it reveal who we are?

To answer these questions we have to go back to the years 1971–1972. We moved to London when I accepted employment as a waiter at Sloane Square Hotel, Knightsbridge, London. The hotel had provided us with a large, single room to use until I found accommodations. After spending 29 days looking for accommodations, as near to the hotel as possible, I found nothing that we could afford. On the 60th day, the very kind hotel manager called on us and explained that, unfortunately, they needed the room, and we must vacate the room by tomorrow. The only possible accommodations we could afford were not near a tube station, and buses didn't run run after 10 p.m. on Sunday, or 11 p.m the other nights. In order for me to make enough money for a family of four and one child on the way, I would have to serve both lunches and dinners. The question was how to return to our flat if the buses were not running after 10 or 11. London was too expensive. I made a drastic mistake thinking I could make enough to support my family in London. I was confident that I could make money working day and night, but I was defeated. "Em, we have to find another way to survive in England." To make matters much worse, the day before we arrived in England, on the 13th of August 1971, President Nixon devalued the U.S. dollar against the British pound, which meant our dollar savings would be worth much less against the pound, and everything now in England would cost us more.

Fortunately, Emily had for some reason the telephone number of an English head teacher with whom we had taken a college course on "Progressive English Schools." That phone call proved to be our savior, our lifeline. I'm sure that Em saved Mr. Francis Backhouse's telephone number because he inspired us, and we admired his intellect, warmth, and especially his philosophy on child-centered education.

On our last morning in our hotel room, we contacted Mr. Backhouse, who lived in Great Tew, Oxfordshire, and explained our dire situation. By chance, Francis suggested that we could purchase a used, small caravan that one of his teachers was selling, and we could place the caravan in his large "garden." We packed up the few belongings we had, phoned Francis to tell him our train arrival time, and he would pick us up at the Oxford station. We flagged a taxi at the hotel and traveled on to Paddington Station. The trains ran every 30–45 minutes to Oxford, and we waited, as an excited family on a mission, at Platform 4 to begin our new lives in England. Francis took Em and the two children to meet Anne while I went to look at the Avondale caravan, which was located in the town of Bicester. The caravan-trailer was about seven feet wide, 10–12 feet in length and seven feet and six inches in height, clean with slightly worn seats and a two-burner butane cooker—tight sleeping accommodations for four people, but it was inexpensive. I did not have a money order or enough English pounds on me, but I was told I could settle up with the seller later. Francis did not have a trailer hitch on his new Renault. He tied a rather complicated series of knots using a double-braided polyester rope that he uses in his rock-climbing adventures. Forty minutes later we arrived in Great Tew with our new home tied to the Renault. With Francis, his two daughters and two sons, Anne, his wife, and me, we pushed and pulled our new home with two tiny wheels into their garden and located the caravan close to the house but far from the outhouse. When I mentioned the outhouse, Anne quickly indicated that we could use their bathroom and shower and kitchen in their house anytime as long as we provided a little advance notice. For our nighttime relieving duties, we used a flashlight (torch), shoes, as the grass was always wet, and didn't drink any liquids after 6 p.m. We settled in rather quickly; our two children, ages three and five, were excited to be on a camping holiday. Em, the stalwart, remarkable, positive wife and mother, was four and a half months pregnant, and we had no clue as to how long we would remain in the caravan. Em had a little over four months before the baby came, and I had to find something. This was my doing, or undoing, as the case may be. This would be our biggest challenge so far, for us as a family and for me as a husband and father, but also a profound opportunity to test our true grit. We eventually succeeded as an all-together family.

One week later I purchased a very used 1964 Vauxhall Victor for 100 pounds. Em learned on a manual transmission, and now she would have a car. After a couple of days in Great Tew, she found a "play-group" for our two children that was operated by an American teacher. This opportunity offered Emily some time to visit schools and volunteer in Francis's school. Often I would ride to school with the Backhouses, and as a volunteer teacher I learned directly from the students and from the excellent teachers at the school. I also spent time in the town of Bicester looking for employment and a place to live.

We spent much time with all the Backhouses. We learned about Francis's workshops in the states and his educational philosophy as an English primary school head teacher. His teaching wife, Anne, bright, enthusiastic and artistic, was an exciting teacher to observe and learn from. What we gained in new knowledge about educational theories, progressive practices, philosophy and psychology would be our educational foundation forever. The more we inquired about English education, the more informed and excited we became about English primary schools and their "progressive" educational practices and theories. I visited many primary schools in and around Bicester and observed some of the most creative and child-centered head teachers and classroom teachers I ever could have imagined. I began to observe the value of hands-on educational experiences, how to determine what experiences were relevant and developmentally appropriate for children, and how to promote and construct ideas and theories through manipulating organic elements found in nature such as sand, wood, water and clay. Many of their philosophical and psychological theories were derived and adapted from the revolutionary pedagogues such as Johann Pestalozzi, Friedrich Fröbel, Maria Montessori, and our own John Dewey. In summary, their aim for education and for children was to develop caring, thinking and responsible human beings capable of creating new things, ideas and theories, not simply repeating what others have done.

In 1967, a significant government-sponsored research publication on primary education called the Plowden Report, "Children and their Primary Schools," gave "official" sanction to progressive–informal classroom methods. "Progressivism" was meant to educate children effectively. It was vital to attend to children's natural dispositions and particularly to their modes of learning and stages of development. Concomitantly, educators could match the interests of children with their sense of wonder. It was Aristotle who stated that the search for wisdom begins with wonder. The Plowden Report called for more attention to children's development and to the factors that affect learning, both in and out of school. "Children and their Primary Schools" noted the importance that the curriculum was to be thought of in terms of activities and discovery and not just facts to be memorized. We immediately recognized the most distinguishing characteristic of English primary schools was that each classroom teacher had the primary responsibility for what happens in the classroom. Teachers needed to think out for themselves what their view of children was and what they believed about the education of children. Teachers were encouraged to demonstrate the relevance of the school experiences in order to promote meaning for understanding through everyday life applications. The teachers I observed allowed children to grow into tomorrow, by living fully today. In this progressive thinking, at the heart of the educational enterprise lies the child. Two of our children were members of this English primary approach and were very happy with their school experience in England. We learned, and our beliefs continued to strengthen and thrive in this child-centered progressive philosophy. These experiences would become our educational foundation for our entire careers in education.

This year also allowed us to spend ample time visiting the Cotswolds in our little black Vauxhall. It was in the Cotswolds that I began my infatuation with and inspiration for the history and architecture of the Saxon and Norman churches and 17th-century tithe barns, which were all within the 800 square miles of this special region of England.

Two months before our third child was born we found a small flat, and I secured a job as a cook-cum-server in the small bed and breakfast in the village of Bicester. From the Bicester Village Hospital, Emily presented us with a beautiful baby girl in December of 1971. Now we traveled in and around the Cotswolds with a complete family, and the joys of slow travel actually began as a family. We took the time to observe, orient, reflect and spend lots of time together eating scones and having our tea.

It was during this period in our lives that we recognized and appreciated what child-centered and relevant education was about. The British primary school movement would motivate and inspire us for the rest of our collective 50 years we devoted to education. Why did American school educators, administrators and university professors from all over the states and elsewhere visit these English schools and write books about how American education should be more like the progressive primary school of England, especially in Oxfordshire, the West Riding of Yorkshire and Leicestershire? In the 1970s the United States was open to a more positive mindset about how children learn and how schools need to be more child-centered and how teachers should follow the children's interests, promote project-based themes and trust children's dispositions. It was a period when teachers should have considerable responsibilities for instructional decisions; the only teacher-proof curriculum was one that the teacher designed and managed. This was the first educational rediscovery and reform since the 1920s and 1930s with John Dewey.

I don't have to tell what happened to this progressive movement in the states. We in America are very concerned about the bang for the buck. We have a habit of not waiting too long before we make evaluative judgments. Results, much like in business, must provide proven evidence of success or change the model for something that will be more profitable. We harbor attitudes toward the conflict regarding the individual versus honoring collectivism or collaboration. Along with the attitude of individualism, we also embrace an attitude of egalitarianism. In the educational setting, on the one hand, we value independence, some self-directed learning, and the promotion of positive self-images; on the other hand, our prevailing social attitudes and teaching targets are often defined by decisions based on what is best for the group, the middle, the average. America's biggest attitude that was difficult to change in American educational thinking was the attitude toward work and play. In English schools we observed and actually worked in, "work is play and play is work," which was a most important attitude distinction from the American culture in which we tend to separate work from play; that learning is a preparation for life instead of a paradigm shift to working to learn. The essential, often political, questions is, Can we evaluate critical thinking, creativity and curiosity, innate dispositions that all children possess? Answer: only if these factors are measurable to produce the defined results. There has to be a more rigid assessment scheme that proves that the children are learning within an established and prescribed curriculum-based assessment scheme. I am reminded of what Alfi Kohn said in "The Schools Our Children Deserve," about the prescribed curriculum and rushing through to cover everything, "We have so much to cover and so little time to cover it. Howard Gardner refers to curriculum coverage as the single greatest enemy of understanding. Think instead about ideas to be discovered."

Education in the states decided to move back to more academic analysis, prescribed materials and instruction and codified teachers' behaviors. Their answer was to measure accountability through standardized and norm referenced assessments and teacher accountability to the prescribed curricula, and that became the overriding educational policy and orthodoxy of practice.

"Open Education," as it was labeled in the United States, was a misrepresentation; sadly, in the states it died as quickly as it began. The United States tried to package informal British practices and classrooms for wholesale distribution, forgetting to adopt the process and to fully understand the theories and psychologies that led to this child-centered outcome, a process that precluded packaging.

Oh, in England this child-centered progressive informal education did continue in some form in some small areas until 1989, when England implemented a national standardized curriculum and exhausting testing of children's progress. It all came to an unfortunate demise.

How did this positive and enlightened English school experience carry over to our return to the states in 1972? Graduate school seemed the most effective and efficient approach to learn more about educational philosophy, developmental psychology and children's growth and development. We tried to fill in all the many blanks that were missing along the way. Our graduate studies became our purpose for and devotion to providing the best learning environment and appropriate practices for children. We also knew that our brief overseas living experience would not be the last. We really wanted to return to England.

After earning our respective graduate degrees in 1974, we knew of one route to return to England, and that was teaching for the Department of Defense Dependent Schools. We applied, but they only had one teaching position, ironically, in the small village we lived in and where our daughter was born in the Cottage Hospital during 1971–72. Bicester American School was located near the American Air Force base and within the dependents' housing. When I asked Emily what we should do, her response was firm and decisive: "If not now, when?" so back to England we went in 1974. During my first teaching assignment at Bicester American School, I was, at first, overwhelmed by meeting 34 children in the morning sessions and 32 children in the afternoon session. Once everything had settled down, the joys continued, commensurate with my child-centered educational beliefs and practices; I immensely enjoyed the time and excitement the children brought into my life. The second year at Bicester I was allowed to teach a combined fourth- and fifth-grade class. This "family grouping" approach was central in the British primary school practice. Coincidentally, the advantages of this multiage grouping arrangement were part of my research dissertation. As there was only one teaching post at the Bicester American School, Emily continued her graduate work at Oxford University. This fortunate employment opportunity allowed us to travel extensively to explore the art and architecture in Great Britain, France and Italy during our two years I taught in Bicester, Oxfordshire.

It was in England, thanks to Emily and Francis, that I began to read the works of John Ruskin, *The Lamp of Beauty*, and his interest in beauty. Beauty for Ruskin was about how beauty affects the mind both physiologically and visually. I often wondered why I felt an emotional attachment to structural proportions and symmetry in buildings and churches, especially Romanesque, Gothic and Baroque. There was also a certain selfish desire to possess it, as I responded intellectually. But what I learned from Ruskin, which was the most pivotal memory I carried with me, was his notion that the only way to possess beauty is to understand it and the elements responsible for it, that is, emotional, psychological and visual. For Ruskin, to understand is to grasp meaning, to see the relationships to other things, to note how it functions, what are the causes, what uses it can be put to. For me, this beautiful idea of understanding meaning would be stamped in my mind, body and soul throughout our future slow travel experiences. We must not only have the experience but also understand the meaning and its connections to other aspects of the world.

Because of an Exceptional Performance rating for the two years with the Department of Defense Dependent Schools in England, I was offered and accepted a three-year teaching-administrative post to southern Spain. Emily was hired by the DoDDS as a "local hire," meaning she could not receive a housing allowance but would have a teaching job. For three years we were both assigned to an isolated region of southern Spain, called Morón de la Frontera, one of the most strategic points (home to the largest air landing and refueling base) controlled by the Americans in all of Europe. It was in this region of Morón de la Frontera that the so-called "Romani" flamenco guitar music was created and firmly established. This mixture of different percussion, rhythms and golpes (finger taps) made an enjoyable lasting impact on our music agenda.

We were treated with enormous enthusiasm and respect from the parents, children and the base commander of the school. The commander provided us with the entire former officer's club building for a school for the kindergarten to eighth graders of dependent children on the base. We continued to provide first hand experiences, following children's interests, and working collaboratively (benefits of family grouping) that we learned from our time with the English primary schools. What an absolutely enjoyable growth experience for all of us. It was also an opportune time to learn about the language, Spanish culture and its history. Our host nation teacher was as enthusiastic about teaching as we were, as he assisted all of us in learning the language and about Spanish music, art and architecture. The children were enjoying learning new things while working collaboratively on interest-based projects that were mostly based on their interests as well as the interests of the three teachers.

Our three conditions for a "project-approach" were: an interest; is the project worthwhile intrinsically; will the project awaken new curiosity and create a demand for information. And we, as teachers, remained as sensitive and resourceful as ever. Interestingly, were we merely responding to the children's enjoyment and enthusiasm and reciprocating or just being the teachers we were? We were deeply aware that child-centered education was rooted in teachers' personal belief about how children learn best.

Furthermore, we were extremely fortunate to be able to slow travel and explore all of the Iberian Peninsula, Italy, France and England during these three wonderful years in Spain. I continued to maintain a daily journal of our planning, procedures, sights visited, costs and general record keeping, as this journal was the only way to "lock up" those experiences in my mind and heart.

Success and purpose sometimes means you have to leave an idyllic family and work situation to move to another more different challenge. Our sense of purpose to travel, discover and explore in our life was what motivated us. This slow traveling, with our family, shaped our goals, guided our direction, decisions and influenced our present and future actions. The Department of Defense Dependent Schools needed me to move for a four-year assignment to the army base school in Mainz, Germany. The challenge for me, very opposite from my post in Spain, was to be an effective leader and administrator of a very large dependent school. For Emily, first as a second-grade teacher, then as the Child Support Service Coordinator, she'd be caring for the daycare and nursery centers. Together we cared for and were responsible to the children and families on the base from the ages of three months to 12–13 years: Mainz School enrolled 1,490 K–6th graders and employed Emily as coordinator for the daycare sites, family daycare and nursery school of approximately 150 children. As a result of determined leadership, new understandings of children's and teachers' learning and teaching styles, and an exciting emphasis on developmentally appropriate teaching approaches throughout these four years fostered what I believed were the best practices in child-centered education that we, as a school staff, could implement.

We managed to travel widely in Germany, Italy, Spain, Morocco, Ireland, Israel, France and back to the Cotswolds of England during these four years. An exciting and memorable time for family, career and travel.

We were overwhelmed and inspired by the architectural sites we visited in Spain (e.g., the Gehry Guggenheim Museum in Bilbao, the Alcázar in Seville, exploring the Alhambra), the Mannerist paintings by Caravaggio in Rome, and the beauty of the Gothic churches in Paris. Of course, the memories of the Gutenberg-Museum, in Malnz, the natural beauty of Germany, and especially Germany's best-preserved medieval city of Erfurt will last forever. In returning to the Cotswolds I discovered there was more to the Cotswolds than rolling hills, pretty villages and grazing sheep; the ancient history and the many periods of architectural style had become a fascination for me to study. These art, history, architecture and culture experiences would become our quests that certainly would provoke future travel.

These ten years of slow travel explorations and discoveries were insightful and important in our quest to learn more about history, art and architecture, and the experience defined our inspiration in terms of realizing that someday we would have many more years of discovery and learning. But when? We realized that our retirement would be a wonderful opportunity, however brief, so when that happens, we must make sure to enjoy it while it lasts.

Emily's mother became seriously ill, and we had to return to the states at the end of our four years in Germany. Family first has always been our mantra. Subsequent administrative posts in Connecticut provided me with a very fulfilling 20-year career in United States education. Emily successfully and enthusiastically took on leadership roles ranging from director of preschools to director of a large childcare center to college lecturing. During this period from 1984 to 2004, we endeavored to be the best educators that we could be.

We still managed to travel to Europe and Asia whenever it was possible, but it was not the same as slow traveling; we were just passing through in time and then back to work. We began to have the mindset, "We work to travel." The essential questions were: Is this true when we travel? Do we move too fast and not feel and observe the meaning of the experience? And do we continue to slow down in order to reinvent an understanding of meaning on our own?

In 1991, Emily went with a small American delegation of educators to learn more about the Italian preschools of Reggio Emilia, soon to become world renowned after a publication in 1991 in *Newsweek* magazine, titled, "A School Must Rest on the Idea that All Children are Different." *Newsweek* claimed in their featured article that the schools in Reggio Emilia were among "The 10 Best in the World—and What We Can Learn from Them." That pronouncement set the progressive thinkers and doers to learn more about this Reggio Emilia approach. This child-centered spirit is still very much alive as a recent article suggests its relevance today: an article published in April 2020 from the *New York Times* was titled, "What are Reggio Emilia Schools? The spirit and philosophy of Reggio Emilia's child-centered, and interest based project approach to early childhood education continues to be a mecca for caring and thinking educators around the world." Emily remembered what Loris Malaguzzi, the founder of the Reggio schools, stated to her: "We do not educate; we are educated in Reggio schools." For me this echoed the English primary schools, with a distinct Italian cultural approach to art, drama, culture and history. The redeeming takeaway for Emily might be explained best when the educators in Reggio Emilia stated that children have real understanding only of that which they invent themselves, and each time we try to teach something too quickly, we keep them from reinventing it themselves.

Reggio Emilia was another critical sign that progressive, child-centered education was alive and well. Emily brought such inspiration from Emilia to all of us in education. A rekindling of the child-centered schools of our earlier learning experiences in Oxfordshire for sure but dramatically different as this is northern Italy, rich in its history, art—many northern Italian painters—and Renaissance and Baroque architecture. As a direct result of Emily's excellent work in getting the Reggio Emilia approach out to the surrounding colleges and universities, we subsequently brought two delegations of teachers and educators to Reggio Emilia to understand, question and reflect on their philosophy and the notion of possibly adapting, not adopting, this unique child-centered method as an inspiration to the many nurseries and preschools across the United States. Not satisfied, we did spend another five weeks the following summer for an educational refresher in Reggio Emilia. Once again we both were actively involved in promoting a positive and relevant mindset that we should always celebrate children's interests, their dispositions of wonder and imagination, their creativity and intellectual capacities. We did our best to foster this philosophy and the accompanying developmentally appropriate practices throughout the rest of our educational endeavors.

Emily always reminds everyone, in her talks to educators about the Reggio approach, that what really matters in the lives of children is how they spend their day at school. As educators, we ask ourselves, "Has this been the best day possible for every child in my class and in our school?" I am sure every teacher asks that question.

The last few years of teaching, a slow change in our country's need for more accountability-based education began to seep into the lifeblood of our beings. This insidious requirement for our country to standardize curricula, systematize children's thinking and make teachers, parents and administrators accountable for the test results was working against our "best practices" and experiential beliefs. How do we embrace something so inappropriate and ineffective into the school lives of children and teachers? With the slow implementation of wrongheaded decisions, practices and policy, we began to ask ourselves: "What, if anything, is anyone learning as a consequence of these counterproductive measures?" The first biting and itching hints of retirement emerged from these counterintuitive operations. Composer Igor Stravinsky once declared in *Poetics of the Form of Music in the Form of Six Lessons*, "The more constraints one imposes, the more one frees oneself of the chains that shackle the spirit." Perhaps it was time to selfishly exploit his declaration in planning our next future. We were aware that retirement meant a suspension of our past, and the past could indeed redefine our future. What from the past 45 years of marriage do we keep and bring forward to our new future together? If education would no longer be our full-time career, then the joys of travel and learning would become our mantra, "If not Now—When?" At this point, we both retired from our past and began to re-evaluate and redefine our retirement future. This could be our own renaissance: Growing older—living younger!

For the next five years (2004–2009) after our retirement, we became the caring and loving grandparents to our two grandsons. We moved to New Hampshire to be near them, because that was what we really wanted to do during these early years of retirement. To share their early years and become their first teachers.

PART TWO

Beginnings: Rome

The Great Recession was a period characterized as a general decline in national economies globally occurring during the years 2007–2009, and the effects of that recession are still with us today. When homeowners began to walk away from their mortgages, the housing prices fell, and people were not purchasing homes. This was a period of great uncertainty, and many people had to sacrifice just to get by.

As it happened, we walked down Miller Street to Market Square, headed to Breaking New Grounds in the center of historic Portsmouth. It features a variety of fresh, roasted coffees, lively and hip baristas and excellently located street tables, both inside and out, perfect for viewing the action around the square. The square is a colorful assortment of old and young locals, college students from UNH, tourists and established residents who have seen their small town become more expensive, from housing to coffee. These kind and caring folks are easily recognizable amongst the backdrop of upscale clothing stores, an independent bookshop, three restaurants, a new Starbucks, a long-established hardware store, a jewelry shop, and a bakery.

Seven-year-old grandson Cole was eager for his "morning glory" muffin and large glass of milk, which he partakes of every time we bring him with us. His younger brother, Ty, when he comes along, prefers a freshly made cinnamon bun with his milk. We secure a prime table near an indoor window, our favorite spot. This table has the best view of the square, perfect for people-watching. I order two nonfat lattes with extra foam, an eight-ounce glass of whole milk and a "morning glory" muffin. These muffins are filled with healthy ingredients like whole wheat, flour, flax, carrots, raisins, honey and cinnamon. I can detect their slight and pleasant scent in the air and love their texture—moist like apple spice cake. Cole really takes his time to savor every bit. When Ty, Cole's younger brother accompanied us, he always asked for a sweet cinnamon bun, and we tried to convince him to try the more healthy version, a morning glory muffin. About ten minutes into our visit, Cole helped me with his muffin and milk. I passed over to Em her latte, sat down with my coffee, and Em utters very quietly...

"I have been thinking for a long time about spending a year abroad, as seniors."

That lit up my neurons. "Where did this come from?" I whisper in return.

"We have certainly enjoyed plenty of our organized tours, but I've had this abandoned feeling of always being rushed, never getting a sense of and depth of the sites."

"I agree, never enough time to really observe anything in detail," I immediately replied.

I do recall in past trips her saying, after a tour, something about moving too fast or not really going deep enough. I reflect for a moment and ask,

"You always loved your trips with Nancy something, that master art quilter, haven't you? Those were slower, right?"

"Nancy Crow. Yes, especially the Provence trip."

I didn't accompany Em on her Provence trip. At the time, we were helping out with the boys' childcare while their parents worked, and it hadn't felt right to leave.

"I keep thinking about how much we enjoyed actually living overseas," Em continued, "and loved studying the British primary schools and the schools in Reggio Emilia. We really went deep back then, didn't we?"

I had to agree. We learned so much about education, philosophy and psychology from the head teachers and the directors at the Reggio schools in Italy. It's true; we really didn't have that kind of excitement anymore. These days, it was more about morning glories and people-watching.

"Yes! Rekindling those sorts of experiences could be interesting, but tell me more."

In the past we did have conversations about what our retirement would be like. One of our goals was to travel as much as possible. I even made a list of places we would enjoy visiting and possibly live for a while.

I asked Em more about her reflections on past tours.

She explained that for one thing, while group tours, including cruises, were useful for sampling a number of countries and helpful during the limited time windows of school vacations, they were too short, giving us only a glimpse of the art, architecture, history of a place and then too quickly moving on to the next site. We just never had the time on those tours to carefully observe, reflect and enjoy.

"Yes!" I replied, "We had the experience but missed the meaning!" We saw, learned a bit, and immediately moved on to something else that was on the schedule.

Kindly set before me was Cole expressing his eagerness to use the toilet, and straightaway he noticed a two-toned black and maroon Citroën 2CV and shouted, "A Charleston CV-2, Poppy!"

He was correct; we both knew our cars. I asked, "Cole, what year?"

"Poppy, you know that they all look the same."

He was right; the Deux Chevaux, produced from 1948 to 1990, had hardly changed over those four decades. Em was looking pleased and relaxed; I, slightly distracted by Cole's keen observation, was still deep in thought. But that was the moment when we began to envision a year of living overseas, "seniors on our junior year abroad" as we liked to joke, rekindling the excitement from our earlier travels and experiences actually living abroad.

"So now where, specifically, do we go to recreate that excitement?" I asked Em.

I continued, "Remember our joys of living in England and Spain?"

"Yes, I realize that much of our enjoyment of our early travel was because we actually 'lived' in England, Spain and Germany."

I thought for a while about how much I enjoyed living in Oxfordshire, England. Our youngest daughter, Dava, was born there. We visited dozens and dozens of schools, learning about progressive educational foundations from the head teachers. I even volunteered as a teacher in one school. But it was just about the schools. My interest in the history and architecture of the Saxon and Romanesque churches was never really satisfied.

Not to be forgotten were the endless weekends we spent as a family in the idyllic Cotswolds. Yes, I loved living in England. I also remembered how much we enjoyed living in Jerez, Spain, and traveling throughout the white towns of Andalusia with the Spanish music and flamenco dancing. And I cannot forget those weekend tapas meals and the delicious pescado dinners! Dinners began at 10 p.m. or so, and our children would play outside until midnight and were never able to sleep straightaway.

This endeavor sounded inviting, even intriguing. My growing excitement was fueled by memories from past enjoyable and meaningful travels. But not every trip abroad was pure joy. Honestly, I wasn't particularly enthralled living in Mainz, Germany. True, living there provided us with endless opportunities as a family to travel to many countries in Europe. On the other hand, Em and I were both working long hours and had tremendous responsibilities: Em as Coordinator of Child Care Services, and I as principal of a large elementary school. Add to that our own three preteen and teenage children, active involvement with students' parents, and our role as productive members of the army base community. Still, I reasoned, much of the issue had to do with our family and careers at the time and really had little to do with the country itself. How different might it be now, free of such responsibilities?

And which countries to focus on? I knew Em would want to return to Italy. She always reminisces about the art, architecture and food of Italy. We both loved living in Spain, and I in particular admired the Cotswolds. And when we visited Paris, Em would tell me that we could live in Paris forever! Actually, Em said the same thing when she first visited the city of Reggio Emilia and their renowned preschools. In fact, she once called me from Reggio and told me that she might just stay there forever.

"Russ, we immersed ourselves in other cultures of where we lived, doing everyday things, and visiting schools. I loved talking to other educators and getting to know other well-traveled people. I just keep thinking: how can we make this year abroad happen? If not now, when?"

I agreed, intellectually, and was energized by the prospect that this adventure would be a new learning opportunity. However, I had real concerns about our children and grandchildren. We'd really wanted to be there for Annika, Cole and Ty; the idea of leaving them felt logistically complicated and almost physically painful.

"Hold on, Em, let's think this through," I said as I reached over into my bag. Cole was just finishing his "glory muffin," and I estimated that we had about a half hour before he'd start to get antsy. I laid out some drawing paper and his favorite ten markers that I brought along.

"You look puzzled," Em said.

"No, I think maybe 'perplexed' is a better fit for my feelings," I retorted a bit curtly.

She replied, "Look, this is a lifetime opportunity to redefine our purpose in retirement, to learn about the art, architecture, history and culture of different countries. The only way to come close to achieving this goal is for us to take a year abroad."

I loved the idea but was having a difficult time comprehending how to come to terms with telling our family, leaving our grandchildren, living overseas on a fixed budget, and making this dream a reality. As my mind lingered over these complexities, I noticed Cole was getting antsy, as he had been drawing cars and trucks and coloring the wheels different colors for over an hour. I was also lamenting that Cole probably memorized every juicy detail that Em and I discussed and would tell his mother before we could break the news ourselves.

We decided to suspend our discussion, providing me more time to contemplate our future and retirement strategy.

The next day the weather is warmer, and the café is humming with activity. The boys are at swim practice, so we have some time alone to talk about our senior year abroad idea. Luckily, we are able to secure our favorite table again. Could this be some sort of karma? Could today's actions determine the fate of our future existence?

I open with, "I'm glad you asked me to avoid talking about our year abroad again until today. You're right; it gave me some time to reflect, rethink and re-examine what this adventure could be like."

"You understand what I was explaining to you yesterday about getting to know a place, to slow travel to another culture?"

I agree, and I'm excited about the possibilities, yet hesitant.

"You have doubts, I can tell because you are looking away," Em says, always the observant one.

"No, I'm looking at you with my ear," I counter, forcing a smile out of her.

"You have to look at me. Listen to what I have worked out so far. Portsmouth is more expensive than we thought when we moved up from Connecticut to nanny the boys. I know we can't afford to maintain our condo here and spend a year abroad on our limited pension. Something has to go."

"You mean the condo … or me?" I smirk.

"If you don't get serious, Russ, it might be you! For now, why don't we sell the condo? We'll also have to sell the car and not renew our teaching positions." (We both had part-time positions supervising students.)

I interject, "That's wonderful. We will be homeless, jobless and carless!"

"We'll take any profits from the sale of the condo, bank the money, and live our year abroad on our fixed budget; that would work as long as we stay on a firm budget."

We do receive a teacher's pension and monthly social security checks. My thoughts drift to making immediate contact with our realtor to see if our condo can sell in this depressed market; the Honda will go to our daughter, Hattie.

I take a breath and pronounce, "Okay, I think I am getting into this adventure."

"I can tell because you're smiling, talking fast and looking at me rather than all over the place," Em observes shrewdly.

But my mind is still confused. I'm excited about our new redefinition of post-retirement opportunities. I subconsciously question myself, however: Do I deserve this? Did I earn this year abroad? It seems so irresponsible. But Em doesn't think so, and I decide to go with that. Our first task, after I contact our agent is to start making a list of what needs to be accomplished for this to happen; I love to make lists, as they help me organize my priorities.

Regarding telling our children about our retirement abroad, we were concerned about their reactions. As their parents, we have been known to make rather impulsive decisions—for example, selling everything and moving to England while Em was several months pregnant with our youngest child. Oftentimes, while working in Germany, we would not tell our children where we were going and visit another country because we had a long weekend. They thought we made decisions without sufficiently consulting with them. We needed to not only explain to them how we felt about redefining our retirement by spending a year abroad but convince them that we had thought it through. Em reassured me that they would be excited for us as they knew how much we enjoy traveling.

OK, I nod. I'm staring at Em; then I ask "the" question:

"Where do you want to live?"

"What immediately comes to mind is Italy," Em replies without hesitation. "There is Rome, Florence and Reggio. I could live in any one of these wonderful places."

When we traveled to Italy in the past, we always said that we would return again in retirement. I remember Em's call to me from Reggio several years ago. It was early in the morning as she either forgot, or was too excited to care, that there was a six-hour time difference. Nonetheless, I loved hearing that she was enjoying and learning every minute she was in Reggio Emilia. She explained how the preschool children excitedly explored their historic center, how they carefully observed and drew the lions outside of San Prospero Church. She said they were happy; they were learning—firsthand—about their culture and city. She talked about the imposing medieval architecture, the emphasis on art and drama at the schools, and on and on. I was overwhelmed with joy for her, and envy seeped in my selfish mind, wishing I was there with her. She left me with a phrase from the founder and leader of the Reggio approach, Loris Malaguzzi, that I would never, ever forget: "nothing without joy!"

It's almost 3 p.m. I need to pick up the boys from swimming.

Three more days pass before we can continue our stealthy plans. We bring the two boys with us to Prescott Park so they can enjoy the outdoor theater production of *Annie*. Our on-and-off conversations are now dominated by where to go after our stay in Italy. We manage to mention two places that we finally agree upon. I really want the Cotswolds: no language issues, and we're fairly familiar with the region. However, Florence and Paris sound absolutely marvelous too. The boys are focused on the lively theatrics. Afterwards I ask Ty who his favorite character was, and he says, "I liked the singing best." Cole indicates that Mr. Warbucks was his favorite.

The next day the boys are at school, and we set off to Breaking New Grounds again, our Portland version of Paris's Les Deux Magots or maybe Café de Flore.

I ask Em, "Do you want a skimmed latte or matcha tea?"

"Please, latte with one sugar," she replies.

We relax, but not at the table of our choice this time, as we are near the barista's counter, which is busy and noisy. Regardless, we manage to have a brief conversation about yesterday's living abroad choices.

"Well, we didn't get much accomplished yesterday, but the boys seemed to enjoy the play. What about Florence and Paris?" I suggest.

"I have been thinking!" Em exclaims.

I interrupt her with something sarcastic like, "Well this could be very interesting."

Em shoots me that look that means "hear me out before you judge." She continues, speaking a bit louder than earlier. At first I think she is angry with me but then realize that she needs to shout above the café noise. But there are no other seats inside or out, so she continues at a higher volume.

"You know when I went with Nancy Crow a couple of years ago, the tour took us to visit another wonderful small town of Uzes, in the Languedoc region, near the Avignon in Provence. This town must come into play at some point in our retirement travels."

I dutifully acknowledge by nodding my head. I remember that Em did call me from Uzes to say that she had found one more place that we could live. She was so excited, explaining the design of the town, the size and spaces for people to comfortably interact with each other, and the beauty of the 900-year-old medieval architecture. She also told me that she spoke with one of the guides, who happened to live in the area, about long-term rental properties. He would send her information after the tour. Many weeks after Em returned she received several leasing properties in Uzes from him. To this day she kept that property list. It was fate!

Just think of it, I pondered—studying and learning about Renaissance art and architecture at my young age. I might just get some actual education that I never had before.

I probe, "So Uzes, for how long?"

"That depends. We could do six months in Italy first. I'm thinking maybe living in Rome or Florence for three months each. We could have the time to at least begin to uncover the artistic treasures and at the same time learn and appreciate."

I'm secretly hoping Rome will come first. We have been to Rome a number of times, always with a tour group, with never enough time to discover over 2,000 years of history and architecture. I can foresee a careful study of the notable architectural achievements inspired by Egyptian and Greek influences and during the Roman Empire. What immediately come to mind are the amazing semicircular arches of the Ponte Sant'Angelo and the public baths in the Roman Forum.

"What about Rome as our first adventure?" I inquire.

"Yes, I'm thinking carefully about Rome, its history, art, architecture, and food."

My heart is jumping. I might be getting my first choice of the Eternal City.

We agree that the café is now too crowded and noisy. Em wants to leave. However, our conversation lingers in my mind.

What I have gleaned so far is: three months of rekindled retirement in Rome and three months in Florence and Tuscany. I'm hesitant to guess what the final "semester" abroad will be, but Em loved Paris and had indicated in the past that she could actually live there, language issues aside. I imagine that I could learn more about those Parisian artists and literary folks of years ago who painted and wrote while in La Closerie des Lilas, Le Select or Le Procope.

Later that evening we can't stop thinking about our newfound retirement purpose. I restart the conversation with, "Did you have a third semester abroad in mind?"

Em replies, "Do you really want to know what I think? I was thinking either Provence and Uzes or possibly Paris for four months, as that would complete our nine months. You loved Paris as much as I did."

My little mind begins to peel away like a red onion. Studying Renaissance art and architecture in Florence. Learning about the Baroque churches in Rome. Hemingway and Sontag, Monet and Renoir and the rest of the Impressionists in Paris. I could be very happy in all of those places, but I also realize I could be happy anywhere with Em.

My only immediate but slight hesitation is our language skills, or lack thereof. We don't speak Italian (Em has some background), but French? Forget about it.

I remark sarcastically, "Sorry, but do you remember some French from high school?"

"We can learn enough French to be polite and friendly and let the rest sort itself out. Language deficiencies should not be a major barrier to us pursuing our dreams of Paris."

Okay, that was easy. The next layer of my onion-like amygdala begins to unfold. I still have lingering concerns and questions. Em has the marvelous capacity to look at the "big picture," a random-abstract thinker, whereas I am more of a linear-sequential doer. I have absolute trust in her making things work out, and I must listen more and think less. My concerns are centered more on our family's reactions and leaving everyone behind for so long. But then I think, the boys will be in school, and they have loving, caring and attentive parents. Do they really need us now in the same way as they did when they were younger?

We had moved to New Hampshire to take care of the boys. We wanted to help out, to be their nannies (or whatever we were called) for seven years. We had the pleasure of taking them to their preschools, YWCA library readings and swimming, walks, hanging out in cafés, hikes, trips to the beach and museums.

I reckon that we will work out how to keep in touch with them on a weekly basis. Em, for ages, has been a master at technology; she has a knack for problem-solving, and I trust her intuition. I feel confident that she will know how to do that. Yes, of course! I forgot that there is Skype to keep in contact with all three grandchildren and family.

We are at the point where we have gone through many transitions into retirement, and this will be another redefinition of slow travel during retirement. Although we are both concerned about what the family might feel about us taking off for our year abroad, I must remember that we shall come back for a while after each leg of travel before our next. Thinking out loud has restored my trust in what Em has envisioned. Yet still, if the boys' parents are not in agreement with us regarding our lengthy excursion to another continent, it's definitely a no-go.

I mention this concern again about our families to Em, and she replies,

"I am positive that they will be happy for us to take on this adventure. They know how much we love them, and they also know we do enjoy traveling."

Later I find out that Em had actually already talked to our family, and they were excited for our redefined retirement plans. As it happened, Cole overheard our conversation at Breaking New Grounds and must have mentioned something about us moving to his mom. So when the subject came up, Em honestly put forth our proposed retirement slow travel plans.

Em, always a thinker and problem solver, knew that I needed time to process this endeavor. Actually, I am very pleased that she went ahead and consulted with the family; I have a limited capacity to be so forthright.

She knew the family and knew that they would be ecstatic for us to enjoy our retirement abroad. I really appreciated her initiative as this had been my only lingering concern.

Worries, or concerns, they feel the same. Now that our family had given their blessings, there were a few other concerns to consider. What about our health? And the sale of the condo, especially with the down housing market and with money tight during these unfortunate times.

I mention my concern about health, and Em replies,

"We will make sure that we are healthy enough to live overseas—and they do have doctors there!"

Actually, we are in relatively good health. My allergies are seasonal and will not be as bad if we travel to Italy in the winter. The other advantages to winter travel are that it is less expensive—the off-season—and there are fewer crowds in the museums. Em has to rest her knees once in a while; I'll have to listen and be aware of this.

Em breaks into my thoughts: "Russ, I'm less concerned about health but more concerned about longevity."

"Wait, I'm confused." Confusion for me is the starting point of thought.

"We realistically have about ten to 15 years of travel at our age. On those tours we took, I do not want to be one of the aging travelers we saw having a difficult time walking, climbing stairs, and not really enjoying themselves. I love that they are traveling, but I don't want to travel that way. I looked up our life expectancy, and it is best to travel now, before we become too frail!"

I feel her urgency to travel now, as it has become quite evident from listening to her. I do remember on our tour to China an elderly man tripped and fell. I walked him back to the bus and stayed with him until medical assistance came. He was OK, a sprained ankle, and I'm sure it was painful. As a result, I recall we both missed the tour of the "Forbidden City" … perhaps another time.

Em wants to travel as independently as possible, and that implies living in a place over a period of time, managing the daily routines and learning about a different culture and language. Again, it's the slow travel concept, not the fast tour concept, which will be just the right speed for us.

Time seems to be moving quickly. Working collaboratively, we check off those actions that are either in progress or completed from our previous "To Do" list:

- Select the apartment from my research findings.
- All financial details, banking, security, fees and exchange rates. She has been banking online for years.
- Make the doctors' and dentists' appointments.
- Arrange for Skype to be available to our entire family.
- Ascertain banking security and methods of money exchanges while overseas.
- Begin to find Italian language courses.
- Work with our realtor on selling the apartment, schedule showings, etc.
- Research multiple sources for renting apartments (then pass along to Em).
- Be the contact person once Em has selected an overseas apartment.
- Find out about the Schengen requirements, that is, length of stay in each country.
- Find out how to have our mail forwarded or stopped.
- Secure medical and evacuation insurance.
- Work on the most economical flights.
- Miscellaneous.

For me, the most important "to-do" was already complete: telling our family. Their positive reactions made me confident now to move on to the remainder of my tasks, which were many. We worked out appointments, including yesterday's encouraging meeting with our realtor. We can store our furniture in our daughter's basement. I did find out that we can only stay in Italy for three months without a residence visa. In France, if we stay for four months, we will have to apply for a long-term (one-year) visa. I understand that obtaining a year-long visa takes considerable documentation and time.

The decision to live in Rome, Florence and Paris energizes my motivation. I still need to continue to research accommodations on SabbaticalHomes.com. We easily agree upon ideal criteria for an apartment in Rome, including such practical elements as accommodations within our fixed-income budget, a location near public transport and availability of public parks. My research narrowed down to four attractive possibilities that matched our criteria from Sabbatical Homes; sadly, not all were within our fixed budget.

My thoughts and heart rate play catchup with each other as I wonder what our specific focus will be. First, in Rome. From our previous travels we enjoyed and appreciated the light and dark style of Mannerist master artist Michelangelo Merisi Caravaggio (named after his native city of Caravaggio). Maybe we'll try to find all his paintings in Rome. Although I was somewhat interested in church art, was the idea of finding Caravaggio's paintings and exploring Baroque churches in Rome a significant enough quest to justify leaving family and living in a foreign country, with only Em having rudimentary skills in Italian?

I questioned myself over and over as I wasn't sure that she would suggest Rome as our first choice. I offer my dilemma to Em; she says, "Absolutely, love that idea. I think there are at least 15 or so paintings by Caravaggio in Rome. Remember you have always been somewhat interested in learning about the history of art and architecture. Certainly, the church art in Rome is extraordinary. Other specific quests will emerge as we begin to study and learn, but our major purpose is to enjoy our retirement, to remain lifelong learners."

The embers of our past travel are to be rekindled into a final blaze in retirement: enjoyment together, slow travel, exploration, discovery, and active learning. "Yes," I bark out, "back to joyful and engaged learning in our redefined retirement!"

Shortly after Em retired from full-time work she enrolled in a graduate art and architecture course at the Metropolitan Museum in New York. Sadly, as I reflect on that time, she tried to get me interested in both, but I was too busy with work. However, I reckoned that her knowledge of art and architecture would be very beneficial in my studies. It is true that I have always enjoyed the museums and galleries of our previous travels, oftentimes with too little time to observe and reflect, however. Isn't it true that architecture is art and art is architecture? I think I could really get actively engaged in studying art and architecture and history. Language, on the other hand, might remain a persistent challenge.

We share our feelings about a number of different thoughts. We will miss our family and grandchildren. Em makes a new point that, as older travelers, it's not as easy to find a group of ready-made colleagues as in the past, as we no longer have any university attachments. She makes it clear, however, that language is not going to be a factor as long as we learn polite phrases and everyday vocabulary. We'll plan to watch Italian movies with subtitles to help us learn.

Em's knees might be an issue, as she must rest them periodically and not push too much without resting. I will have to be very sensitive to her condition and avoid pushing her or overextending our outings.

As we enjoy each other's company and chitchat, Em talks about how in every place we've lived overseas, we took the opportunities to visit the host nations' schools, and what we learned became pillars of our educational philosophy. She pointed out that it was important to recognize that there are many different ways to learn and that there isn't only one right way to teach and learn. I remember what a head teacher told me several years ago. She said to keep these seven words in mind when promoting child-centered environments: "Children learn from the company they keep." Accordingly, Em mentioned how in Reggio teachers know how to listen to children, how to allow them to take the initiative and be able to guide them in productive and collaborative ways. Reggio preschools also successfully challenged the many false and misleading dichotomies like child versus adult and enjoyment versus study. These were indeed important pillars of our pedagogical and epistemological beliefs. The question might be, are these educational pillars relevant to redefining the joys of travel? I learn in different ways, and perhaps a more hands-on, observing and thinking approach might work best for my learning style. Em is multifaceted; she learns by thinking, analyzing, evaluating and is guided by her incredible intuition capacity. We shall see how our learning modalities stay the same or become modified or adjusted based on our discoveries, explorations and observations in Rome.

One last item we discussed to relieve my last bit of anxiety was about our financial status moving forward. I said, "Just brief me on our financial status now and in the future—this has been bothering me."

"Our main source of income while overseas will be our teacher's retirement account," she replied. "The condo has a certain amount of equity, and we have been excellent savers over time. We are planning to spend nine months overseas, so upon our return to the states we might have to rent for a while. Russ, we must stay within our fixed-income budget. I will prepare a budget based on our resources, and we will adhere to it."

"Absolutely, yes, dear, I'm with you 100 percent. I'll place that requirement at the top of my 'Must Adhere' list along with respecting your knees and learning rudimentary Italian."

Our purpose this year abroad is to live our retirement to the fullest capacity possible. Thoreau said, "I wanted to live deep and suck out all the marrow of life." What would our next chapter be like if we "sucked all the marrow out of life"?

Em is always thinking ahead, the stalwart and problem solver in our family, and her cautious and positive optimism regarding discovering and exploring the wonders of travel was an inspiration indeed. Em's authentic gifts are what educator Lillian Katz called dispositions or attitudes about learning; that is, her curiosity, playfulness, perseverance, and confidence were the motivating factors in our relationship and in slow travel. In retirement, we will have the time and motivation to once again rekindle our previous enjoyment of European travel experiences. A couple of questions were still with me such as:

- How do we rediscover the joys of learning and discovery we experienced in our previous years abroad?
- Will our retirement somehow make learning new things enjoyable and sustainable?
- What did our 50-odd years in education teach us about travel and the value of research, exploration, reflection, and further study?

Hopefully these and other questions would be answered in the coming year abroad. To help with my organization, a collateral aspect of my past administrative endeavors, I make several simplified lists, for example: A master list for long-term goals; a weekly project list, a high-impact list (need to do now). I always make lists for everything, like shopping lists, laundry lists, to-do lists, lists for what to do after the to-do is completed, blood pressure records list, inventory lists, book and music playlists. I'm like that, perhaps a bit over prepared.

After the families were delighted and encouraged about our year abroad retirement endeavors, Em explained in detail the financial aspects of this endeavor; next on my list was to contact our realtor and sell our condo. My thoughts, as we discussed the possibilities of a sale, were perhaps in a year or so our apartment would be purchased, and we would sail off to our retirement in the skies. I think about my favorite Italian song, "Volare." The lyrics from "Nel Blu Dipinto Di Blu," were reminiscent of my thoughts at the time: "Flying, oh, oh." Who knows, maybe by that time we might even have a different plan for our retirement years.

The call is to Brad, our realtor, who originally sold us our flat. Brad, a clever and knowledgeable, born and bred New Hampshire outdoor enthusiast, told us without seeing it that he could sell our apartment within four weeks. I didn't share our tentative year abroad plans with Brad, as I felt that could indicate that we were desperate to sell and might not be in our best overall interests; perhaps a bit paranoid on my part? The next day Brad came over to have a look at the apartment. While waiting for Brad, from our third-floor window I observed that he was driving a new Volvo S60, beautiful and expensive, and said to myself that he must be a success in the industry (no judgment, please). He was impressed enough with our apartment to reassure us that "you have an excellent property for this current market."

Brad further indicated that Portsmouth was becoming a "hotspot" for investors, and as a convention center, new hotels are needed. New apartments and hotels were in their planning stages, and Brad said that the zoning commission had already given their approval to build. I had one incomprehensible and inexplicable buried belly of hope in my abdomen. Let me explain: The gut is directly connected to our brain and lined with more than 100,000,000 nerve cells, making the gut practically a brain unto itself—and that was our one-bedroom apartment, which was in excellent shape, minimally furnished to show off the late 20th-century carved-wood details on the arched door moldings, polished oak or maple floors, a neat cove-like kitchen with a functionally sized pantry, and the apartment was within walking distance to the lively iconic Market Square. I had hopes that our museum-like display of our four large, colorful floral watercolors, two Tuscan landscape pastels, and a few oil paintings from our past European travels would feel warm and look inviting on those freshly painted white walls. Come to think of it, the artwork was mostly our memories of Rome, Florence and Tuscany, Paris and Provence. Was that the inexplicable bit that was incomprehensible in my gut?

As the sale of the condo was completely out of our control, we continued to discuss our plans. Next on my list was to research and locate a few rental properties in Rome. I started a new list: "Possible choices of apartments to live." I learned from one of my influences in college to list the problem or condition you want to solve or improve upon and proceed with the following steps.

- Origin of the problem, in our case, is finding property in Rome that is within our budget, near public transport and with public parks.
- What criteria would we use to solve this dilemma: within our budget, near public transportation and parks.
- Analyze the situation in terms of researching online sources for accommodations.
- Possible solutions: Home-Away, Airbnb, looking through the classified sections in *The New York Review*, VRBO and Sabbatical Homes.

We shall be leaving our grandchildren, I thought. I reflected on how we prepared them for their early childhood experiences. When they were young, but ever so adventurous and enthusiastic grandchildren, we supplied them with an ample supply of maple wooden construction and building blocks for constructing farms, barns, castles, Roman forts and the Eiffel Tower. Along with the building of structures came pictures and children's books of ancient Rome, the Royal Forum, the Colosseum, and the Pantheon, which provided questioning, stimulation and motivation for them to seek out more. Accordingly, books about building, ancient Rome in particular, were being read to them, and they were enthralled by the horrendous happenings in the ancient Colosseum. Art and architecture, Em's silent passion, was always interpreted as a gateway to the understanding of history, culture and living. The results were more books about art techniques, painting and drawing were in abundance, all present and accounted for. We constructed a mini-classroom in the boys' parents' basement. We replicated the enjoyable classroom environment that we had set up for the many children we taught years ago.

"The past is always present," John Coe, our colleague and an English primary advisor, would always tell us when we inquired about HOW–Loris Mallaguzzi and the Reggio approach; Friedrich Fröbel (founder of kindergarten) who emphasized the value of play; Johann Heinrich Pestalozzi, whose pedagogical methods emphasized that instruction of any type should always proceed from the familiar (concrete) to the new (abstract) and stressed group and collaborative work as opposed to children learning alone; Dr. Maria Montessori, who proselytized self-correcting play and individualized learning pace; John Dewey, who maintained that schools are looked at as a community and emphasized the integration and connections of subject areas; and Jean Piaget, who supported a developmentally sensitive approach to learning and advocated hands-on exploration of all types of materials. He influenced the British primary schools movement and developed his own philosophy and educational psychology. In "Learning Theory," he would say, "They all brought something exciting and new from their past that allowed us to interpret their beliefs and pedagogical practices into what would be best for children and their motivation and enjoyment to learn for today." In other words, I guess, the past is always present today.

Before the boys actually attended nursery schools, we commandeered their basement and sectioned it off into bays or sections, including an art and drawing area with a stand-up easel, a child's old swimming tub that was used for water and sand play, a section for modeling clay and play dough. The largest center of the basement was reserved for construction and block building, Cuisenaire rods, Legos and Lincoln Logs, which were designed by the son of Frank L. Wright. We also included an area for found objects such as chestnuts, pine cones, rocks, stones, marbles, pieces of driftwood, beeswax and seeds, and anything the boys found and wondered about there was room for. Nearby was the science center with a small microscope. A small camp tent stood alone in the corner near the window in case either one, or both, wanted time away from me or to be by themselves. We always had room somewhere for Hanna, their black Lab.

Two shelves with an array of relevant picture and reference books and a display area were mounted neatly against the whitewashed wall alongside the stairway for their art and crafts projects. I carved out a small desk space for my notes and lists in order for me to occasionally check if the boys spent some time in each of the prepared learning center areas during their week.

This is a "third teacher" environment; that is, the environment is viewed as the third teacher along with the child and the teacher, an essential component and arrangement in the Reggio Emilia schools. Loris Malaguzzi believed that social learning preceded cognitive development and stressed that the environment plays a central role in the process of making learning meaningful and relevant. The many Reggio Emilia classrooms we observed and studied were flexible environments, responsive to the needs for children to motivate and inspire creative learning together. The environment we created in the basement reflected the values we wanted to communicate to the boys.

The interest-learning centers or bays were a throwback to the exciting and child-centered English primary schools of the 1970–80s and the notion of children learning by doing. Children's motivation was increased through activities that offer opportunities for collaboration and to become aware of different points of view. What we created, essentially, was a nursery-preschool environment relatively complete and developmentally appropriate (for their age and stage) for their exploration, discovery and enjoyment.

Evaluate each solution (accommodations) and compare by using the criteria (B) to solve the issue. We talked about the possibilities. Em reported that "more research was required in order to make an informed and practical solution." So I continued with this pleasurable task.

Finally, the solution was to narrow the choices down to three or four. Use Google Maps to eyeball each neighborhood, keeping in mind that the apartment had to be practical, cost effective within our fixed-income budget, and within our time frame of no more than three or four months away.

After exactly three weeks and one day, an offer was extended for our apartment.

Brad told us that he thought the offer was too low and recommended that we counter, which we did. Three days later our counteroffer was accepted. Since the couple, both University of New Hampshire employees, were renting at the time, they wished to close on the deal and move into the apartment as soon as possible. We were, of course, excited. I was uncertain about how to proceed but thrilled that the deal was a cash purchase.

After the initial shock, we thought and reflected on what had just transpired.

"Em, this happened, and so fast, I cannot believe it."

"I know, and we were so very fortunate to have this place sold given the lingering effects of the housing crisis."

The couple, expecting their first child, purchased the apartment on the third floor without an elevator and the washer/dryer in the basement; they miraculously really liked our place; that made us very happy.

That gave us approximately four to six weeks to pack up our bits of furniture and carefully bundle up our small collection of paintings acquired over our years of travel. Our daughter invited us to store in her basement what we did not give away. If the apartment was sold, how about our Honda? Our oldest daughter could use a very reliable vehicle, so the car went to her. Three factors had been settled: The apartment was sold, with furniture stored, and the car gone.

For the first time in our 45 years of marriage we were to be homeless, jobless, and, after handing over the keys to our daughter, carless. Was the feeling of freedom or despair?

Still for me it was the best of times, and it was also the worst of times. This could be the new age of wisdom and knowledge, or this could be the age of foolishness and despair. Perhaps this was the season of darkness but also the spring of hope. We chose hope and knowledge as our motivation and a new wisdom for our aging development.

Exactly what did a new age of knowledge and discovery have to do with our purpose to leave family and grandchildren? Our discussions continued.

"We will find our purpose through our experiences abroad," Em reiterated.

I countered with something like, "I think we should have in mind our purpose before so we know what we are searching for." Listening to Em, after many abrupt and often extensive conversations to this essential question, we arrived at a compromise, important in our relationship, and that was to focus on art, architecture and culture. Em's final outburst of wisdom was, "Let's just enjoy to the fullest our year abroad in Europe, as we have the time and the resources as long as we stay within our fixed income budget." She always puts things right.

Of course, another lingering thought I had was I do not speak Italian. It was helpful to me that Em's Italian was basically rudimentary, at best; at least it was a language somewhat familiar to her. Sadly, I have always had difficulty learning another language; however, I absolutely agreed to learn some polite phrases and necessary vocabulary.

The decision to spend our year abroad as seniors in Rome meant that my persisting anxieties moved from my mind to my abdomen.

Reflecting on what Em had said about our purpose, I tried to keep a positive mindset, a growth mindset, about how to continue to develop within our positive growth. How do we reestablish the joys of discovery and learning that emerged in our previous years aboard? I cultivated the thought of how our retirement travel would promote learning new things and be sustainable in our exciting years to come. And will what we learn through slow travel teach us something about the purpose and value of education? Do our many years of teaching educate us on the value of motivation, research, reflection, study, discovery and exploration?

"A list," Em said to me. "Please make one of your composite lists or a problem-solving rubric so we can analyze and evaluate our next steps." Through our collaborative efforts, we made excellent progress in terms of the research, planning and preparation, which, although enjoyable together time, was time consuming. Time was built into our retirement plans. Not knowing that time was the difference between time measured with a sundial and time measured with a clock, I chose a clock; we have the time, so let's get on with it. The tremendous assistance for us, of course, was the wider scope of research that information technology provided. Back in the day, we didn't have search engines or mechanisms to expedite our travel plans. I began my problem-solving metric.

- How many months in Rome? Situation identified.
- Possible solutions to the length of stay in Rome was based on finances and time away from the grandchildren.
- Evaluation of the solution: If we locate a flat within our fixed budget and spend only on what we need, we can manage three months in Rome.
- Solution: Three months in Rome on a fixed income.
- Always ask ourselves if the solution is practical, cost and time-wise?
- Answer: affirmative.

I just kept adding to the original rubric as each problem was identified and possible solutions were satisfied.

The first aspect of slow travel to a country that would be foreign to us was expenses and finding an apartment within our budget.

List: Problem: First search for a flat that will be within our budget.

Possible solutions: To keep the expenses manageable we need to search in an area outside of the center of Rome (too expensive) but close enough to the center to use public transportation.

Evaluate the solutions in terms of the flat within our budget.

Next step: List the possible apartments from an Internet search to work out what housing was available for three months and within our fixed income that had a park-like location and access to public transport.

The search took only a few days as our choice of accommodations was restricted or prescribed by several variables, such as long–short-term rentals, cost, utilities included, availability, size of apartment, location near parks (we knew that we would need parks and nature to relax and for reflection, and note-taking after spending most days in the museums, galleries and churches in the center of Rome), and what the reviews say about the accommodations. We never lived in Rome, but our previous European residences were always in the local economy, so we felt relatively comfortable outside of the center of Rome. Knowing that Em is really an expert at problem-solving, finding bus routes and locations would play into her amazing capacity for such issues.

Possible solutions: For example: A two-bedroom apartment in the Prati neighborhood near the Vatican for $2,500, excluding utilities, plus a $2,500 security deposit. Our reaction: super location, too large for the two of us, and too expensive for three months. Example two: "Center of Rome's historic center. Near the Piazza Navona and Pantheon." Further scrutiny provided these gems' hidden comfortability or uncomfortability such as on the fourth floor, with a small patio, no elevator or air conditioning, modern furnishings, recently restored bathroom and shower, bookcase, desk and a studio apartment. Advertised cost for the three months was $9,000, but it included utilities and free Internet. Super, but really not for us. Here was my favorite from Sabbatical Homes: "Historic building apartment in the heart of Trastevere composed of a main house with bedroom, a little living room convertible in a little bedroom, living/dining room, kitchen and bathroom, there is a big equipped terrace (200 sq meters) and no utilities." The price was 2,000 euros per month or at the present exchange rate about $2,450.

I asked Em if any of these apartments indicated if there was a washer, as I knew that dryers are not included as they would be costly; electricity is expensive. We did not worry about air conditioning as we were to spend the three months in the winter: cheaper, less tourists, museums and churches aren't overrun with people as they would be in spring and summer.

Em was getting to the real point of finding accommodations; she does that quite well. Found: Outside of central Rome, near parks and access to public transport. Within hours, she found what turned out to be the best possible apartment for us in terms of the cost, location, parks nearby and public transport. I heard a resounding "Found it!"

Another list I prepared was for additional problems and their solutions.

- How do we manage expenses which we are unaware of, such as exchange rates, euros exchanged for U.S. dollars, or the other way, U.S. dollars exchanged for euros, that's right. A currency lesson was my job, although Em is much better at finances and budget minding than me. Solutions: The higher the euro the lower our dollar's value for purchasing goods in Europe. For ten years we lived in England, Spain and Germany, and based on those experiences, we made an educated guess that foodstuffs, produce, dairy would cost either the same or less than we paid in the states. Past experience told us that kitchen items like aluminum foil, paper products, and laundry products would cost more than what we were used to in New Hampshire. I put a note on my weekly list to account for and review these possible discrepancies along the way and make the adjustments as needed.
- Problem: Can we stay up to 90 days in Italy without a special visa? I had this problem solved immediately as I knew colleagues who took the sabbatical in Spain and France were allowed 90 days without a special visa. However, I cross-checked to make sure requirements did not change and read the Schengen Agreement, a treaty comprising 26 European countries that have abolished all passport or border controls. As United States citizens, we are exempt and do

not require a visa for Italy. To stay longer than 90 days, one needs to apply for a long-term visa, with strict requirements to ascertain such a long-term visa. No problem to solve.

- Problem: What about inexpensive flights? The criterion for solving this problem was cost. Analyze the problem after research proved direct-fly cost more; one stop or multiple stops cost less. To save money we evaluated if there were any advantages to flying nonstop, making the eight-hour flight a little easier on us? What about a one-stop flight? We found out that a one-stop flight from Boston to Dublin and on to Rome cost little more than one with multiple stops. We chose a one-stop in Dublin, a less expensive flight than the direct flight. We hypothesized that perhaps due to competition and comparative search engines available, European flights were relatively less expensive than we ever imagined. Em, again, found the best flight for our tentative flight to Rome.

- What about money exchange and extracting money once we are in Europe? A thorough research job was required with the different banking schemes that provide no fee for exchanging money and a set fee for the bank transactions. Which credit/debit card company would provide us with the lowest or no charge on foreign transactions? We found a bank that did not charge any transaction fees for debit withdrawing euros or bank fees using our credit card for purchases. This was a practical solution that should have immediate benefits in managing the budget. I did not list the problems in ascending order, but this problem was huge in order to make permanent arrangements for Rome. Was our health good enough to live abroad for a long period? Solution: Schedule physicals immediately. Problem: What about health care in Rome if we need it? Solutions: After extensive research, the solution would be if you need medical assistance, you pay the doctor in euros because our stateside medical plan does not pay for overseas doctor visits. The other alternative we chose was to buy medical insurance in the U.S. that covered all possible emergencies. We followed up with physicals, checked and cleaned our teeth, had eye exams. I needed a new prescription as I am nearsighted. We requested and received three months of prescriptions, updated our immunizations as a preventive measure. Thanks to our excellent doctors, we were "classified" as healthy and "certified" for slow travel abroad.

- What about our language skills or lack thereof? We already had decided to learn polite phrases and some essential vocabulary. Em was further along in both polite phrases and vocabulary than I. My emphasis would be to learn several Italian phrases to appear polite and friendly; we certainly did not want to offend our host as we were foreigners in their country. We were also fully aware that we would not be able to carry on any lengthy conversation. Em instructed me to learn these phrases, and she would help me along the way: good morning (buon giorno, buon pomeriggio), good afternoon, good evening (buona sera), thank you (grazie), hello (ciao), you're welcome (prego), excuse me (scusa), I'm sorry (mi dispiace), please (per favore), my name is (mi chiamo), where? (dove?), right (destra), left (sinistra), how much (quanta costa), and finally, HELP! (AIUTO!).

- What type of clothes should we bring, and how are we to dress in these new foreign territories? Does it matter? We had many years of overseas travel early in our work overseas; clothing and "the right" apparel was not a concern. As long as we dressed appropriately and did not stand out, we were confident in our wardrobe for our junior year abroad as seniors. Also, if we really need clothes, we can purchase them from open markets or department stores. Also, we always travel light—two carry-ons and backpacks or duffel bags, that's it. When we use only those luggage containers, we're careful as to what clothing is essential and which is not.

• Our conversations about our regrets over leaving our three grandchildren for three months were minimized dramatically by the positive mindset and unconditional support we received from the grandchildren's parents. "Travel, learn and enjoy, it's your retirement years," were the loving embraces we clung to when we felt sad about leaving them. The grandkids were a bit too young to understand where Rome was in comparison to New Hampshire. A world map, Google Maps, books about Rome, which they had in their basement library and a few in their bedrooms that we read to them, and finally, online virtual simulations of Ancient Rome proved to be the comfort zone to make the "real" connections for where we would be for a while. We explained that the Colosseum was not going to be our "go-to place" nor would we be living near there while in Rome. Our biggest booster for our reluctant confidence to stay in touch with the three of them was Skype. The "Stay in Touch" telecommunications application specializes in providing video chats between computers, tablets and phones. Skype would solve the communication problem without having to analyze and evaluate it any further.

PART THREE

Living in Rome

I heard a resounding "Found it!" Yes, Em had found a one-bedroom basement apartment with a ground-level patio priced a tad under budget but utilities not included, near three parks, shops, and buses and trams. We researched the neighborhood of Trieste, and that provided us with the three essential solutions to our accommodations:

- The cost for three months was within our budget.
- We wanted to be in a residential area with parks and green areas, walkability and away from the liveliness and busyness of Centro Storico of Rome.
- Easy bus or trolley access.

Em's like that: Give her a problem or situation, and she will find the best method to solve it; she doesn't need a list.

I anxiously read the description: one bedroom, bathroom with shower, kitchen, study room, and small patio. Near public transport and the Villa Borghese and Museum. That's it; we can walk to the Borghese anytime we wish.

I read some of the reviews, the latest ones first. Here is one: "Simona and Giuliana were the best of hosts and were always prompt in responding to any requests," dated December 2009 from a chap from Australia. Another review was earlier, September 2008: "The hosts were very friendly, the area was safe, and the public transport stop was five minutes from the flat. A 15–20 minute walk to the Borghese and to two other parks nearby. We had a wonderful 3 months stay. Thank you Simona and Giuliana." The three additional reviews were as reassuring as these.

I immediately emailed the owners at 6:01 p.m. our time to make sure the apartment was available for our dates, January to March. I, for some reason, thought I would receive a reply in a few hours, but nothing. Em reminded me that there was a six-hour time difference, meaning that the owners received my inquiry at 12:01 a.m. She's like that.

Next day at 2 p.m., a reply. I had been checking my email every 30 minutes because I didn't want us to miss out on this opportunity; also, I was really excited about this property to rent. The email reply was straightforward: yes, the apartment was available for the three months of January–March. If we were interested, we must confirm the arrangements by sending a "holding deposit" that would be used against the first month's rent. The security deposit of one month would be given to the owner upon arrival. The email was signed, "Regards, Simona and Giuliana." What brought confidence into my perpetual realm of suspicion was that their English was perfect. I read the "Member" notation that accompanies Sabbatical adverts, and it said that Simona and Giuliana were both graduates of the University of Rome, one in classics and the other in international relations. They both have done research studies in Paris, Cambridge and Princeton. Well, that answered the question about English; it would mean we could converse with them in English about any queries we might have. I asked Em, "Are they partners or sisters or shared owners?" She said, "Does it really make a difference? We can have the apartment—that's all we can ask for at the moment."

As instructed, the "holding deposit" was sent at 10 a.m. our time in order to arrive at their bank at 16:00 hours their time. They requested we send payment via PayPal to their address, and a receipt would immediately follow, and it did. The owners sent us the address of the apartment: 3 Via Adige, in Trieste, Rome. Em immediately suggested that we use Google Maps; we used the street person to look up and down the streets in and around our location. The neighborhood looked residential, lots of graffiti on the walls. "What the hell," I responded. Directly across the street from number 3 Via Adige looked like a café or restaurant. "That would be super," I exclaimed, as I'm easily pleased.

Over the next few days we communicated to them about how to get from the Leonardo da Vinci International Airport to the apartment. What are the temperatures? I could have looked that silly question up on AccuWeather. How much are the utilities going to be for three months? Is there a supermarket nearby? Every response was clearly framed with precise directions from the airport to the apartment and addresses of the nearby pharmacies and supermarkets. The question regarding utilities was a bit more difficult for an accurate reply. They indicated that electricity is expensive in Italy, and the heating, hot water and washer were operated by electricity; the stove was gas. So, it depends on how much you use electricity and cooking. I didn't need to ask such a dumb question, but I did.

We have three days before we leave from Boston to Dublin to Rome.

From my list of everything we need to do, we checked them off to make sure: passports, identification-license, computer, cords, credit and debit cards, 200 euros purchased from our bank (placed in my neck pouch along with a copy of our passports and credit card numbers), and a few books, notebooks, pen and ink. Those items fit safely into my Safepac backpack. Clothes, toiletries, travel scale, etc., went into the carry-on bag. We received a wonderful and caring acknowledgment that Simona and Giuliana would be pleased to pick us up at the airport and take us to the apartment. We were elated. I was concerned and jittery about taking other alternatives such as the Roma Airport Bus or the Express train nonstop from the airport to the Termini Station and finding another bus to our apartment. They did not recommend a taxi, as it would be expensive. They mentioned where we should meet them at the arrival Gate IA. We, in turn, provided them with the flight number and our time of arrival.

We spent the remaining two days with our daughter, son-in-law and the two boys, trying to hide the fact that we would miss them terribly. We Skyped our son, daughter-in-law and granddaughter, Annika, told them how much we would miss them, and promised to Skype every Sunday. And finally, our daughter, the oldest and cleverest of the lot, had nothing but best wishes for us as we started our quest to study and learn as seniors in their year abroad plans.

We arrived at Boston Logan International Airport via the C&J Bus Service at 2:45 for our 5:45 flight #1745. Fortunately, no delays, and after eight and a half hours, we arrived at 7:00 in the Dublin Airport. An easy flight, but I continued to have jitters and a headache. We left Dublin at 07:00 to arrive in Roma at 11:55 on Saturday; I still had jitters. Em's just fine; she's like that! It was a long walk to reach the Passport Control. I didn't have my passport out ready to show the officer, and he looked a bit annoyed, and more jitters. We were lugging our carry-ons and backpacks and purse bags through the overabundance of duty-free shops: liquors, cigarettes, jewelry, bookshops, Prada, Armani, Gucci, Zegna, Valentino, and finally found Gate A1 in the Arrivals. Em made sure that I did not get too far ahead and get lost, as she is like that, thankfully. Behold, along the line of chauffeurs, family and acquaintances waiting for their passengers, we see our first names written in Renaissance Chauncey Italian script on a 12" × 12" white cardboard. It was love at first sight, as I also write my notes using an Aurora fountain pen with a broad oblique Italic nib, which produces a similar semi-cursive script.

I love fountain pens. I have a small collection: two English pens, a Conway Stewart and Osmiroid; one Parker, once manufactured in America, now in France; a French Waterman; a German Pelikan; a Japanese Pilot Kakuno, and my Italian Aurora. Each pen has unique characters and nib variations to reflect my mood. Fountain pens translate your mind and heart. Moreover, a well-kept fountain pen can replace hundreds of disposable pens.

Standing behind the cardboard sign were two handsome, well-dressed women in matching scarves, leather boots (one in a shorter version, the other in very long boots), one in a smart black down coat and the other in a tan mid-length coat. Introductions were made—they were sisters—and we set off. I thought, respectfully, Giuliana and Simona were older than the picture they had sent to help us recognize them at the gate. But who am I to talk about looking old—that would have been Em's reply to my sometimes implicit biased thoughts about age. The sisters were perky and energetic and insisted that they push our luggage to their car. As we walked to the car park, we chatted briefly about the weather, as it was cold and cloudy at 08:00 hours. But "this is winter in Rome," Giuliana replied to my silly questions about the weather in winter in Rome. Em's thoughts: "How lucky we are to be able to live in Rome after retirement and on a fixed income." I had looked up the average weather for January–March in Rome. It was on my list of "Weather for Rome: January–February–March": The average temperatures in Rome in the winter are 45 degrees Fahrenheit or 7.5 degrees Celsius, and at night there, temperatures could easily go down to 0 degrees Celsius. Thinking ahead, not always the smartest thing to do in my case, I'm trying to guess the make of the car. What car would be able to carry four adults and essentially four bags and winter coats? Perhaps a European Ford, Volkswagen or Lancia, not really sure what brand these two urban-hipsters would be into.

OK, here we are—a red Fiat 500, a small two-door, four-passenger with a length of approximately 12 feet. I checked it out—I'm curious. They requested that since we had a long flight, we get into the car as they miraculously placed the two carry-ons and handbags in their small Fiat 500 trunk! Well, not entirely, as the two handbags were propped against the rear window, resting uncomfortably against my head, and it was impossible for the driver to see out the back window. I was jittery, cold and didn't want to talk but respectfully did. The drive from the airport to Via Adige took about three hours; it seemed like that but actually was about 45–50 minutes, not sure of the time as I tried to observe everything during the drive from the airport to the beginning of the center of Rome. I noticed that there was little traffic—when I asked about it, Simona said, "It is Sabato, a non-workday." Loved the surroundings: magnetic and energizing colors of crimson red, yellow ochre, burnt-orange, and plenty of graffiti melting into the patinated walls.

When we passed what looked like a brutalist, Neoclassical white building in the near distance, Giuliana said it was "the EUR business district of Rome."

"How old? And why build it out here?"

My first moment of wonder and joy in Rome. The building turns out to be the Palazzo della Civiltà Italiana, which is in the Esposizione Universale Roma (EUR).

"About fifty years, was built as the site for the 1942 world's fair, and Mussolini planned to celebrate his 20 years of fascism," she said, as her voice sort of trailed off to almost a silent whisper.

I said to myself: Myself, you will learn more about the EUR during our three months in Rome.

Arriving at 3 Via Adige, I helped unload the bags while the three women proceeded to unlock the hallway door, descend eight stairs, and employ the same set of keys that unlocked the hallway door, using a shift triple-lock maneuver, to spring the heavy black door open. These will be our living quarters for the next 90 days.

Tired, almost exhausted, not physically but mentally—so much new information to accommodate (i.e., to modify or change in my little mind so new information can fit in and then to assimilate this new information and add that information to what already exists in my mind)—mind-blowing! A new continent, country, city, history, culture, and a new definition of retirement.

Giuliana took over the explanations of the apartment while Simona apologized that she had to leave. The two most important aspects for us to know, Giuliana explained, were the triple locking of the door—two turns left, one turn right, key back to the center, and they locked, but double-lock. Is this an ominous sign of something I don't want to explore in my mind? She demonstrated three times. Em did it correctly on the first go; it took me three times, but my effort looked good. The second were the utilities and where the meters were located. Down under the hallway stairs, she showed us where the two meters for our apartment were located, the ones with the name "De Rossi." We can monitor our usage by checking the meters whenever we wish. However, I do not know and was afraid to ask how we determine the usage cost based on the meter calculation? I guessed this would be a trial and error or wait-and-see method until the first reading in two weeks. Lastly, Giuliana provided Em with the Internet password and mobilized the phones and computer. She was planning ahead for our Sunday Skype connections with family and grandchildren. She's like that…

The apartment: How fortunate are we to lease this somewhat eccentric basement apartment. Let me count the ways: The ten-foot ceiling in the living room–cum–sitting room, the largest room. Placed in the middle of the room near a long wooden table was a marble table with three Roman emperor busts, two of Marcus Aurelius. This bust seemed like he was trying to convey to anyone that paid attention to him, I, Marcus Aurelius, was a great philosopher; hear me out and reflect: "The happiness of your life depends upon the quality of your thoughts." I think that I will be talking to you as I read more about you, I said out loud to myself (I do that). The other bust of Aurelius had a stoic meditative quality in his profile. The third bust was a mystery, as many emperors kind of look similar. From the huge library of books on various subjects including art, history, architecture, international politics, social anthropology, and ancient medicines, I found a book about Roman emperors. I began in chronological order, starting with Augustus Caesar, all through to the last Roman Emperor, Flavius Romulus Augustus. I pick Flavius as the name of this bust that we'll be with every day for three months because I liked the movie *The Last Legion* with Colin Firth and Ben Kingsley, a great movie about Flavius. The room was dark, a deep-green paint, patina-looking wooden baseboards and door frames. I suppose someone might call this charming. Lamps were scarce: one stand-up with two bulbs and one small reading lamp with a 40-watt bulb on the side table near the rather "used but not abused" two-person couch. The oak kitchen table was equipped with three soup-bowl-size candles. On the walls were eight dark oil-colored landscape paintings, including forests, streams, trees and mountains and terraced fruit or olive trees, with no perspective. Perhaps candle smoke residue had something to do with the filmy coating on the artwork. In front of the couch was a small gas fireplace, I assumed to augment the two electric heaters on the opposite walls. Off the back of the sitting room was a single door leading to roughly 250 square feet or approximately the size of a one-car garage. Because we are in a basement apartment, the patio is lower than the sidewalk, consequently no view. It being winter, the several large terra-cotta planters hosting sleeping leeks, radishes, and other promising green plants are at rest and not attractive to spend time with. In the far corner is a splintered, small-length garden hose and a water spout with an old bucket hanging off the faucet. I noticed that there wasn't an awning to cover at least a portion of the patio. What does one do when the brilliant, hot sun is out over the patio? Just use the patio when the sun doesn't shine; now that's silly! No, we will see how the sun shines on the patio at different times of the day, like Impressionists who painted their focus point of a painting at different times of the day. A beautiful find, in a wondrous way, at the front of the patio hidden by the unattended English ivy, I think, was a pint-size Miele laundry machine. No directions on the machine. If I cannot find a user's manual in the apartment somewhere for this "garage find" machine, Em will know how to work it; she is like that.

Italians do not require large kitchens to produce great traditional and nutritional meals. This kitchen, in its original 1960s form, was functional with adequate counter space and the utilities accepting every bit of space. Perfect for one person in the kitchen. I guess Em and I will just take turns; she is like that. An electric stove and the dormitory-size refrigerator are tucked under the cabinets. There was no pantry and very little storage space to build up an inventory of everyday products. Perhaps we have to purchase enough food for a day or two and shop again; it sounds like fun shopping at the open markets and specialty shops.

I am making a list of questions concerning the patio, like when to plant and what to plant in the garden. Another list suggests the possible cost of using the electricity for heating, showers and the other heaters in the small study and bedroom. In addition, another list has ideas on how we could possibly make more efficient use of the utilities. This was in anticipation of the first electric and gas meter reading in two weeks. I'm like that.

Bathroom, mold free! I am allergic to mold, dust and a dozen or so trees and grasses. The poor lighting over the sink will be a challenge for shaving and makeup preparation. No tub, of course. Single-person-size functioning shower; I'm thinking we can save on water heating with this small arrangement.

The small study or drawing room, half the size of the patio, was made smaller with the floor-to-ceiling book shelves complete with Italian mystery, art, architecture and history and photos of the two sisters in different stages of their lives. There are an Ikea desk, lamp and chair.

The bedroom, the last room in the apartment, is the size of two study rooms, with two wardrobes, a queen-size bed with a bamboo carved headboard, a relatively firm mattress, and two soft pillows. We brought two hypoallergenic pillowcases; we always bring them. Em indicated that if the pillows are not right, we can purchase different ones at Rinascente that she saw when coming from the airport. Once again, the two floor-to-ceiling bookcases absorb most of the room. However, it's a very interesting array of books ranging from university textbooks, lab books and reports to Italian, English and American fiction and nonfiction, mostly history books. A library for everyone! Exciting.

I am a little paranoid about robberies. It has never happened, but I'm an American living in a neighborhood with graffiti on every wall; streetlights are nonexistent, and we're in an apartment building with eight apartments, people we have not met, in fact we haven't heard a sound as yet.

At the airport I withdrew 200 euros to have available when the electric and gas bills arrive (no credit cards) and in case some establishments don't or won't take credit cards. That was a lot of money, and I had no idea how long that sum of euros would last. How could I? Anyway, I brought with me a cutout, old, hardcover book (*A Tale of Two Cities*) cut larger than the U.S. ten-dollar bill to fit my euros in once I was at the apartment. I placed the euros that were in my neck pouch into the cutout book and placed it on the second shelf between Dickens and Twain over our bed. That assured me that our money would be safe from any intruders. Every day I would simply take out enough euros that I thought we would need, put them in my neck pouch, and on my list I'd place our expenditures for each day until I got a reasonable handle of cash flow.

Giuliana indicated that they both lived nearby, gave us their mobile number, and told us to call them if we needed anything. As I walked with her to the hallway door, I noticed that the noise level in and around our apartment was negotiable, so far! I said to myself, sure it's dinnertime on Saturday, but what happens after dinner? Car horns, motor scooters and bikes, they are the loudest, and the all-night parties! We unpacked, placing our boots and winter coats in one wardrobe and the rest of our clothes in the other one. Em's watercolors, paper, pencils went in the study along with my notebooks and Aurora fountain pen. Everything in its place for our long stay. We are staying on local time even though we have been up all night and half of today without any sleep. Staying on the country's time seems to allow us to avoid jetlag. Still, one last item of business before we collapse is to get something to eat now and for breakfast tomorrow. I made a list: fruit, milk, tea, cookies, breakfast cereal, sugar, yogurt, bread and cheese. Simona mentioned where the supermarket was located, three blocks past the tabacchi and across from the farmacia. I remembered this part as I made the clever association of the word tabacchi with tobacco and farmacia with pharmacy but forgot how many blocks and which way. Em remembered—she is like that!

Entering the small sub-market, we picked up a wire basket. Em previewed my list and said she would look around while I should pick some fruit.

The produce was just inside the entrance door, not a large selection I deduced since it was winter. I carefully observed: the apples—Fuji, Golden Delicious, and Granny Smith, Clementines, persimmons, pears, lemons, grapefruits, and some other kinds I wasn't familiar with. I thought we'd get a couple of Granny Smiths, Em's favorite, and two pears. I began to touchy-feel the pears until I got scolded by another shopper in a language I didn't understand but knew that sound when my grandmother would scold me for all sorts of misbehaviors. She pointed to the plastic gloves hanging right beside the produce bags. I get it, but I guess she didn't want me to contaminate the food with my grumpy hands. I adroitly laid the glove on my right hand in an effort to show that I had done this before but merely forgot this time and selected two apples and two pears; I looked around to see if Em had caught the act. Em's an excellent food shopper. In her own basket she had the milk, Parmalat 2%, Twinings Earl Grey tea, cereal (nutrition e fibre), demerara sugar, two La Fermiere yogurts—vanilla bean, a small Italian cheese sampler. We both selected the same Abbracci cookies; I suggested we take two, but "one is enough."

Not going straight to bed after the long flight and drive from the airport actually gave us both a "second wind," as they say. Mentally exhausted but physically managing quite well. We got in line where it said "cassiere" for checkout. I noticed the cashier was sitting down, not standing up to make transactions, a brilliant idea. I noticed too that most people had their own bags and were bagging their goods themselves. I was also aware that an older woman cut in front of me and smiled; I smiled back but didn't mean it. I would put on my grocery list to bring shopping bags next time. We get to the cashier and carefully place the apples on the conveyor belt when the woman says to me in perfect Italian something like, "deva pesare la melly." Em said, "You forgot to weigh them and put the price on the bag." Before we could proceed, I had to go back and find the picture chart of all the fruits and vegetables, find Granny Smith, weigh them, wait for the price ticket to emerge and do the same for the pears. Back in line, there's some chatting with customers before she gets to me. After I bagged, gave her the Visa card, and said "grazie," we sauntered back, elated to get back to our flat.

Quick showers, "Your future depends on your dreams, so go to sleep" (M. Barazany), and we did.

At 08:00, the phone rang. Giuliana wanted to make sure we were fine; her kindness and reassurance were a wonderful way to start our time in Rome. Em was excited; I was anxious to explore our neighborhood.

Across the street at number 16 or 18, part of the number was blurred with graffiti, was Marco's Café. Marco, the owner we presumed, was a short, well-built chap who gave us a friendly "buongiorno." Em ordered due cappuccini and a small, almond cream tart. He did not speak English, but Em worked out a conversation about what to see around here. He pointed out a neighborhood called "Quartiere Coppede." I had thoroughly researched this area on the Google Map before we left, and it indicated about a five-minute walk from the apartment. Our first area of discovery and exploration as slow travelers in Rome was just around the corner in the Coppede neighborhood.

The Beatles jumped into this Frog Fountain in the 1960s.

We entered through a rusticated gate along Via Salaria to the middle of Piazza Minco, where there was an interesting fountain of the frogs (Fontana delle Rane), a two-tiered basin decorated with shells and human figures and at the rope were eight frogs sitting on the edge. Straight on was the Fontana delle Rane. As this was built in 1924, the style is in keeping with the architecture of the neighborhood. A rough count of perhaps 35–40 villas, named after fairies, and buildings are in this neighborhood. My personal reaction was it is perhaps an interesting and insightful entry into a fairyland. Em read about this neighborhood and pointed out the eclectic Liberty style that was designed by Gino Coppede. "Rome's best examples of Art Nouveau are found here," I commented. Em pointed out a dash of Greek influences, Liberty, akin to Baroque, touches and other playful and amusing details. Summing up, this compact quarter was a mishmash of Tuscan turrets, Baroque sculptures, Moorish arches, Gothic gargoyles, frescoed facades and palm-fringed gardens—all designed in the 1920s. We saw an estate agent's for sale sign that had a four-bedroom house in this area for a cool 8,800,000 euros. That is only about 10,000,000 USD; mind you, no garage and parking is on the street!

Whoa, for our first venture out, we shall continue to learn more about this neighborhood, I mumbled to myself.

Together, we made an "option list" of what and where we might do and go the first week or so in Rome. I suggested the first couple of days let's explore our neighborhood. Em confidently indicated that if we are to discover and explore the historical center of Rome, we need to use public transport. Looking through the three-page folder that the sisters left for their tenants that contained recommended restaurants, cafés and markets that were close by, I found what the previous tenant from Australia had left for the next renter: a detailed bus schedule, bus pickup locations and bus numbers to almost every area of Rome. In addition, he left a hand-drawn map of the bus stops and bus routes to various tourist attractions. Em is amazing at working out bus schedules and numbers, but this will provide her with a heads-up. On the list were the possible options for the week:

- Orient and observe the immediate neighborhood, from locating shops, cafés, and tabacchi to purchasing bus and tram tickets and tickets for the Borghese Museum.
- Purchase bus tickets and head to Piazza Navona.
- Find two Caravaggios at the Popolo church.
- Visit across the river to Trastevere. "Basta"—enough for this week!

Tuesday, 41 degrees Fahrenheit, perfect for a long walk to the largest park in Rome. "Buongiorno Marco, due cappuccini, e due cornetti, por favore," I proudly proclaim my much-practiced Italian phrase. Cornetti is a little horn-shaped croissant. We wanted to establish a friendly relationship with Marco, as his coffee is fresh, tasty, inexpensive and just across the street. For today, we mapped out roughly the trek to find the Borghese Gardens. Em's great at this sort of important task. We walked the 1.3 kilometers to the Borghese Gardens and Museum. First, we'd secure tickets to see the massive collections of Ancient, Renaissance and neo–Classical art. We were politely told that we need to schedule a time and date for entrance. I assumed they did not wish to have too many observers in the gallery at the same time. We scheduled our date and time, paid 30 euros for the two tickets; satisfied that we had accomplished that, we set off to enjoy the gardens.

As we lingered to explore the gardens, we found three "secret" spaces and gardens: one with trees with an eagle fountain in front of the adjacent mansion; the other was the flower garden, laid out in a formal garden design. The third garden was in front of the aviary, near the Meridiana mansion, which a plaque explained was designed by one of the leading Baroque architects of the 17th century, Carlo Rainaldi. We knew that we would visit these gardens many times during our slow travel stay, take the slow stroll back to Via Pinciana to Via Allegri to Via Po to Via Tagliamento and down the street to #3 Via Adige. For our second day in Rome, we felt energized, confident, although I still had jitters, and finished off the enjoyable day with a quiet meal at our oversized wooden table together. I made a list of those sights and events and what to revisit.

It's cold, 40 degrees Fahrenheit—no sun to warm us up today. We stop at Marco's; he appears pleased to see us. "Stesso ordine"? Same order, I nod, as I recognize ordine as order. Em goes to look at the fresh pastries and orders due cornetti instead of one. We spend time sitting here, our little cozy café, as almost every customer stands at the bar where the coffee espresso is half the price. We work out what we plan to do and how to accomplish it. From my list we planned to purchase bus tickets to Piazza Navona. We had learned what some of the major attractions around there were, but we wanted to discover more.

Right! We head to the tabacchi on Via Chiana #44 to purchase bus tickets. I know from research that we can purchase an ATAC—the monthly pass—for about 35 euros or $44. The individual 100-minute bus ticket cost 1.50 euros or two at three euros for approximately $3.45. If we use the bus or tram 13 times per month, we break even; any more usage is basically free rides. We planned to use the bus as often as required to reach sites too far to walk.

I noticed that the tabacchi are open long hours, and the attendant was very efficient as he asked me, "possibly aiutarta signore"; before I could take out my phrase list to ask for a monthly bus pass, he was off to another customer who was buying cigarettes. From my list of phrases I said, "buongiorno, vorry acquire un mensile a tac." Well, that was not the correct accent from the actual written phrase, "vorrei acquistare un abbonamento mensile ATAC." The very kind man somehow figured out what I was asking for, and I gave him a 50-euro bill, and I had our monthly tickets and my 15-euro change. I was sweating when I left; it was 40 degrees Fahrenheit outside. I just told her that "it was very warm inside the place." Em found the bus stop on Via Nazionale bus #64 stop at Corso Vittorio Emanuele, and we'd walk 1,000 feet to Piazza Navona.

A 30-minute ride, 20-minute walk, and we see the 15th-century oblong square, a former sporting stadium built in 86 BCE. From my list we are to find Sait' Agnese in Agone, a 17th-century Baroque church. But first, we were overwhelmed by the Fountain dei Quattro Fiumi, the most famous fountain by Gian Bernini. The fountain represents the major rivers of the continents where papal authority have spread: the Nile, Danube, Ganges and the Rio dela Plata, South America. Unfortunately, I didn't check the opening times for the church—I will add that column (opening-closing times) to my ever-growing list, and that Baroque beauty was closed. Not to worry, as we spent our time lingering, observing, and enjoying more fountains (e.g., Fontana del Moro and Fontana del Nettuno, both creations by Michelangelo's student, Giuseppe Porta). The day was getting short, and I did not want to miss our bus, so we walked to the Pantheon, built by Augustus as a place to worship all the gods. We just stood still and admired this 125 CE Roman temple, knowing that we would observe it more closely soon. Returning to our bus stop, Em remembered exactly where it was—she is like that—and 60 minutes later we are in our cave ... I mean basement apartment. Time for Em to play with her sketches and me to rewrite my lists and notes.

Marco's—our silent friend doesn't ask; he just intuitively knows for the past five days we always order the same—and I nod, "Si, Marco." We had planned to bus over to the Piazza Popolo. Em uses our detailed, designed map left by that brilliant Austrian chap to guide our public transport: the bus stops and routes to these touristy locations. A "molto gracies, chao" to Marco as we left. As we were walking to the bus stop to wait for our #63 bus, Em explained that I just said thank you very much in half Italian and Spanish; you say, MOLE-TEH–GRAHT-SEE-EH. I'm embarrassed, but I know that failure is instructive, and I'll do better tomorrow, I promised myself. A short bus ride to the next stop, and we wait 15 minutes for bus #19 to Piazza del Popolo—the People's Square; the buses were very busy due to the early morning departure, I deduced. We entered through the third-century Porta, and smack in front was the Egyptian obelisk, one of 13 in Rome. From our readings, it was brought to Piazza del Popolo in 10 BCE from Heliopolis in lower Egypt during the reign of Augustus. But we wanted to see the Caravaggio's in the Santa Maria del Popolo. However, we were drawn like a huge magnet to the center of the square where a large fountain, gushing with fresh water, and two giant lions had been guarding their home for centuries. We are walking further away from the Caravaggios at the church of Santa Maria del Popolo by walking to the north gate, which was once the gateway in the third-century Aurelian wall and one of the major gateways into the old city. Standing majestically were Santa Maria dei Miracoli (1597) and Santa Maria di Montesanto (1675). The two churches look very similar from our distance, but as we drew closer, careful observation told us differently. We learned that a design adjustment, due to space considerations, had resulted in one church, Santa Maria dei Miracoli, having an octagonal dome, whereas Santa Maria di Montesanto has a dodecagonal one. However, for us, the square's major church is Santa Maria del Popolo (1442–47), one of the best examples of a Renaissance church in Rome. The church was a treasure trove of art, including: sculptures by Bernini; Apse designed by Donato Bramante; exquisite work by Pinturicchio; Raphael's design of the Chigi Chapel; and two of Caravaggio's most religious paintings in the Cerasi Chapel, "Crucifixion of St. Peter" and "Conversion of the way to Damascus" (1600).

We observed, lingered and felt how the art was so compelling. John Dewey mentioned, "art is the most effective mode of communication that exists"; it moves you in a physical and emotional sense that is hard to explain. This was our destination for today, to have the good fortune to observe these magnificent structures and appreciate those masterpieces of Mannerist art. Two buses back, and we are back at the apartment. We have lunch, Em works on her drawings, and I write my notes in my reflections: The Peoples' Square was a pleasure to enjoy and wonder what all these people are seeing and thinking. I commented on the masterful art we observed today: Caravaggio's, Bernini, Bramante, and Raphaels.

I reflect: Devotional art was not meant as a work of art but for a religious purpose, usually in a religious setting. Religious art in a church provides a context to assist observers to understand the works and how they were meant to be seen. The question I have is, should devotional art made for churches be taken and placed in a museum? What would be the argument for devotional museum art to be returned to the churches where they were originally made for hundreds of years?

A 40-degree Fahrenheit day greets us as the sunshine makes us happy. We stop in to see Marco, his wife, Benita. I make a decent attempt to order due cappuccini e uno cornetto, which must have worked, as Benita brings my order over to the table. Em asked, "dov'e Marco?" She responded, "con duo padre" and hustles to attend to a line of

These "twin" churches, located in the Piazza del Popolo, are Santa Maria di Montesanto and Santa Maria dei Miracoli, designed by Rainaldi and revised by Gian Lorenzo Bernini. They look similar, but with careful observation there are differences both outside and inside.

customers. We have our plans to visit Trastevere. We reflect on what slow travel means, to take the time to carefully observe, orient and study the environment, whether it is a building, neighborhood, café or park. The purpose and value of learning comes from discovering and exploring the world around us, and that is our motivation to continue to seek out learning opportunities. We take bus #63 to Trastevere. There are a number of ways to get to Trastevere (which means "across the Tiber River"). We chose to walk to the Ponte Fabricio, the only original bridge in Rome, that connects the island from the northeast side. Trastevere is a character place and full of energy. Isola, the island that has existed since 293 BCE, now serves as a hospital.

There's a café smack in the center of the Piazza San Maria in Trastevere and directly in front of the Basilica. We luckily found two seats in front of the wall of oranges, as the essence seemed to be everywhere. Caffè delle Arance, as the name implies, oranges are in abundance.

Fifteen steps from the café is the Basilica of Saint Cecilia in Trastevere dated from the ninth century but rebuilt in the 18th century. Some highlights:

The Byzantine mosaics, 12th-century stuccos and 16th-century frescoes, were remarkable masterpieces. When I looked down, I discovered an intricate tapestry of Carrara marble, glass and precious stones swirling in patterns of serpentine, circles and squares—Em says, "It's the Cosmati floors." During this time period churchgoers stood up to receive the message; therefore, the floors became an important visual attraction as they certainly were today. The magnificent marble carpeted floors by the Cosmati brothers are present in many of the churches in Rome.

Our first restaurant lunch since we arrived, Da Enzo's, a family-operated trattoria at Via dei Vascellari was wonderful, their food, services and atmosphere.

Every opportunity to take a detour is a surprise when we slow travel. After a leisurely walk over Ponte Sisto, we find San Nicola in Carcere at Via del Teatro di Marcello, near the Teatro Marcello. We learn that San Nicola in Carcere was built in the 11th century in the ruins of three temples. The oldest temple (observed by the remains of Doric columns) was built in the second century BCE.

A fabulous day—from the beginning to the end.

Saturday. Wash and clean day. Just like everyone else. We had nothing planned as we do not know how long the wash would take or the cleaning of the flat. Em worked out the

People-watching with ambiance.

operation of a tiny washing machine. The capacity was one top sheet, socks, and two dish towels—that's all. The setting was for "lavaggio veloce." After 55 minutes, the machine rattled to a stop, we placed the sheet on the drying rack with the two towels and socks. Next load, next.... By lunchtime the cleaning, vacuuming, bathroom, mirrors, dusting and general sanitizing of the shower and toilet were completed; the wash continues. After the last load, Em indicates that it is time for a walk; I love "walking in rhythm, moving in sound, humming to the music, trying to move on…"; the Blackbyrds' lyrics are stuck in my little brain. Yes, I'm walking in rhythm. We have three parks within 25 minutes of our flat, having not explored Villa Torlonia, a 20-minute walk from Via Adige to Corso Trieste to Via Nomentana through a classy and tidy residential neighborhood. Sights seen: Former residence of the Mussolini family, used in 1944–1947 the property was occupied by the Allied High Command, various species of palm trees and the Casina delle Civette. The House of Owls was designed in 1840. The motif of the little owl was used widely in the decorations and furnishings. The 20 rooms include 54 pieces of Liberty-style stained glass.

Reflections: This park was lovely. Small children ran around the statues, some climbed onto the statues, others ran around the walkways. Plenty of benches to meditate the time away and relax and reflect in the silence of time. Hopefully, the last load will be finished.

Sunday. Our Skype day—six-hour time difference. We arranged to phone both our son and daughter at 12 our time, 18:00 their time. The grandchildren sounded happy with their school, Lego sets, friends, climbing trees and recess. One grandson showed us his landscape watercolor painting from his art class at school. Everyone was fine, not really missing Emmy and Poppy, just being young children.

It's our first day that we can do some thinking, writing, researching, planning, and reflecting. The neighborhood is very special due to having three large parks, Via Ada, the largest park in Rome, Villa Borghese (Museum Borghese), and the park-gardens of Villa Torlonia. I made sure to add on to my to-do list to include putting some plants and flowers on the patio when temperatures are appropriate for plants and flowers. I'll research the proper plantings for spring.

Several essential questions that we often discuss and think on: What is our purpose or reasons to rediscover the joys of travel? What are we giving up to slow travel? What are the benefits? Is traveling a passion or a purpose?

John Dewey, an American philosopher, psychologist and educator, one of my influencers in my educational endeavors, reminds me "that we do not learn from experiences alone, we learn from reflections on those experiences" in *Experience and Education*. In other words, we, Em and I, must reflect on those interactions of events, sights, objects of art and people if we are to learn and gain an understanding about art and culture. We cannot fall into the "had the experience but missed the meaning" sort of behaviorism; that is, we don't learn simply by a response to environmental stimuli; we must think about thinking.

Purpose and passion are often muddled together, as if they were aligned as one impact that encompasses peace of mind and happiness. Our purpose, our reason to slow travel, as it was many years ago, is what we were placed on this earth to do, an outward WHY impact that compels and motivates us to enjoy every reflective moment. Our passion, it seems, is more a WHAT, an inward impact that leads to our excitement, emotional charges, and motivations that transcend from traveling and interacting with art and architecture. The What and Why will meet together at some point—the purpose of why and passion of what will realign. We have accepted the truth that learning has no end beyond itself; for us it is the end.

The wash is still hanging on the two clothes racks that were provided. The cotton sheets took ever so long to dry. Em and I took turns ironing to help the drying process along. Fortunately, we had another set of sheets while the others dried.

We used the three electric heaters attached to the three walls but could not get the clothes racks close enough to dry the sheets. The wall heaters did work well for the socks, underwear, shirts, etc. It's Monday, so we need to do some grocery shopping. From my list I had three markets close by: Carrefour, Coop and Standa. Slipping the cloth shopping bags around my arm we walked six blocks, and we are at Carrefour. I have my list: fish, fresh produce, dairy, canned and frozen goods. We need peanut butter (if available fine) and a spatula. Mondays might be the best day to shop as every shelf was packed and fewer shoppers than expected. I even found a small jar of Skippy peanut butter, expensive at $7. That will have to last until June, I say to myself. I had learned to always use a glove, when they were available, before exploring the maturity of the fruit. Overall, it's a wonderful experience to shop with a manageable list so we don't buy goods we don't need.

Finished the ironing, so the rest of the day is ours.

The day begins with temperatures in the 40s degree F. An exciting day as we are off to Villa Borghese and the Galleria Borghese. Our timed and dated tickets are in hand, and 35 minutes later we are at the entrance of the Borghese. The gallery of art, for me, was a numinous moment to moment experience. What initially began as a lingering observation of the Greek and Roman sculptures and artifacts turned out to be an even sweeter surprise as the Musée du' Louvre lent 60 of their famous masterpieces dating from the sixth century BCE to the 17th century to the Borghese. When Napoleon was emperor of France, also king of Italy in 1807, his sister married a Borghese. Being a king, he took those 60 masterpieces and placed them in the Louvre, where they are permanently kept. These 60 pieces made an already impressive gallery even more special. We lucked out for sure. Too many painting masterpieces and sculptures to mention, as we need to study more about the artist and period. However, we shall return with more information and a study about the artists—paintings—sculptures. We were allowed 45 minutes, and they were strict about it. The entrance line was drifting far past my vision of sight.

As we approached the east side exit from the Borghese, we saw a nursery—preschool—half in and half out of the garden. The entrance gate was open, and I decided to go in and see if anyone spoke English (parla-inglese). At first, the guardian at the door, signor Sergo, said, "NO!" Em intervened in her determined, yet very pleasant smile and attempted to explain to Sergo, along with a couple of teachers and parents who were present, that we were early childhood teachers from the states. After words of encouragement were related to Sergo, he let us go in with one of the teachers. The teacher, Matteo, spoke a few words in English, basically, "venire" (come). Matteo showed this new preschool in the Borghese park that overlooked the Galleria and the beautiful gardens that surround the Galleria. The school playground was actually in a garden of oregano, basil and snowdrops and anemone. The school was clean, bright, colorful and even had snowmen and snowwomen made by the children displayed nicely in a row on the manicured display board. In the middle of the visit we met another teacher, Gianna; she spoke perfect English, and away we went as she told us about the school serving the children in the immediate neighborhood. The school (Scuola dell'Infanzia-Giardino Incantato) "enchanting garden" is a commune of Rome-county preschool (ages 3–5 years), not a state school. We intuitively recognized the way the classrooms, the low, open shelves, and the Montessori-designed sensorial materials were neatly and orderly in place. Asked about the school's philosophy, Gianna smiled brightly as she mentioned that the school was a sort of blending of Montessori with a Reggio Emilia spirit! We observed the prepared environment and Montessori pink tower, arithmetic boxes, sandpaper letters, cylinders and rods but could not discern exactly where was the Reggio Emilia "spirit." If we are invited back with children, we might be able to observe the Reggio Spirit in action. Gianna offered us to come back next week when she would be at the school only in the morning. Just another diversion on a slow travel day that always seems to foster a revelation and an occasion to learn something new and exciting.

"We will take bus #603 to Tagliamento, and bus #106 to Via Corso and walk to the Pantheon," Em is on it.

The Pantheon has to be one of the absolute favorite structures in all of Rome and for good reason. From our readings, the Pantheon is the best-preserved example of an Ancient Roman monumental building and has influenced Western architecture from at least the Renaissance (e.g., Brunelleschi's dome of Santa Maria del Fiore in Florence, completed in 1436). From the 26 coffers' panels to the round oculus streaming sunlight to the basin below, the Pantheon is special in every way. Interestingly, it was converted to a Christian church in 609 CE; therefore, its long survival as a place of worship kept it from being destroyed. However, the gilt bronze roofing tiles. Constantine (633) stripped the gilt bronze tiles and sent them to Constantinople, and Pope Urban VIII (1625) melted them to cast the Baldacchino about St. Peter's altar.

Studying the exterior design, Em's an art quilter, has a keen eye, and is a competent

Reconstruction on the Pantheon (pictured) in Rome began with Trajan and was completed with Hadrian in 125 CE.

mathematician as she points out that the exterior height is exactly equal to its diameter, with no supporting structures. The monument also houses the tombs of Victor Emmanuel II and Raphael.

The classical symmetrical design of the Pantheon can be detected in many buildings of the 19th and 20th centuries such as numerous city halls, universities (e.g., University of Virginia and Columbia University), and public libraries (e.g., Manchester Central Library in England), which replicate its portico-and-dome structure. The dome-and-portico design we see over the world all began here at Rome's Pantheon.

Another cold but sunny day awaits us with temperatures ranging from 40 to 52 degrees F. As is our de rigueur routine, we pop in at Marco's. He nods, I nod, and he brings over the coffee and cornetto and sits down. Something was different. I imagined that Marco would want to charge us for all the times we sat in the dining area and only left the remaining change from the 2.80-euro coffee and cornetto. We always go to the counter to pick up our coffee and cornetto; it's the polite action to take. Marco says, "incontrare mia moglie, sia da Cuba" and looks over his shoulder to the bar. Em worked out that his wife, behind the counter making espresso, is from Cuba, and Marco wants us to meet her. "How do I say pleased to meet you?" Just say piacere—slowly please— pi-a-cere and smile. I stand up, and we meet Benita, a handsome, tall woman with long golden-yellow red hair in a bun gracing her smooth skin. She instantly smiles, and her bright, perfect white teeth are very noticeable and beautiful. She replies with a friendly "buongiorno"; it is busy, and she moves adroitly to make coffee while Marco talks to his regular customers. We were putting our bus numbers down on the file card; we keep the bus numbers and station stops on file cards so I can put them on my expanding bus list. The bus routes and stations that were left in the apartment were super starters to the major tourist sites, but we know that we are moving behind those particular sites if we are to explore Rome and other parts of Italy. We also remarked that Marco was our only Italian acquaintance, and we are thrilled, language barrier aside. I said we can teach Marco some English, in turn, Italian to us.

Only one incredible sight is planned, unless some diversions take us to another opportunity to discover: to observe Raphael's 1514 frescoes cycle that occupies two levels of the horizontal beam of the loggia arch in the Chigi Chapel of Santa Maria della Pace. The frescoes represent the Prophets and Sibyls.

From my list of opening times, Santa Maria della Pace was supposed to be open on Fridays from 9 a.m. until 12. However, it was closed when we arrived at 10:30. "We shall return," I exclaim!

Surprise! The Bramante Cloister is adjacent to the church. The cloister was perfectly sheltered from the busy historic center. The cloister was built in 1504 and reflects Bramante's earliest Renaissance concepts, like the simplicity of harmony and handsome proportioned spaces. Those Renaissance ideals of the rebirth of Greek and Roman aesthetics are obvious in this architecture. But, for me, it was the effects of light and shadow created by the arches and the columns on the upper mezzanine. Fortunately, the cloister was a perfect stop of due cappuccino, free Wi-Fi and an eagle's eye view of the harmonious cloister below.

Still cold in the mornings and at night (40 degrees F); afternoons are around 53–55 degrees. We are somewhat getting used to the rhythms of the weather and the culture of Rome.

Itinerary: I wrote two months in advance to secure the very limited entrance to

the Palazzo Farnese. This huge palace usually is not open to the public, but with a written request, if accepted, you can visit. My research indicated that this Palazzo is one of the most impressive High Renaissance palaces in Rome. We must seek out this opportunity.

Via Giulia, named after Pope Julius II, was designed by Giacomo Barozzi da Vignola, with guidance from Michelangelo in the 16th century, as a plan to build a square of roads near the Vatican. A wonderful street to stroll and linger on as you cannot get lost—straight as an arrow—and is wide enough so you do not have to dodge cars and scooters. We started at the ivy-covered arch, designed by Michelangelo, and walked to the Palazzo Farnese. The Palazzo Farnese (1517) was designed by Giuliano da Sangallo, a favorite architect of Lorenzo de' Medici and heavily influenced by Brunelleschi. The structure was built of huge blocks plundered from ancient monuments; it has to be one of the most magnificent palaces of Rome. The two-hour guided tour was in French, but we were so in awe of the paintings that it did not matter. Knowing that the guided tour would be in French, we did read about the history of the palace and the frescoes ("Love of the Gods") by Carracci beforehand.

On the great halls and Galleria Carracci frescoes were masterpieces painted by the Bolognese painter Annibale Carracci and his pupils. They are considered to be a major influence from Renaissance Mannerism to the new Baroque style in the 17th century. After the extinction of the Farnese family, it passed by inheritance to the King of Naples. Since 1936 it has housed the French embassy and the French school of archaeology of Rome. When Sangallo died, Michelangelo in 1589 finished the palace, adding beautiful cornices and the third floor. The magnificent courtyard was designed by three great architects: Sangallo, Michelangelo and Vignola. Most impressive—indeed.

Today is our "reality day," or meter reading day. Two weeks in the apartment and Giuliana will come to read the meter, and we will pay the huge fee, cash, of course. Giuliana is a cheerful and elegant woman. She's dressed in Max Mara winter attire, not exactly L.L. Bean. I have surveyed the meter downstairs, recorded on my list the movement of the numbers from our first day, but they mean nothing to me and I stopped. Giuliana shows me the electric meter readings on the left, the gas on the right. She showed me what the readings were when we arrived; evidently, she had copied those numbers down, but I did not notice. Amazingly, she computes the electricity cost: number of kWh used per day at 02.5 kW = 90 euros for 14 days. Whoa, at this rate we will have to economize or find some efficiencies to reduce the electricity cost. The gas bill was 50 euros, paid in cash. One hundred and forty euros or $160 for two weeks is astounding; we will begin immediately to reduce our utility consumption. Upon further review, Italy's electricity is produced mainly from natural gas, which accounts for more than half of the total. Italy, regrettably, has few energy resources, and most supplies are imported.

I make a list of possible efficiencies:

- Turn off radiators when we leave during the day;
- Turn radiators off at bedtime;
- Take shorter showers;
- Use water bottles for feet at bedtime;
- It will become warmer, less heat use and spend more time out of doors.

Wash, cleaning and dusting are on our agenda today.

Sunday is our Skype day. We hear that the grandchildren are flourishing at school, home, climbing trees, block building and hanging with their friends. We are so happy for them; they probably don't miss us. The wash is still hanging on the racks, window's open even though it is 45 degrees out.

I questioned our purpose and our passions; now I question what is educative, what are those conditions that make meaning, to understand?

A list in order:

- Identify our interests. We enjoy very much our continuing interest in and discoveries about art, architecture, history, music and literature.
- Is interest enough? Do our discoveries and explorations foster emotions and desires, like passions? Lost for words most of the time, we just want to experience more.
- Are these experiences, events, and objects we observed each day in Rome transitory, or are they enduring? Here we must come to terms with a related question. Are our interests mainly one of excitement and inspiration, or are they thought involved—do we think, study and understand their interconnections?
- Are the activities we seek out worthwhile intrinsically? Do we see a consequence beyond the immediate pleasure of a Raphael or Botticelli that engages us to further research and study it?
- Are we grasping the real meaning of an event, object or situation to see it in relation to other things (e.g., how and why are brush strokes applied to a painting, how do the barrel and fan vault or flying buttresses operate, what causes new movements in art, literature, music and culture, what can we learn from these experiences, and how can we put them to use during and after our slow travel time in Rome)?
- Are we thinking about thinking (metacognition) during these exciting times? What is our awareness and understanding of our own thought process?
- Finally, do we have a mechanism to monitor our progress in reaching our skill base, that is, real knowledge of visual arts and more? How do we improve and set up strategies to overcome these challenges and others.

Shopping at Carrefour, Em notices that the baby food jars contain foods such as horse meat, lamb, kidneys, carote e salmone, chickpeas and pumpkin, lentils, rabbit, veal and regular vegetables and fruits. Just in case we need a light snack, I guess?

On Sundays Marco's is closed. The wash we spread out over the racks and chairs in hopes they will at least dry enough so we can iron to completely dry them; we head off to our second-favorite café-cum-restaurant, Café Bartaruga. Playing continuously is an enjoyable assortment of jazz, disco, doo-wop and opera—we sat for two hours watching the tourists marvel at the fountain, which was just outside of the café. The fountain is of late Italian Renaissance style built around the 1580s. The bronze turtles are attributed to either Gian Bernini or Andrea Sacchi in 1658. The fountain is also on the Jewish walking tour; we shall return. Nothing without joy!

The weather is surprisingly sunny and a tad warmer at 48 degrees Fahrenheit. We were excited this morning to return for the second time to the Chiesa di Santa Maria della Pace, not far from the Piazza Navona. It is open, as advertised, and we're admiring the exterior of the church, and the adjunct Bramante cloister is energizing. But it is about the Chigi Chapel and Raphael's "Sibyls and Angels" (1514), four sibyls accompanied by angels in living and vivid color. There are only two other people in the church, so we have all the time to observe and linger. The interior of the church is rather unusual

Santa Maria della Pace (pictured) was decorated by Raphael and Peruzzi—architecture by Pietro da Cortona.

in that it comprises a short rectangular nave and an octagonal domed section. Also carefully observed is the elegantly painted "Madonna with Saints" by Baldasare Peruzzi, who worked with Bramante and Raphael.

Marco's: A "good morning" in English, no way! Marco is far ahead of me. "Molto bene, Marco," I replied. We're planning our next adventure to the Palazzo Barberini. The morning is rather cold, rainy and no sunshine, with temperatures ranging from 41 to 53 degrees F. For the past 15 days we have enjoyed coffee at almost every place we have been but not lunches or dinners. As we are on a fixed budget, we are still trying to adjust to the costs of transportation (monthly bus passes), museum entrance fees (most with no riduzione per pensionato), food and utilities of electricity and gas, which are still unknown. Our small basement apartment is heated by electricity, and the temperatures in the winter are chilly to cold; the electric bill will represent those temperatures. By having the meter read every two or three weeks (upon request) we will have a better sense of those expenses as well. As the temperature reaches a point where reduced electricity is required, eating out will be more manageable.

Today our itinerary looks busy. Sunday's wash is almost dry. We need to purchase our February bus and tram pass at the Tabacaria around the corner and bus to the elegant Piazza Barberini. Adjacent to the Piazza is the imposing and gorgeous 17th-century Palazzo Barberini, designed by Bernini, and its Galleria Nazionale d' Arte Antica. From our readings, we learn that the painting collections are the most important in Italy. We were first entertained, then entered into a learning mode to put other experiences together, when we reached the upper floor. Borromini's famous helicoidal staircase and his false-perspective windows are revealed. Borromini's windows are set in a false perspective that suggests extra depth, a feature in architecture that had been copied into the 20th century. Flanking the hallway are two sets of stairs and Bernini's large, grand squared staircase; both are masterpieces in design and function. The old masters from the 12th century to the 18th century are hung to perfection in the huge gallery. We are beginning to assimilate artists to the Renaissance and the Renaissance to the architecture, one of our major learning themes during this time in Rome. I think *absorbed* is the word to describe the paintings by Raphael, Caravaggio, El Greco, and Hans Holbein.

We returned after seven hours to find our wash hanging on the clothes rack was not entirely dry, although what do you expect if the radiators were off for seven hours? It is still too cold to open the windows to dry the clothes, so it will be another day before they are completely dry. This is what I call "need adjustment" in a foreign country. We don't need a dryer; it's expensive to operate. "I'll iron them," I mention silently to Em.

Two of my highlights, of many, were the special temporary exhibits of the 16th-century painter Giovanni Francesco Barbieri, better known as Guercino (1591–1666). As I read, he was heavily influenced by Caravaggio, but his paintings seem more expressive, a dramatic use of white without abandoning idealism; I'm feeling the connection here. And I'm having two of the greatest Renaissance architects, Benini and Borromini, who they say were once colleagues, then enemies, side by side to interpret for me.

Coffee with Marco. We learn that Marco and his wife, Benita, have two small children, and his father lives nearby. Em got this—"ho due figli e mio Padre vive nelle vicinanze." (Someday we hope to meet the children.) From my "possible site visits" list we selected to walk up the Spanish Steps (1723) to one of Rome's highest churches, Trinita dei Monti, but it's actually one of five French churches in Rome. The French Gothic elements, the pointed arch and cross-vaulted ceilings are easy to spot. The bell towers on each end give it symmetry and proportion. The interior is replete with period works of art by Daniele da Volterra and frescoes scenes of the Old and New Testaments by the Zuccaro brothers. We did not have a clue about these artists, so we researched to find out more. The purpose and value of learning new things comes from the world around us;

here was our new world. Daniele da Volterra, a Mannerist (style from the end of the High Renaissance to the start of the Baroque style) painter and sculptor (1509–1566) became a student and close friend of Michelangelo. Federico and Taddeo Zuccaro painted during the same Mannerist period. Although the brothers had similar styles, their differences were distinct (i.e., whereas Federico created a clear, detailed and carefully staged composition, Taddeo was more free-spirited, spontaneous and bold in his approaches). Learning about these differences and careful observation of their frescoes demonstrated which one did what. What fun! What enjoyment! We count that day lost if we don't learn something new about history, art or architecture.

Marco's was extremely busy, but we had a later start than usual. We are happy that his business appears to be very successful. I think the dapper gentleman in the impeccably ironed white shirt, blue blazer, with a pale blue double triangle fold, arranging the pastries is Marco's father. I made a note to put on my "to return" list to revisit the Galleria Nazionale d'Arte Antica as we only visited the Palazzo Barberini, not the Corsini Gallery. The gallery was across from the main entrance to Villa Farnesina. The Corsini seemed much smaller than the Barberini but certainly had equally impressive works of art. Whereas the Palazzo Barberini's collection was from the early Renaissance through the Baroque, the Corsini's collection displayed works from the 16th through the 18th centuries by such masters as Ruben, Jan van Eyck and Fra Angelico. Our favorite, though it's totally ridiculous to have a favorite, was Caravaggio's St. John the Baptist. We take a coffee and light lunch stop at Caffetteria-Bistrot at the Chiostro del Bramante. The setting of tranquility differentiates this café from all the rest as it is located on the top floor of the elegant Renaissance Chiostro del Bramante. We experienced friendly service, and the woman who took our order was very patient with us as we tried to decide our lunchtime treat. Three small portions of mozzarella and tomato baguettes, a collection of fresh tempura vegetables, and a bottle of water for 30 euros certainly will not break our bank. An enjoyable and very special day in Rome.

It's a cold 41 degrees Fahrenheit with pioggia forecast for the day. With this raining forecast, we will look at my list to select "A site using the bus." We dress for the cold and wet day ahead and slip over to have coffee at Marco's. His business seems to be better than ever as he only nods—same order—and "buongiorno" exchanges, and I pick it up at the counter. I learn a new phrase directed at Marco and Benita, "buona giornata," as we leave.

Em selected the MAXXI Museum at Via Guido Reno, 4a. This is the first national institution dedicated to contemporary art and architecture. She is a genuine fan of this period of art and architecture. I reserve my opinion until I learn more and understand more. The real adventure is getting to the MAXXI Museum. Em is a marvel at bus locations as three buses were involved to reach the museum.

The neighborhood we explore is northwest of the historical center of Rome. It is located at the 1960 Olympic Village. One must wonder, how have these neighborhoods remained the same since the Olympics? Nonetheless, we love these neighborhoods, as this is part of Rome that tourists and visitors miss partly due to their location and the difficulty getting to this section of northwest Rome.

The MAXXI building is an example of extraordinary contemporary architecture. The wet, soaked, gray, drab concrete building, not my favorite building material, was huge. Their permanent collection has over 75,000 drawings and projects. The travel adventure getting to the MAXXI was adventurous and thrilling. Em got us here!

Remarkable. The building was designed by the great architect Zaha Hadid, a celebration of her long-lasting relationship with Italy through an exhibition presenting both architectural and product designs by one of the most inventive and ingenious architects of our time. In fact, *The Guardian* hailed it as her finest work, a masterpiece fit to sit alongside Rome's ancient wonders."

On the trip back we stopped in the neighborhood of Parioli, one of the most expensive residential neighborhoods in Rome. Em worked out to get to Parioli we would take bus #53, then #13, and tram number 3 to arrive at Cingoli Caffé Pasticceria at Viale dei Parioli, 16a. We read, and the sisters both suggested as a special treat: to go to this local favorite café-cum-pasticceria. The cappuccini and due ricotta cannoli were absolutely fabulous. With this quality of coffee and pastries and tony neighborhood, the cost was about three times what we pay in our neighborhoods. However, we are beginning to taste what the good life for some folks is like in Rome.

Saturday: our ubiquitous wash, clean, dust day. Since I have both seasonal allergies and am very allergic to dust, I must vacuum several times a week and thorough dusting on Saturdays. For the first time, Em has a slight issue with her right knee. She twisted her knee several days ago and didn't feel any pain. We will have to watch and wait on this condition. We have gotten the wash down rather well. First the bottom sheet, socks and underwear in one load. Hang the sheet on one rack and other items on the second rack that was provided. The next load is top sheet, shirts—hung on our newly purchased third clothing rack. The rest of the laundry, dish and bath towels, etc., go in the last load. We do not want to use the radiators to dry the clothes, but opening the window a bit might help to dry. Ironing takes a while to finish off the drying process.

We are confident enough to let the washer run on its 55-minute cycle and go out and explore the wonders of Rome. I just don't want to be bound inside by the wash.

As for cloisters, many years ago I visited the Met Cloisters museum in Fort Tryon Park, New York, and from then on I have tried not to miss any cloisters (or cemeteries) from England to Spain in our previous travels. My take on cloisters, located usually on the south side of the church, is for their practical and religious purposes. You have a garden, open to light, oftentimes a cloister fountain, a sanctuary to meditate and pray, and a walking quadrangle surrounded by covered passages to move from place to place. A place to contemplate how fortunate we are to be able to live and slow travel in Rome. As Pope Francis stated, "How great is the joy and prophecy proclaimed onto the world by the silence of the cloister!" Nothing without Joy.

Marco's is closed on Sundays. We found Rasty Sas on Via Chiana a few weeks ago. Rasty Sas is favored by locals, and we just try to fit in as best as we can. It has become our coffee–cum–research home away from Marco's. Another chilly but sunny day. From my cloister list, Em indicates that we take bus #63 to Trastevere to observe two little-known 12th–15th-century cloisters:

- The cloister of the Nuovo Regina Margherita Hospital
- The cloister of San Giovanni d' Genoves

One of our recurring quests in Rome is to see all the hidden cloisters in Rome. After much research and Google Translate, we are off to discover and explore. Em mentioned that if we were in the Trastevere area, we might locate what the sisters reckoned to be the "best pizza" in Rome at Dar Poeta, at Via Bologna in Trastevere.

The first cloister is not that easy to find at the Nuovo Regina Margherita Hospital, a former monastery turned into a large hospital complex in 1970. Apart from the hospital staff, patients and families, few people know that the hospital grounds contain two spectacular cloisters. The first is medieval (1100s), the largest in medieval Rome, and the most impressive. Roman columns, ancient inscriptions and sarcophagi are scattered over the lawn. Beautiful orange trees will be blooming. The second Renaissance cloister is highlighted by twin columns, narrow brick arches, basins, and filled with fragments of ancient Roman inscriptions.

Among the maze of medieval buildings in the Trastevere district, off a side street, is the headquarters of the Brotherhood of St. John the Baptist, where I think is one of the most beautiful, hidden cloisters in all of Rome. The only access is via the church through a tiny door in the left-hand wall. It is so secret that the warden checked our bags very carefully, warning us not to take photographs. Em held up a pencil and sketch pad, and a dramatic and emphatic side to side nod meant no! He, just doing his job, carefully watched us the entire 55 minutes. If this becomes a tourist attraction, the place will be a monument in no time, as it was a haven of peace and silence. The ground floor has harmonic arches, the proportioned buttresses bridging into the octagonal columns that are bonded elegantly into an inspiring upper story. At the center is a remarkable 14th-century travertine well, set off by two ancient columns in Ionic style. Fragments of ancient Roman marble are scattered about. Most interesting for me were the painted walls covered with graffiti designs, inscriptions, ship outlines, and dates by the Genovese sailors. We were wondering what the graffiti was about and guessed perhaps the sailors were commenting on the quality and support of the hospital. This 15th marvel is a fantastic find for any tourist-cloister junky.

The day was growing short, our wash was probably rusting in the machine.

It's Sunday: Skype to everyone. The grandchildren only want to tell us about their playdates, tree climbing, Lego sets, and swimming lessons. Their friends and social time are developing into lasting enjoyment and happiness for them. We are so pleased; are they finding our replacement?

Sundays in Rome are family days, and everything slows down, especially in our residential neighborhood. It is a wonderful time to stroll and be happy.

Sundays are also our time to relax, rejoice, and think about our thinking as it relates to redefining our retirement purpose. We spend five or six days a week discovering and exploring the treasures of Rome: the museum art, church art, architecture, parks and the Italian culture; we look forward to slowing the pace and amplifying our reflection time.

There has been little known about learning styles or preferences for older adults like us. There have been studies to determine the learning preferences of older adults. D.A. Kolb's Learning Style Inventory was used to identify the learning styles of over 150 adults. The styles were called Accommodator, Assimilator and Diverger. The results indicated the age group 55–65 preferred the Accommodator, learning by feeling and doing. The 66–74 age group preferred the Diverger style, that is, feeling and watching, and the 75 and over age group preferred the Assimilator style, or learning by thinking and watching. What are our learning preferences? Em states her style is a combination of thinking and doing, whereas my style would be watching, doing and thinking. Not all learners are active, hands-on learners, but rather, with age, there is a tendency to become more reflective and observational in the learning environment. Whatever the age and learning preferences, we need to keep learning.

Marco's. Marco has been absent from the café for three days. Em asked Benita, "dove e Marco"? Her reply, "con i bambini." Sweet, he has time to spend with his children, I mumble. From my ever-expanding and detailed list, today is our scheduled day trip to the American Academy of Rome. The weather is chilly and cloudy, but the forecast is warmer in the afternoon with temperatures reaching 50 degrees. A great day for slow traveling. This event required an advanced written request, and we were fortunate enough to have been invited. The American Academy gazes out over the Eternal City from its setting high on the Janiculum Hill. It was a dynamic community intimately connected to the ongoing transition in the arts and humanities in Italy, Europe, and around the world. Today, we observed the painstakingly beautifully restored buildings, the mid–17th-century Villa Aurelia and the meticulously maintained gardens and grounds, which was a reminder of all that was and is in Rome. At these very gardens of Casa Malvasia in 1611, a reception was held to honor Galileo and his newly invented telescope. The next morning, with the use of Galileo Galilei's new telescope, the guests were able to read the letters on the Archbasilica of San Giovanni in Laterano, several miles away from this garden site; an astounding revelation occurred.

The Academy is a leading American overseas center for independent studies and advanced research in the fine arts and humanities. As we were waiting for our guide, we read carefully the Academy Visitor's Guidebook and various literature pertaining to the past and current residents; for example, Anthony Doerr, we learn, wrote *Four Seasons in Rome: On Twins, Insomnia* whilst at the Academy.

The American Academy in Rome began as a collaborative effort in 1893 and merged in 1911 the American School of Architecture and the American School of Classical Studies into the Academy. The Rome Prize fellowships support up to 30 artists and scholars who live and work in an atmosphere that breeds collaboration as well as individual achievement. Each year, artists and scholars working in areas such as ancient, medieval, Renaissance and early modern, modern Italian studies, architecture, landscape architecture, design, historic preservation and conservation, literature, musical composition, and visual arts are chosen by juries of experts in those fields.

This was the most rarefied creative and learning environment we have ever experienced. In addition to internationally recognized authors, architects, musicians, painters and thinkers, renowned chef Alice Waters was an invited guest at the Academy and complained that the food at the academy was not up to Italian cooking. She immediately established her second Sustained Food Program in 2009, and since then the food served at the academy is outstanding, as reported by the honored residents of the academy. Just about every well-known thinker and fine arts doer has been either a guest-in-residence, a Rome Honor recipient or performed here at the American Academy of Rome.

We experienced a memorable and enjoyable three hours of new knowledge and admiration from our terrific guide. Sakura, a Japanese-American, is a graduate of Smith College and has lived in Rome for nine years. Her mother is a teacher at the International School in Japan and was inspired by the Reggio Emilia preschools of Italy that we have studied in earnest for ten years. Needless to say, our conversation and connections were enhanced because of our mutual admiration of both Japan, Japanese culture and Reggio Emilia, Italy's educational approaches.

A very peaceful, creative and energizing community of very talented teachers, learners and producers will bring forth new and great advances in the fine arts and humanities. Advanced planning is essential to benefit from the many free events that are available in Rome.

Marco is back and happy to see us, and we are pleased to see him. He shows us his new pastry from the kitchen, an almond custard tart with raspberries. Marco decided for us: uno crostata di creama pasticcera alle mandorle con lamponi e due cappuccini. Grazie molto—we agreed.

I'm off to find two ways to reach the Piazza di Spagna and the Spanish Steps. One way we already discovered was to go through the Sports Center where the underground Metro entrance is, turn left and take the escalator, at the end turn left and follow the signposts to the Spanish Steps and wind up at the bottom of the steps. We love this way as we see all types of people in all kinds of attire. However, I discover an alternative that will take me through the Borghese garden. I head south from the Villa de Borghese Gallery, walk to the first fountain, turn left past the Piazza di Siena to Viale di Popazzi at the temple, turn left to Viale della Casina id Rafaela, turn right at the Piazza di Cantanti intersection, turn left to Viale d' Magnolie, and turn left to Viale d' Medici, and I'm at the Spanish Steps. A two-hour and a half adventure, with time allotted to jot down the directions in case we ever want to use this approach again. We could simply take bus #116 to the Borghese and then follow the above walk; you see everything, and you can't see enough of the park.

Off to Marco's. It's colder than yesterday; never mind, it doesn't matter—we are off to the Galleria Nazionale d'Arte Moderna E Contemporanea at Viale delle Belle Arti, 131. Em loves this museum. This museum was completed in 1911–15 and houses the largest collection of modern Italian art. We learn that the museum has over 5,000 works of art and sculptures from the 19th–20th centuries. I love the designed space allowed in all the 55 or more rooms, as human space allows time for careful observation, even with many visitors in each room. All of Em's beloved artists, such as Giacomo Balla, Gustav Klimt, Antonio Canova, Amedeo Modigliani, Vincent van Gogh, Giorgio de Chirico, Lucio Fontana and Gino Severini, all of them are an inspiration and enjoyment for all … except me. I did develop a sense of curiosity, confusion, and wonderment from the collection of art from the Futurism period. This artistic and social movement that originated in Italy in the early 20th century emphasized speed, technology, youth, violence, cars, airplanes and the industrial city.

We had the rest of the day, and Em had read about a very special restaurant in Trastevere that she was eager to experience. The Trattoria de Gli Amici was operated and staffed with people with disabilities. Their menu explained their purpose, their beliefs about how every person has different intelligences and capacities. Absolutely wonderful! The service—caring and thoughtful and the food fresh, tasty and enjoyable. The Amici was situated in the lovely and peaceful Piazza di S. Egidio. I was so happy that Em found this restaurant, and we enjoyed the total experience.

While we were in Trastevere, we strolled around until I found a Sicilian bakery called I Dolci Di Nonna Vincenza. Em mentioned, "We shall return to this idyllic spot."

We brought back one almond and one lemon cannoli.

Che Bello! The temperatures are warming: 41–51 degrees Fahrenheit.

We notice that the city is constructing barriers at the end of Via Adige and are wondering if these barricades will affect Marco's walk-in business. We don't ask him. How would he know at this point? Itinerary: Although we plan ahead, one of the advantages of slow travel is that we can take a diversion at our will at any time. We started off to see the Guggenheim exhibit at the Palazzo delle Esposizioni at Via Nazionale, 194. Along the way to the Quirinal Hill (one of seven original hills in Rome), we had to pause, linger and explore two famous churches: San Carlino (Borromini's master design) and his architect opponent, Bernini's Sant Andrea al Quirinale. We wound up doing the agenda in reverse; we got sidetracked as usual.

Borromini's San Carlino Church is considered a masterpiece of the Roman Baroque and an illustration of Borromini's genius. Also, a few hop-skip-jumps down Via Quattro Fontaine is Sant Andrea church. We notice that the church's design is diametrically opposed to Borromini's church. It's a wonder and pleasure to visit these two Baroque churches because of their architectural designs (proportions, perspectives and ratios) used to produce these harmonious structures. For the entire 17th century, Rome was the protagonist of Baroque architecture and art. Baroque was a direct response to the Lutheran Reformation. Indicative of this architectural design, the nave is unique as its focus is on the altar and on the communicative part of the public worship.

A stroll through the park led to the Via Nationale and the Guggenheim exhibit. The city of Rome owns the exhibition hall, cultural center and museum. The Guggenheim exhibit, directly from New York's Guggenheim, was devoted to Constantin Brancusi, who produced an innovative body of work during the 20th century that diverted the flight path of modern sculpture. His work in non–Western European traditions must have led to new and divergent thinking in terms of Western art and sculpture. The other theme was the art movement in America from 1945 to 1980. All the key players during that time were exhibited. The insightful cultural-historical context was reflected within the different artistic periods (e.g., post expression to abstract to pop art) and dramatically illustrated our artistic and cultural directions after World War II. It was a great exhibit with a huge crowd, even at midday (Italian lunchtime).

Marco is not available to tend to the fewer-than-normal coffee seekers this morning. We wish Benita a good morning; she prepares due cappuccini, one cornetto with grace, smile and ease. Em read that there was an exhibit featuring Damien Hurst, "The complete spot paintings, 1986–2010." She worked out the bus route to the Gagosian Gallery, a converted bank. The only names I recognized were Hurst and his dots and Cy Twombly's free-scribbled, calligraphy and graffiti large works that I had seen somewhere. Combined reactions: The brilliant spot paintings by Hurst did grow on me, thanks to Em's perspectives. ("Each dot of a different color could form a unique quilting pattern. Observe, no two spots touch, no color is repeated on the same canvas." She continues, "Since no two dots ever touch, there is no narrative or friction between them. The dots don't really form an image, like, say, Seurat's pointillism.") Twombly's work is masterful. We took bus #603 to return to the apartment. Well done, Em.

This is our one-month anniversary in Rome. We are supposed to have a meter reading today; we waited and waited. We missed Marco again today. Business seems less than two weeks ago. It's wet, damp and chilly. We are at the end of our first month in Rome. It's interesting to note that the weather does inform us to the extent of our flexibility regarding our slow travel destinations. We just adjust and enjoy whatever happens—merely one of the valuable benefits of slow travel. "I want to carefully observe and study every Caravaggio painting in Rome," I exclaim. "OK, there are about 16–20 of his works here in Rome." I brought out my list of locations where we have seen Caravaggio paintings: Three we shall see today in the Church of San Luigi dei Francesi, six in the Borghese Gallery, two in the Palazzo Barberini, one in the Capitoline Museum, two in the Church of Santa Maria del Popolo, two in the Doria Pamphilj (on my list for tomorrow), and "John the Baptist," at the Corsini. We could have studied up to 16 Caravaggio paintings after tomorrow. We'll try to visit the Casino Ludovisi; the Vatican has one. There's one more in the Church of Sant'Agostino; that will be almost 20 of Caravaggio's late Mannerist-style paintings. In European terms, he's probably the most influential of all 17th-century painters.

The Church of San Luigi dei Francesi is close to Palazzo Navona; the Church of San Luigi dei Francesi was built in 1518 and is the national church of France in Rome. In the Contarelli Chapel, the fifth chapel, there is a pictorial narrative of three works by Caravaggio. His Mannerist style is unique—the viewer is actively involved with the painting. He creates an illusionism of realism, his faithful details grip the viewer's attention, and he is a master at imitating nature, suffering and revenge. His paintings are dramatic, as in theatrical, to realism. Through his use of chiaroscuro (shadows—light, dark) he produces the dramatic appearances in his painting illustrations such as emotions of mystery, drama and solitude. Caravaggio directly influenced subsequent masters such as Ribera, Rembrandt, Ruben, and Orazio Gentileschi.

The barriers are around Marco's Café. We must walk to the end of Via Adige and back down to reach our Italian friend. Our energies are to continue our quest to find two Caravaggios at the spectacle seventh-century Villa Doria Pamphili, the largest landscaped public park in Rome. The Doria Pamphilj Gallery at Via del Corso was our focus, but we took the time to admire an amazing example of a naturalistic English landscape garden. The gallery was airy, large and open. The two Caravaggio paintings were elegantly displayed against the white walls of the gallery: "Mary Magdalene" and "Rest during the Flight to Egypt."

Our viewing of the paintings is becoming more of a "study" as opposed to just observing. I began to see how Caravaggio masterfully uses white to reference certain symbols and define areas he wanted the viewer to "study."

We arrived at the apartment at 4 p.m. to relax, reflect and redefine what we are learning, and are rediscovering the joys of retirement. Dammit, we missed our 12 p.m. Skype! I was so anxious to visit Pamphilj, I figured we would be back sooner than 4 p.m. to call the grandchildren. It's the first time in five Sundays we missed. Too late to call home. I cannot let my selfish desire to discover and explore interfere with contacting the grandchildren. We'll call tomorrow at 12 p.m.

We are both developing, growing in our depth of experiences but not necessarily our knowledge of art, architecture and history. Always students, we are being educated, and education fosters human development, the ultimate goal of education. Reflecting on our growth development, we are reconciling a deeper understanding of this physical, social and moral universe. A thing understood is a thing with a meaning; that is our motivation, relevance, and the joy to our retirement. Learning must be in conflict with what we already know, or what would be the purpose to continue to study and research? For us, "active aging" works best for us rather than lifelong learning, as being active represents a more emotional and embracing framework in our enjoyment of retirement.

Early morning meter reading. Giuliana arrives at 9 a.m. sharp. We chat a bit about how we spend our days and if we need anything. The utilities are a little less this time but still more than we had hoped; warmer temperatures will be coming. I must admit waiting for Giuliana to calculate the cost is like waiting patiently for the results of a potential root canal; please, no work needed.

At Marco's we visited earlier than usual, and his business was steady. We had to wait longer, but the coffee and cornetto are always consistently excellent. We planned to leave early in order to make our Skype call close to our 12 p.m. arrangement.

We set out to discover a neighborhood of Garbatella in the postindustrial grit of the district of Ostiense, south of the historical center. However, Em changed her mind while on the bus because she read an advertisement on a local bus that read, "Roma al tempo di Caravaggio Exhibit" at the Palazzo Venezia was to close this week. Em is always on the cutting edge of discovery. "Roma al tempo di' Caravaggio 1600–1630," realism extraordinaire. Slow travel allows us to make this diversion and go tomorrow to Garbatella. Reflections: Michelangelo Meredith da Caravaggio (1571–1610) was one of the brightest shining stars during this time in Rome and influenced so many of the artists during his time and much after. The exhibit featured 140 works brought together from all over the world. For us, the exhibit brought together the works of those artists who influenced Caravaggio (Guercino, Giuseppe Cesari) and those who were influenced by him (Ribera, Rubens and Rembrandt). We read that the exhibit would not travel outside of Rome as the works of art were borrowed from churches, museums and private collectors from around the world. Slow travel fosters unplanned exploration, surprises and excitement. Bus #63 and back at the apartment by 12:30.

We Skyped everyone; nobody missed our Sunday call. The conversations with the grandchildren are getting shorter and are basically about their school play, friends, out-of-school activities, Lego sets, tall tree climbing and swimming. Super happy for them. I mumbled, "They really don't miss us." Em's response was that it is an indication they are active, happy and focused on what is "in their moment." I feel better.

Marco greets us with a big smile and hands us a brochure about an exhibit called Rinascimento Roma. I'll definitely put this exhibit on my list. Since we were happily detoured yesterday, thank goodness, we are off to the southern region outside the city center to explore the neighborhood of Garbatella. I read about their political leanings and thought it might be an interesting discovery. What a marvelous surprise! A whimsical suburb, with lush communal courtyards, eclectic architecture and colorful left-wing graffiti. The neighborhood is intriguing and of a distinctive design, a garden city. The district's historical center was developed in the 1920s, with different architects developing different blocks, injecting medieval, Renaissance and Baroque accents. This is somewhat like New York City's Meatpacking District but with more architectural cool and calming greens—just my opinion. Reflections: The umbrella pines rise high from the courtyards, flowerbeds and green areas to represent this neighborhood on Rome's southern edge. Planned and built in the 1920s–30s, this amazing human-scale project was the first garden suburb for the working class. Perhaps this is why the neighborhood is a proud bastion of the left. Unfortunately, the hammer/sickle and aerosol art proclaiming workers' rights are a bit of an eyesore within these distinctly upscale and tidy haunts; could we be understanding a bit more about Italian politics and workers' rights? It is only three metro stops from the Colosseum, but we prefer to take two buses, and we're 50 minutes from our apartment. Seemingly, this neighborhood is rapidly becoming a rarefied, gentrified, hip area complete with one of Rome's cultural centers of art, architecture, and gastronomy.

Morning cheers from Benita; Marco was fussing with the pastries. A few of the workers from the street or sewer repairs were lined up at the counter. When Marco was free, Em asked him what they were doing with all those barriers and noise. Em worked out this from Google Translate: "Cosa sta succedendo fuori?" Marco said, "tutti I rotti devono essere sostituti, e un problema." So they are replacing the underground pipes, and it is a problem. Does he mean this disruption is causing his business a problem?

Having both reread Jake Morrissey's *The Genius in the Design: Bernini, Borromini, and the Rivalry that Transformed Rome,* we wanted to explore a little less-known church that Borromini designed.

The book tells a remarkable tale of how two geniuses with extraordinary vision schemed and managed to get the better of each other but in the process create the spectacular Roman cityscape we experience today. The book further surveys the trials and tribulations of the greatest architectures during the 1600s. A long story short, they were total opposites in terms of their personality, style and creative bend. That is our single focus for today unless something else happens along the way!

The church of San Giovanni of Florence at Via Acciaioli, 2. We read somewhere that Borromini and his mentor Carlo Maderno designed this church. However, after further review of the literature, we learned that this was incorrect. Yes, Borromini was involved with the design of the sanctuary; that was all. The architects were Carlo Maderno, Antonio da Sangallo the Younger and Giacomo della Porta. After many design iterations, the governing commission went to Sansovino. The church was a keen example of all the flair and energy that was represented during this particular 16th-century Baroque era. The recognizable feature of Baroque was an elliptical ribbed dome that sits on an octagonal drum. The interior decorative scheme is set off with white and gray, expertly carved stone sculptures, with the side chapels much more richly decorated. This was Borromini's last work (sanctuary) before he committed suicide at age 37 years. He and Maderno are buried under the cupola. Although this was not exactly what we thought it would be, it turned out to be a marvelous find. This church was near Castle Sant'Angelo, but there were no tourists inside, such a shame to miss this Baroque masterpiece. We continued to observe and linger through the old back streets behind the Piazza Navona. The Florentine district was once occupied by merchants, craftspeople and artisans. A transformative day! We are beginning to see the architectural connections, and that area is increasing my ignorance and desire to learn more.

Good morning to Marco and off to Trastevere. We have my list of tentative plans ready each day. However, we do not have to sit at Marco's to plan every day. I feel much better not taking a seat in the sitting area, although it is not used very much, as his establishment isn't a library or a Starbucks. There were two sites on my tentative list: The Jewish Ghetto—Portico d'Ottavia and Basilica Santo Spirito in Sassia, near Vatican City. Although we have spent countless hours in this fascinating and historic district, one can never really appreciate the tragedies and hardships associated with this neighborhood. We learn that the Jewish community has been living in Rome since early Ancient times, and today's ghetto is where the Jews moved to after they left Trastevere in the 13th century. The Portico d'Ottavia has been the heart of Rome's Jewish Ghetto; it's a chunk of urban surrealism that one finds only in Rome. The 2,000-year-old portico thrusts into the dome of the Baroque church of Santa Maria in Campitelli. However, a few steps from the Roman monument tourists dine, as we have, on the restaurant's terraces amid fresh artichokes. The ghetto was a tightly confined area with many narrow streets and alleys with plenty of neat shops and kosher food outlets. Since the end of World War II, over 2,000 residents were deported and never returned; several remembrance plaques have been placed on buildings. The ghetto district is now very pleasant, filled with historical buildings and a lively neighborhood. The Jewish school is heavily guarded by police, and plain clothes police are everywhere. This is a very significant place to reflect and redefine one's thoughts and beliefs.

The Church Basilica Santo Spirito in Sassia is a Renaissance church designed by

Antonio da Sangallo. Sangallo also designed the Baroque church we observed yesterday. My research on the church's opening days and hours was inaccurate once again. The sign on the door indicated that the church was only open for a few hours on Mondays, and today is Saturday. Nonetheless, we admired the original 12th-century church's exterior; it has been rebuilt in various architectural styles since, however. We find out later that the organ (1556) is still used today. Not ever to be disappointed, we always say we shall return. Instead, we merely walked to St. Peter's Square and saw the unbelievable huge lines to enter the Basilica. All bags, of any kind, were being checked before entry. Well done. We plan to visit soon. A slow walk to the lovely neighborhood of Prati to take tram #19 to the apartment. Lunch in the park near our flat.

Sometimes we do our washing on Saturday and dust and clean day as well. Sunday often is our work day. Em has the wash down to a formula, and I want to Skype the family before 12 p.m. Em tells me to finish the dusting and vacuuming first. At the designated time, we Skype—two of the three grandchildren are swimming, and the other is on a birthday playdate. The explanations are that the boys are participating in a scholarship fundraiser for their school, and our granddaughter was invited to a birthday party along with her schoolmates. Not to worry, the hugs and kisses will be directed appropriately, both mothers and fathers assured us.

Marco's on Monday was the busiest we have ever seen it. Coming from our apartment across the street, we saw a line waiting to enter the café. By the time we walked to the end of Via Adige, a ten-minute walk due to the barriers along the street and beyond, the line was just about gone. Marco's heart-shaped smile and his sincere, warm greetings always make us feel as if we, in a very small way, are helping his business and family. Most of the tables in the sitting area are occupied, so we stand at the end of the counter where Benita is refilling the pastries. She smiles; we smile.

We return back to the apartment to finish washing and ironing the shirts, pillowcases and towels until they are completely dry.

Upon reflecting on our present happiness, I have no anxieties about our future. In *Portraits from Memory and Other Essays*, Burton Russell reminded us of the two dangers to guard against old age: (1) "undue absorption of the past, (2) one's thoughts must be directed to the future; not easy, as the past is gradually increasing in weight." The present is our focus, and if we value our health, finances and love, we must "measure" or be accountable for these values. I made a list of what we value:

First was health. Em's knee requires periodic rest; that means no five-hour walk-a-thons.

Second, my seasonal allergies will be triggered once the weather warms and the trees and flowers begin to bloom. I will take appropriate action before this occurs.

Third, eating healthy, which is very easy in Italy, and controlling portion sizes: splitting pasta or pizza and one pastry once a day seem to work for us. We have not gained any weight, but we really work at this as it is too easy to put on extra pounds.

Fourth, exercise: We have been walking an average of four to five miles a day. That has had an effect on Em's knee, and we will have to adjust to a different form of exercise, such as more yoga and stretching. We purchased a mat, light hand weights, bands and used a number of excellent YouTube videos to motivate and inspire us to continue to exercise.

Fifth, finances: We value our fixed-income budget, so we measure the daily expenditures. We make adjustments to accommodate large spend days (e.g., monthly bus passes, museum tickets and infrequent eating out). We save money by eating the majority of our meals at the apartment or having picnics in the park. Em is an excellent cook, which she learned from her Sicilian mother.

Lastly, we value our good health, as without good health, our relationship might be somewhere different, I would imagine. What I am learning about our relationship from living in a foreign country, with no language acuity, is from a stalwart partner whom I rely on and have confidence in for my survival and happiness.

Many theorists have written about an answer to strengthening a loving relationship. One particular notion mentioned in the literature is something called emotional endurance, which is the acceptance of what is truly important and the realization that this is a precious time. That being said, love is certainly an emotion, yes, but it's the action of love (i.e., showing and doing) that makes love more meaningful and deeper than simply saying, "I love you, Em."

The renowned Zen Buddhist monk Thich Nhat Hanh teaches us that to love is a learned "dynamic interaction," as we form early our patterns of understanding to love ourselves before we can truly love and understand our partner/wife. I learned there are four components of truthful love: loving kindness, compassion, joy, and mental composure. I am still very conscious of the fact that I need to place more effort on the kindness and composure aspects, but I am making steady progress. What this year abroad has taught me is that there are no boundaries to love—Em's happiness/sadness is my happiness/sadness, and my happiness/sadness is hers. Our slow travel abroad, with our individual and mutually designed purposes along with the many daily challenges that arise living in a foreign country, has brought out this capacity in me to truly love her through my actions of love such as: respecting her feelings and thoughts, demonstrating kindness, giving her the attention she deserves, compromise, and active-affection and listening.

In other words, actions (of love) are the operative words: live fully in the present, show her that I appreciate everything she does for me, and for us, and demonstrate my love for her by actively listening, compromising, and respecting that she knows what is best for our happiness.

I'm finding that my inflexibility, one of two of my most annoying bits of my personality, is being minimized by our slow travel in Rome. From the former "No, let me think about it" to "Yes, but" seems to be more comparable to our relationship. Therefore, I think before speaking. The second personality design fault is my impatience. Before living in Rome, I was always easily irritated at delays and slow responses to things and restlessly eager for something or to do something. I needed to find situations and places to learn to curb my emotions when forced with things I can do nothing about. My solution has been to focus on what I actually can control: my options, impulses and adversity, instead of external displays of frustration or impatience. Rome, with its ambiguities, illogical behavior patterns, and Em, with her patience, understanding, and love have taught me to be a kinder and better person than before the slow travel in Rome. Since we have been slow traveling in Rome, I have become more patient with Em, people, and cultural norms that are sometimes in conflict with my own. I must accept slowness as a cultural norm, and indifference and lack of kindness to people is not acceptable. I cannot react to situations that are out of my control that make me frustrated and cannot show that frustration. Now that I am more cognizant of these shortcomings in my personality, I have been acting and thinking more like a cooperative, respectful and loving companion. I think it took this kind of living experience together in a different culture and close living conditions to make me realize that I must make these proper adjustments to my life and for Em. I do feel like I have a more positive and growth mindset and am making steady progress. Coming to terms with my emotions now allows me to re-engage with new and different situations with an open mind, body and heart and new terms of endearment for Em.

By midafternoon the wash was finished, ironing almost done; we must take advantage of the still cool but sunny rest of the day. Several blocks from our apartment we locate Café Amelie at Piazza Verbano, 17–19. At the café and its newly expanded outdoor setting, we find a spot. With the warm sun at our backs we enjoyed the Illy caffé; Illy blend is 100% Arabica. This is a people-watching kabuki theater. Happy folks were dancing and singing, but no costumes were observed. Today's coffee prices certainly represented the new renovations. We enjoyed the time together.

Marco's for coffee, a polite buongiorno, grazie, and buona giornata, and we bus ride near Trastevere and the Jewish Ghetto. We began to poke around the back alleys until we found the amazing Palazzo Mattei di Giove, a hulking brick townhouse whose corners mark the edge of the Ghetto. One of the greatest showcases for the loot that was plundered during the 1500s was placed in this palazzo. The palazzo was built by Rome's famous architect Carlo Maderno (St. Peters, also). Not far away from the palazzo was our beloved Fontana delle Tartarughe (Fountain of the Turtles.) Adjacent to the fountain we discovered the Centro di Studi Americani. Established in 1936, this property houses a nonprofit institution where historians, politicians, essayists, novelists and actors hold conferences or study in the huge library. Our amazing quest is to find new and different interests that are always available in Rome; just have to keep digging.

Weather today: 40–51 degrees Fahrenheit. A rather cold morning, and we felt it straightaway. Brought along an umbrella as rain was forecasted.

Our itinerary was to visit The Rinascimento a Roma (The Renaissance in Rome) at the Museo Roma at Palazzo Sciarra located off Via Corso.

A fantastic Renaissance retrospective that Marco recommended included 170 works, including sculptures, paintings, drawings and engravings from this epic period of art, architecture, literature and music. The collections came from several continents. After 1530, many artists drew inspiration from the styles of Michelangelo and Raffaello, and the rest is history. The show also featured a host of items from everyday life in Rome, demonstrated through works of art, floor tiles and ceramics. Our reflections: This has been our most inspired exhibition so far in Rome. The authentic sense of the beauty and proportions that represented the Renaissance period was clearly a once in a lifetime experience. The exhibition will leave Rome in two days as the collections belong to other museums and private owners and must be returned. We were very lucky to catch this exhibition. Thank you, Marco, for suggesting it.

Marco's not very busy this morning as the noise and dust are everywhere. Evidently, the workers must be digging deeper than they were a couple of weeks ago; more barriers were placed near the sidewalk entry of his café. We hope this construction does not last too long for Marco and his family's sake.

Our itinerary was far south of the historical center of Rome to the EUR or Esposizioni Universale di Roma and the Basilica of Santa Maria Maggiore. The EUR was the same sight I saw and asked Giuliana about when coming from the airport.

After a 40-minute bus ride, we arrive at the extravagant, monumental white travertine marble, and the wide avenues remind one of an imaginary city of fascist modern architecture. This is a large business/financial district a distance from the Centro, similar to La Défense just outside of central Paris. The initial project was presented in 1938, the design inspired by Roman Imperial town planning, with modern elements of neoclassicism. The EUR is a quiet, yet energetic community. Large sidewalks for walking, many shops, and huge marble, tufa and limestone buildings. This grandiose plan in the 1930s was the dream of Benito Mussolini. The most iconic architecture is the Palazzo della Civilta Italiana (1938), also known as the Colosseo Quadrato (Square Colosseum). The palace has six rows of nine arches each. The inscription on the four sides of the building read: "A people of poets, of artists, of heroes, of saints, of thinkers, of scientists, of navigators, of voyagers." Dramatic, historical and a time warp of the 1930s. I'm excited; my first site of curiosity upon arriving in Rome has come to life.

We wanted to see another of the ancient four major Roman basilicas, the Basilica Santa Maria Maggiore. Moreover, this is the Papal's major basilica and the largest Catholic church in Italy. A basilica has certain privileges conferred on it by the Pope. The other three major basilicas are Basilica of St. Paul Outside the Walls, Basilica of St. Mary Major, and Archbasilica of Saint-John Lateran.

The imposing Basilica is a huge structure; however, it's not as large as St. Peter's. The original church site was in 432 CE and has been a church ever since that time. The façade was a Baroque art lesson for me: classical harmonic forms, enlivened dramatic sculptures, and the broken lines of pediments interplay with the openings in the loggia porches. The Cosmati floors are a marvel in craftsmanship. The image of many thousands of pieces of marble placed in dramatic styles, colors and patterns was simply overwhelmingly pleasing to the eyes, mind and heart.

Morning sunshine, cool temperatures in the low 50s. We skipped Marco's today as the second sidewalk entrance opposite the end of the long sidewalk we walked to had been barricaded as the digging work seemed to be expanding. Also, the noise and dust was too much. We felt bad; we didn't want to abandon Marco and his business. Em said skip coffee, and we will have lunch at Marco G. We walked to the Villa Borghese. From there we hopped on bus #116 to Ponto Sisto and walked through the northern part of the Trastevere neighborhood until we reached our lunch destination, Marco G at Via Statilia, 12. This small, family-operated lunch stop had excellent Mediterranean cuisine. Marco (ironically) and his entire team were very attentive and friendly. We ordered fresh, made-to-order spinach ravioli and a finocchi-olives-orange salad that we split. We also shared a freshly made tiramisu that was a great, tasty treat. Em's knee was "talking to her," and we found bus #83, then #63 and to the apartment. A wonderful and enjoyable day of slow traveling.

Nearing the end of February, the temperatures are creeping up ever so slightly. We are comforted by the mid–50s and the consistent sunshine. Marco's is not open this Friday. No sign, just the door locked. We forget the coffee and cornetto and take the bus near Piazza Navona. Diagonally from the Pantheon is Rome's only Italian Gothic church architecture, that being the Santa Maria Sopra Minerva Basilica at Piazza della Minerva, 42, designed by Carlo Maderno in 1370. The basilica acquired its name because it was built directly over (sopra) the foundations of a temple; also, it's one of the most important churches of the Roman Catholic Dominican order in Rome. The fascination is the Gothic elements within the Renaissance and Baroque churches throughout Rome. In researching this church I found out that Galileo Galilei, the father of modern astronomy, was tried for heresy in the adjoining monastery, where they renounced his scientific theses in the church in 1633. I'm totally absorbed in Michelangelo's genius for details and his genuine love in crafting his marble statue of "Cristo della Minerva." The rest of the interior brought us to our knees, figuratively and literally! There were the penetrating and intriguing frescoes in the Carafa Chapel by Filipino Lippi (1400), many finely carved funerary monuments, especially the one of Fra Angelico, as Saint Catherine of Siena was buried here, and tombs of many of the Popes. Fortunately for us, there was a lovely high mass with a Gregorian chant characterized by the monophonic texture, inharmonious, lacking in rhythm, an unaccompanied sacred song. Reflective, relaxing, meditative, and enlightening.

As we stepped outside we found another genius, Bernini's marble elephant sculpture, somewhat disharmonious with the Egyptian obelisk on its back, in front of the church. This is just another example of why Rome is such an interesting and inspiring city. Rome's everything is opposite to something else: Gothic meets Baroque and greets Egyptian. Romans took culture from the Greeks, building roads and bridges from the Etruscans, and obelisks from the Egyptians. Unbelievable. Em tells me that if we continue our flaneuring, a few blocks from Piazza Navona we can just make it to view Sant' Agostino Basilica, where there is an exhibit you don't want to miss. Inside, the feature exhibit was Caravaggio's "Madonna of the Pilgrims" (1604)—Barefoot Virgin on a pilgrimage. Magnificent, of course—it is Caravaggio, is it not? After carefully observing this masterful painting, we walked once again to the little church of San Luigi dei Francis. The Mannerist style is brilliantly illustrated by the paintings by Caravaggio. Inside in the Contarelli Chapel are a trio of walls of Caravaggio's famous paintings: "The Calling of Saint Matthew," "The Martyrdom of Saint Matthew," and "The Inspiration of Saint Matthew."

Extravagant beauty! We have now observed, in slow time, 16 of Caravaggio's paintings, excluding those we saw in separate exhibits. His paintings emphasize realism, drama, chiaroscuro and extension of action in space. This was quite an accomplishment as we were motivated to study more about Caravaggio's life, how he inspired the Baroque era, his radical naturalism in his paintings and his tremendous influence of subsequent artists.

A long day and a long walk back from the Via Corso, autobus fermata #630, back to Tagliamento fermata, left us off a few blocks near our apartment. The great news was that Em's knee was not bothering her. Taking buses to the nearest site is the best approach to resting for her knee.

The morning sunshine greets us as we look across the street to see if Marco's is open. Behold, a sign is centered in the middle of the glass and double glazed door. I walk down Via Adige, turn right and walk back down Via Adige to read the sign on the door. It reads "Vacanze di ritorno presto chao, Marco e Benita." I got the vacation but not the return date. We will continue to wait for their return. Frankly, we are not missing our coffee and cornetto. We miss supporting Marco and his family, but we certainly are fine without the morning java. We decide to spend the entire day outside since it is such a beautiful day to walk, linger and reflect. We were going to the Capitoline Museum but thought it best to take advantage of the sunny day. We picked up a couple of olive rolls, burrata cheese, and semi-dried tomatoes, and had a picnic lunch in the Villa Ada, the second-largest park in Rome and just north of our apartment. We have spent considerable time in the Villa Doria Pamphili, located in Trastevere district, Vatican City, the Villa Borghese, the most beautiful park in Rome, and our nearest park, Villa Torlonia. The Villa Ada was a wonderful location to relax and admire the stone pines, huge pond and quiet openness. A wonderful day in the beautiful Villa Asa in the Emerald City.

"Elephant and Obelisk" by Gian Lorenzo Bernini. Of Rome's 13 ancient obelisks, only one is carried by a pachyderm.

Sunday—Skype, washing, cleaning and enjoying our stay-at-home day. Em really wanted to spend the entire day at the apartment to rest her knee and continue with her Rome watercolors, knitting and reading. I enjoy the cleaning of the apartment as it is small enough that it doesn't take all that time, and we keep it very clean during the week.

The wash takes the entire day; drying the clothes and bedding takes a couple of days. Very soon the temperature will be favorable to hang the sheets outside on the patio. We Skyped the family and spoke with the grandchildren. They did not have too much to say other than they like school, have schoolmates and are playing in the snow left by the past Nor'easter, that snowstorm with strong winds. We are happy for them.

We spend part of the day reflecting on how our retirement has provided us with such joy. We are learning, that is, constructing understanding of reality through our interactions, observations, and hands-on experiences. Reflection is the logical outcome of those interactions, observations and questioning. The more we experience, the less we actually know; therefore, this imbalance promotes our quest to restore the balance. These experiences living in Rome, especially our focuses on art, architecture, and the nuances of Italian culture, are what is the essence of our sense of purpose.

Our learning is educating our minds and our hearts.

We must renew our monthly Metrobus electronic card for March. Although the initial cost is pricey, we wind up saving about $85–$90 at the end of the month. We receive unlimited journeys within the city of Rome during the charged calendar month. Furthermore, we often use two and sometimes three buses each day, and our pass covers all bus travel.

Marco's was still closed, and he was still on vacation. We wanted to finish the laundry and ironing before we set off to visit Naples tomorrow. We had due cappuccini at Caffé Amelia, at the corner of Piazza Vernana, then returned to put the last laundry load in the tiny washer, finished ironing the pillowcases, hand towels, and shirts and blouses. Since we are to receive our utilities reading soon, we know that we have been diligent in our efficiencies, so we decide to have lunch out of the apartment.

We passed La Madia at Piazza Zama many times, seeing fresh food being served, and that is where we enjoyed a terrific lunch. A large menu is not always an indication of a good restaurant, but their large menu was all about pastas and pizzas. There was not one of the local customers speaking anything other than Italian. The service was spotty due to the number of patrons, but friendly. The food was excellent. We enjoyed this special lunch date.

From my planning list we had placed a visit to Naples early before the heat and tourists arrived. I looked up the temperatures in Naples, and they ranged from 37 to 58 degrees Fahrenheit, an excellent time to visit "Citta del Sole." The primary purpose was to view Caravaggio's "Seven Works of Mercy" at Pio Monte della Misericordia.

Marco's was still closed when the bus picked us up at 7:30, and we were at the Termini Station at 8:10. We purchased EuroStar tickets and went straight to Gate #8 for the 9 a.m. departure. We arrived at Naples Central Train Station at 10:10.

We have been to Naples twice before, but we never applied the slow travel time to visit the historical center of the city. Today, we followed a walking tour from our Michelin Green Guide and spent six hours visiting the major churches, cultural highlights and notable small shops and artist workshops. Naples, we learned, boasts the highest number of churches in the world, "City of 500 Domes."

The highlights listed were: the Chiesa del Gesù; the Cloisters of Clares (with remarkable majolica masterpiece tiles around everything); Sant'Angelo a Nilo—a tomb designed and partly sculpted by Donatello; the small chapel of Monte di Pieta; Naples Duomo; two major Napoleon churches (The Basilica of Santa Maria della Sanita–1600 and Curtis of San Martino–1325); and Naples University.

Finally, at Pio Monte della Misericordia, we viewed Caravaggio's "Seven Works of Mercy." It's a huge oil painting, illustrating the seven acts of mercy in seven different scenes. As with all of Caravaggio's paintings, the action is rough, complex with a strong chiaroscuro emphasizing the divine light. What we love about his paintings is that his characters are all portrayed as common people; he didn't particularly believe in the charity of the upper class. Art (architecture) is inexplicably intertwined with the mind and heart.

Our reflections: Such joy! There is history, art and architecture galore in this ancient city—perhaps "overwhelming" might be the word. Naples is often called the "blood city," not because of the mafia but because of the religious rites associated with the city. Naples, for me, would be classified as a city with chaotic charms: gritty, edgy, lively and spirited. Remember that the city sits at the base of one of the world's most dangerous volcanoes, Mt. Vesuvius. The Romans captured Naples from the Greeks in 326 BCE, leading to its rich and varied past. Naples took many bombs during World War II, and evidence proves that they are still rebuilding. Great pastries, coffee, and, of course, Neapolitan pizza.

Coffee stop: The famously old Caffè Giovanni Scaturrchio, established in 1905. Samples of some of the glorious and creative pastries—Baba, Ministerial, and Sfogliatella. Tasting these pastries is like taking a walk through the history and customs of the Neapolitans. "Tradition is Culture," as they say at Scaturrchio.

Meals: We should have taken more time to spot a pizzeria, but we fell onto the first one that was off the tourist route and seemingly frequented by local residents. However, their specialty was fried pizza with fresh buffalo milk cheese inside, something like a calzone. Well, long story short: Unfortunately, we cannot eat such a large portion of deep fried foods, and, sadly, we left a great deal of the pizzas on the plate. We made a wrong choice for the renowned Napoli pizza. Our fault—absolutely!

We departed from Naples at 19:00 hours, arrived at Rome's Termini at 20:03 and went home on bus #86 at 21:00 hours. Feels wonderful to be back in Rome!

First day of March: Weather is still very cool in the morning and at night. Temps: 61–39 F. We received our February gas and electric bills from the beautiful sisters. Good news, as we used much less than expected. We shall continue to be vigilant with respect to using the utilities carefully. We paid Simona in cash, and Giuliana said the temperatures will become warmer as we head into March and April, and that sounded very hopeful.

Itinerary: After our full day yesterday, today is open-market shopping and general food shopping. We shop every day for fresh produce, fish, bread and a few pastries. I brought the shopping cart from the apartment to the open market at Piazza Crato, merely eight or nine blocks from our flat. Upon my return I saw some action in Marco's; I didn't investigate.

Reflections: It is getting warmer earlier in the late morning, so we can skip the heavy, early morning traffic. By the time we are out, the temps are more appropriate for walking and waiting for buses. The open markets are the best buy for the money—always fresh and seasonal produce. The supermarkets provide the staples for everyday living in Rome.

Is this magic?! Today the temperatures at the beginning of March range from 50 to 63 degrees Fahrenheit. This is a surprising and rapid change in temperatures and a cost savings on utilities as well. Now we have to decide exactly how many layers to put on and immediately take off. Turns out to be the best weather day since we arrived.

The barriers are beginning to come down on the north side of Via Adige, the side closest to us. Hopefully, these new accesses will stimulate more walk-in business for Marco. There was no one inside his place this morning, as the vacation sign was still attached to the door. Evidently, the sisters forgot to inform us, or I didn't hear them, that the patio cleaners were to power wash the patio this morning! We heard a rather thunderous knock on the door, and I responded with "chi e" (who is it?) and "buongiorno" knowing full well that it wasn't one of the sisters. "Pulitore per patio," Em senses something about the patio. I open the door to see two older-looking men dressed in matching blue denim jumpsuits and red worker's caps. "Buongiorno" and they look towards and point to the patio. I unlock the patio door, and they look around, talk to each other and come back. "Dobbiamo prendere la tua attrezzatura!"

I simply nod "Si." I'm thinking out loud. Do we remain in the apartment while they clean the patio, offer them coffee, or ask them how long they will be?

Em's comment was, "We have many things to do in the apartment, and we will just let the time go by."

The men bring in a large vacuum-like machine and another similar-looking pressure machine with hoses and brooms. Since we are in the basement, everything they require to do the patio must come through our basement door. I just leave the door open as they keep coming in and out for most of the morning. "Power wash," Em indicates. Luckily, we haven't purchased any outside plants yet. Notwithstanding the mild disruptions, we are pleased that the power washing will eliminate the mold and algae that has grown over the past year. This is a hopeful sign that after a couple days we shall be able to use the patio, buy some plantings and enjoy sitting outside in the late afternoons. I'm also allergic to mold.

Em mentioned an insightful tidbit that since we are living in such a densely populated residential neighborhood, apart from our motorbike neighbor, the noise at night is minimal, at best. We know that after 10 p.m., when the motorbike neighbor comes back to roost, we don't hear sirens, horns or gunfire.

I needed about an hour to clean up after the patio power wash chaps as they brought half of the patio residue back through the apartment. No worries, spring is almost here, so we can place some pots of flowers on our clean patio, my love.

"Good Golly, Miss Molly," Marco is back! We welcome him back; he looks the same as before his holiday, whatever that means. Em asked him where they went for vacation; his reply was, "ho appena laboratory in casa," just worked around the house. A few regular customers were standing at the bar counter. Benita was grinding the fresh Lavazza coffee beans; the smell evoked emotions like comforting and pleasing. Excellent coffee, no cornetti today, he said. Nothing had changed in the café; it was just closed for the vacation. From my "must take time to observe and study" list, we are focused on two unique, founded in the fourth century, much admired, oldest-in-Rome architectural buildings: Church of Santi Quattro Coronati and Basilica di San Clemente, both near the Colosseum but up the long hill from major tourists. First and lasting impressions: Standing at the Church of Santi Quattro Coronati's entrance, the dark, chunky, bulky, thickly walled façade looked like a fortress rather than a church, a simple structure that wouldn't get the attention of passersby who would easily dismiss it as simply another of the over 900 churches in Rome. This was evidenced this morning as there were only a handful of visitors in this magnificent structure. It seems that with every attraction in Rome, you can always find a legend behind it. In the case of Santi Quattro Coronati, which means "Four Crowned Saints," they refer to not one but two groups of martyrs. The Basilica was originally built in the fourth century and then enlarged and renovated by Pope Leo IV in the ninth century. There are some remains of those frescoes in the chapels, but in the Saint Sylvester's Chapel, we observed the beautiful 13th-century frescoes. The secret: The cloister is accessed from a door in the left nave. The inspiring and delightful cloister, with an ornamental basin, a manicured garden and small Ionic columns, is offset by capitals decorated with colorful water lilies.

Not far from Santi Quattro Coronati was the Romanesque Basilica de San Clement al Laterno was another revelation. We entered the atrium and viewed the simple austerity of this medieval building. Our attention was immediately drawn to the Paschal candlestick columns (twisted) of very fine 12th-century master work. The dramatically designed Cosmati floors (12th century) are the best preserved in Rome. Moreover, there were devotional relics of Saints, 12th-century colorful, preserved mosaics in the apse so very rich in symbolism (dove, fish and pelican), as are 11th-century frescoes in the nave. Beneath the basilica were the remains of a small temple—3 BCE. Although we have been in this church a couple of times, we, however, are now definitely becoming more acute at observing, studying, and reflecting on their extravagant beauty. Art and architecture are interconnected with culture and all the surroundings in which they happen to be.

Since we are feeling a little less budget pressure because our utilities were less than expected, the warmer temps will make even less usage, and finally, with the warmer temperatures, we will be outside more and use less gas and electricity. The rationale was enough for us to have lunch at Café San Clemente at Via di San Giovanni in Lateran, #124, across from the Basilica St. Clemente. A very tasty, gluten-free pizza, wonderful attentive service, and outdoor seating with a plain sight of the Colosseum. I took a photo of our lunch with the Colosseum in the background for the grandchildren.

A rest and recovery day for both of us. Em's knee needed a rest, and my allergies flared up. I am convinced that the dust, ash and the other pollutants in the city are beginning to take effect in my sinuses.

Temperatures are reaching 47 degrees in the morning, up to 57 in the afternoons. As long as there's sunshine, the weather is perfect for everything we do or see.

What better way to enjoy Rome but to walk to the Villa Borghese Gardens: Our slow and peaceful stroll was an organic treatment for what was ailing us. I'm not sure the blooming of the trees and flowers are a treatment for what ails me, but I enjoy such a contradiction, or I could just not leave the apartment. We walked to the Spanish Steps from the Borghese, using the shorter path of the two, then took the bus back.

Em loves this park, and she did a few really detailed sketches of statues in the park.

This morning we did stop and have a coffee and a cornetto at Marco's. We were a little later in the morning than usual, and only Marco and his father were there. The one customer: the same local chap with an oversized baseball cap with a red "B" on the front we always see at the counter. Because I did not order one cornetto, he brought two cornetti along with our coffee; "grazie," we enjoyed both, and paid for two.

From my "like to do list," which for us would take a two-day tourist binge, we decided to take the Archeobus—a hop-on/hop-off bus routed exclusively to explore an area unknown to us before. The tour took us to Rome origins: the Appia Antica park along the ancient Appian Way. Our second venture would take us to the Termini, Rome's major train station, in order for us to purchase train tickets for our short trip to the Emilia-Romagna region at the end of this month.

Reflections and highlights: There are 12 different on-and-off sites along the route.

The road runs through attractive landscapes, semirural oases, aqueducts, catacombs, cypress and pine trees and sacred ruins. The Appian Way was built in 312 BCE. This smaller bus can make this journey on the narrow road, as the regular buses cannot. Although the road surface is rough (some with actual Roman cobblestone), the views of a Roman countryside were painted with ochre reddish-orange tones and the burnt-orange and browns of the ruined aqueducts blending in with the dark emerald greens of the cypresses and umbrella pines. We had a two-day pass, which makes for another day in the park—that entire area is 2,300 years young. The next day we did the same tour to listen more attentively, with fewer people on the bus and a different tour guide, who was excellent.

Sunday—Skyped the family and grandchildren. We learned that the two boys have the flu, but our granddaughter is fine; thank goodness. The washing machine is at it again, cleaning the sheets and clothes. We are very happy to have this machine on the apartment's patio. This was the first time that we opened the back window to help speed up the drying processes. We know that the wash time will take an hour or so but still decided to head over to the nearby neighborhood of Parioli. The coffee and pastries are outstanding, and costly, but we can sit for hours even with a bottle of water.

While at the café we made up a list of "surprises in Rome!"

- quietness
- easy and inexpensive public transport
- number of Italians who speak and understand English
- expensive, depending upon the weakness or strength of the exchange rate (i.e., the value of the dollar vs. the euro currency)
- graffiti (mostly political as we Google to translate) all over buildings, signs, buses, and trains. There appears to be little to no effort to clean it up, even on newer and fashionable buildings. It just happens and stays there. They say that this has been happening since Roman times and even before; Romans like to leave their mark.
- parking situation, anywhere that the car fits is ok
- abandoned motorcycles, cars and mopeds are left all over the street corners, sidewalks, sometimes behind the trash containers and in parking spaces along the streets. No judgments here, made up from our observations throughout the places we have visited in Rome.

After the Surprise list, we constructed the 10 Best Words to Describe Rome list:

- Ancient
- past
- provocative
- seductive
- red
- burnt-orange
- small-city
- beautiful
- sanctity
- livable

What about the wash?

After another coffee and pastry, we devised our first word that comes to mind:

The Top 15 list of Rome.

- frescoes
- galleries
- colors
- weather—sunshine
- blood oranges
- neighborhoods
- architecture
- paintings
- cafés
- riding the buses
- pastries
- pizza
- pasta
- specialty shops
- Marco

Then came our Top 5 Foods list of Rome: this was most difficult to cull down to just five:

- Gelato
- pizza with spinach-zucchini
- greens (escarole)
- fresh pasta (Bucatini all'Amatriciana)
- cream-custard/chocolate pastries

That was really fun and made us hungry! We returned to attend to the wash, dust, iron and vacuum.

Later on during the day, as we were still in the analysis and assessment mode, we worked on a collective observational statement:

Rome is a conglomeration of varied visual modes of expression which cross our line of vision each day. For example, there are ads for everything on buses, free newspapers handed out on the street, advertisements on every billboard, and, above all, the endless graffiti that's splattered across all of Rome. Is the media the message?

Now, Em has more issues with graffiti than I do. Agreed, some of Rome's side street scribbles are mindless and senseless. And yes, others are objectionable, especially on older Renaissance buildings. Some, however, rouse one's curiosity about what were they thinking (or not), while others induce admiration due to their quasi-artistic qualities. We love discussing such benign notions as these, and I learn from her analysis and assessments.

The weather outside is sunny and the morning delightful, and we are off to Marco's to review our plans for the day. At 08:00, Marco had one customer, the same chap that always sits at the same seat at the counter. We order, and Marco brings over our due cappuccini and une corretto. Surprisingly, he sits down with us. He doesn't have a happy face. I'm jittery; what do I do? How do we converse with Marco in Italian? How do we translate his conversation to English? Em has her Google translation app ready to use. Marco explains to our translator, "I miei affari non vanno bene, i miei affari da due anni vanno male." She repeats back to me, "Basically his business has not been good and for the past two years very bad." Em replied, "ci dispiace, pensi che andra meglio?" (We are sorry; do you think it will get better?) He continues, "incomparable l'economia, ha detto, ma soprattutto la costruzione gli e costata molti affari e la gente trova altri caffè." Em's rough translation: "The economy is not good; most of the problem has been the construction and cost him business and people find other cafés." We have been saying that his business is a walk-to café, as Via Adige is very narrow and there are only a few parking spaces, two assigned to his business, no parking on our side of the street. The construction certainly prevented direct access to his establishment. We are speechless: What do you say? Do we hug him? Do we say, "everything will work out, not to worry." No, neither one of us knows exactly how to reply. During this few seconds of silence, Marco gets up to attend to the only other customer in the café. We will continue to support his business and family every day.

After this disheartened start of the day, we continued with our plan to visit San Francesco d' Assisi a Ripa Grande church, dedicated to Francis of Assisi, who stayed at the adjacent convent. The Friars began to rebuild the church in 1231; the present church began in 1603 and was completed in 1681. However, it is what is inside that brings us back for the third time. In the Altieri Chapel, above the altar lies Bernini's masterful marble funerary monument, "Blessed Ludovica Albertoni," who was a 16th-century noblewoman, beatified in 1671. Observe, linger and wonder—behold, the beauty of perfection. Hold on! Can perfection really exist? Perfection is about something faultless, meaning there is no room for mistakes. But perfection is also a construct open to one's idea of perfection, and in my perceptions, Bernini was perfection.

In addition, the garden had an orange tree in the tradition of St. Francis and places to meditate and reflect; we have spent many hours in this church.

Marco's was closed today. No sign. The barriers are almost all down. Did this happen last night? Today it is supposed to be warming up to 55 degrees Fahrenheit. We stepped outside, and the weather was chilly, cloudy and without sunshine. This is probably our first or second non-sunny day to this date. Nonetheless, the weather doesn't dictate our destinations. We are off to seek out an attractive Neoclassical, fourth-century CE Basilica of Saint Paul Outside the Walls, in the bustling immigrant quarter called Esquiline—one of the original seven hills of Rome. The Basilica of San Paolo Fuori Le Mura was situated outside the original Aurelian Wall and had an interesting history, architecture and art.

This basilica is one of only four major basilicas in Rome. The other three are Saint John in the Lateran, Saint Peter's and Saint Mary Major. Its historical significance attracts visitors and pilgrims from all over the world. Supposedly, St. Paul's body was buried here, and the church was built over the tomb in the fourth century. The building was sacked in the eighth century, and a fire in the 1800s almost destroyed the entire building. The humongous new building (completed in 1840) is brilliant in color, structure, proportions and, as expected, grandeur. Frescoes and paintings of the 12th century are superlatively restored. Especially interesting was the 12th-century candlestick, a remarkable and unique piece of Romanesque art. Also, the bronze gates were made in 1070 in Constantinople. South of the transept is the 12th-century cloister with double columns, inlaid with golden colored glass. I thought the windows were of stained glass, but reading their booklet indicated that they were translucent alabaster—still stunning! Looking carefully at things, old or new, with intelligent interest vastly increases the enjoyment and pleasure; we are learning every single day to appreciate our good fortune.

What happened to the sunshine? Chilly outside means cold in the basement. More heat is required, and Em does not like to be chilly: "I'm Sicilian," she retorts. All the barriers are down; people are walking down Via Adige and some even to Marco's. Marco, Benita and his father are all busy when we come in. Marco makes coffee for the few customers, while Benita places fresh cornetti and croissants in the pastry rack, and Marco's father, whom we never met, is busy cleaning the dining area and wiping the tabletops. As we walk to the sitting area, he pulls out a chair for Em, smiles, and sends an inviting and sincere "buongiorno" to us. We reply in kind.

I went up to the counter to retrieve our due cappuccini and uno cornetto, and Marco, in English, said, "Good morning, have a nice day." I'm flabbergasted. Marco has taught us a few Italian phrases and vocabulary when he was not busy, and we respond with English phrases like, "good morning" and "have a nice day, no worries, and how's it going." We are all learning something new and appreciate his kind and considerate words of encouragement. That is, we must continue to learn more Italian in order to communicate without using the Google translator. Em wanted to spend some time to see the Salvador Dali exhibit at the Capitoline Museum at Piazza del Campidoglio. The piazza was designed by Michelangelo. Em has always said that as a person he was quite a character, and as a surrealist artist he was renowned for his technical skills and bizarre images in his work. Em loves his work, but there wasn't enough; unfortunately, his most famous paintings were not here (e.g., "Self-Portrait," "The Persistence of Memory" and "The Burning Giraffe"). While Em was thoroughly enjoying the Dali exhibit, I took a slow walk to tour the Forum, to linger and reflect on over 2,000 years of history, architecture and culture.

I had the Dali experience but missed the unconscious and creative potential meaning in my conscious mind. Em explained what I missed and why Salvador Dali and the Surrealist movement impacted art, literature, culture and, to some extent, politics. The sisters did mention to try I Dolci di Nonna, nearby. This incredible establishment meets every pastry craving you could ever imagine: Cannolo Siciliano, Santo Natale, Merenda Dalla Nonna, marzipan fruit, croissants, and Lavazza Italian coffee. Thank you to Simona and Giuliana.

Marco seemed to be a bit more upbeat as all the construction barriers were down; we thought that this new situation would reestablish his past business. We are doing our small bit.

The day's temperature ranged from 47 to 56 Fahrenheit. A cloudy day, perfect to visit a new neighborhood for us. We roamed and lingered around the famous Monti quarter, dating back to ancient times of the Forum Romanum. We happened to find the "King of Tiramisu," Pompi, another recommendation by Giuliana, and she said, "Rome's most famous dessert restaurant" is located at Via della Croce, 82. After Nonna Vincenza yesterday, I didn't think anything could be better. We looked at the wonderful selection of pastries and their famous tiramisu. However tempting, we decided to try the tiramisu at another time.

The Monti neighborhood, situated in the center of the city, is a few blocks on foot to the Colosseum and included the Basilica of San Giovanni in Laterano and the Baroque Church of Santa Maria ai Monti. We passed these imposing buildings to reach the famous Pompi Tiramisu and backtracked to spend slow travel time in the neighborhood outside the walls of Rome. Such a groovy quarter with plenty of boutiques, shops, bars, trattorias, hip wine bars, cafés and parks but a long journey since we got lost for only the second time; slow travel, for me, minimizes the anguish of getting lost.

Our reflections: This eclectic Monti neighborhood of Rome was full of bohemian elements and youth energies, making for a great place to observe, linger, and reflect on how fortunate we are to have this amazing slow travel opportunity in Rome.

There seems to be a new, festive, spring spirit in Marco's. Perhaps it is the glorious sunshine this morning? He appears to be happier, singing to us, "good morning and have a nice day." Benita is singing a Los Zafiros tune, Bossa Cubana: "Sabadabadaba Papapapada Bossa nova, ven Cubanita primorosa," and we're also grooving to the doo-wop-inspired close-harmonic Cuban music. I fell in love with Cuban music while we lived in Spain, a departure from the flamingo guitar music! Benita was from Cuba, and I am sure her parents must have listened to the Los Zafiros music of the '60s. Em's knee needs a rest. It's a quick bus ride to the Borghese gardens where she can sketch and watercolor all day long. The beautiful and peaceful park was embraced with the magic of the burnt-orange and ochre-colored 14th–15th-century building in the brilliant sunshine. The Villa Borghese is where Em loves to sketch, especially the fountains and statues. I leave her by her by the Fontana dei Cavalli (sea horses), one of the most poetic fountains according to P.B. Shelley. The fountain stands tall in the glowing sunlight, encircled by tall stone pines and box hedges. Em indicated she would like a couple of hours, "se tu per favore." I am in favor of whatever she wants.

A few weeks ago I found two secret gardens of the Renaissance and Baroque periods within the Borghese park: I had the time and inspiration to revisit the one garden with stone pines, cedars and plane trees, all of which will provide me with a trigger to my allergies in a couple of weeks. On top of the Piazza del Fiocco arch is an eagle statue, linked to all sky gods and a symbol of pride and royalty. The other secret garden was the Flower Garden, laid out in a formal garden design. There are over 250 varieties of plants within the Villa Borghese that, soon, surely will set off my allergies. The third garden that I didn't take the time to explore the first time led me to the Sundial Building, a masterfully decorated sundial made of marble and stucco created by one of the leading 17th-century Baroque architects, Carlo Rainaldi. Nearby, another Baroque masterpiece by Rainaldi was his Casino della Meridiana. By not taking the time during my previous walk, I didn't look carefully at these Baroque structures; I'm sure happy I did this time. While I meandered back towards Em's sketching fountain, I see another garden containing a replica of the Shakespeare's Globe Theater built in 2003, and his plays are continuing to be performed. Em can't wait to return to the apartment and work on her sketches. I can recognize her energetic effort in her work.

Benita is working a number of customers, while the four barstools are taken with matching blue jump-suited city workers, all wearing the same classic Ivy caps. No sight of Marco. As we looked out the sitting room window that faces Via Adige, Marco, and then his father, pulled up into those two reserved parking spaces in front of his café. Marco drives a newer Lancia Delta S4 and his dad a Fiat 500L; I know my cars! We surmise that Marco's father was here to help in the café as business has been steady, at least while we have been here.

Em wanted to rest her knee and work on her watercolors from yesterday's Villa Borghese sketches. I am on my own to discover how the shop owners secure their business premises. Every shop or café has a shutter, or serranda, that closes from top to bottom to secure their establishment. This morning I went around our neighborhood to see firsthand how it works. I have not seen these shutters in other countries, but I did not grow up in the city, so I never saw them until we moved to Rome. Most of the 27 shutters I looked at just before the shops were open were metal, all galvanized with graffiti.

Some shopkeepers even had "semi-professionals" paint or place "sticker-art," something more pleasant on their shutters. Most of the serranda were very colorful with flowers or angels, some with the name of the shop on it and a couple with "fu-k Bush." A key was used for the electronic system to raise and lower the metal door. I did not observe any shopkeepers opening their shutters by hand. They use the funghetto or mushroom (makes sense) that acts to lock down the serranda. They put the key in and rotate the mushroom sideways so the shutter can't be raised. In case a system doesn't work or help is required, one is not far from stickers advertising serranda repairs, along with their telephone number.

Marco is closed on Sundays. The same well-established routine for clothes washing, cleaning and ironing is upon us. This weekly event works well as by 12 p.m. we are half-way finished with the dusting, vacuuming and general cleaning, and we Skype our family and grandchildren. We are relieved that the boys are over the flu and back at school. Our granddaughter is very well and thanks us again for the books. The grandchildren said they loved the books about Rome we sent to them from the Anglo-American Book-shop at Via della Vite 102. Seems the boys' favorite was the book, "*The Rotten Romans* (Horrible Stories)," and the hilarious part about the emperors. Our granddaughter liked "*Madeline and the Cats of Rome*," and she loves animals. Happiness and joy through books!

Interesting weather forecast for today: 39–56 degrees F. It still remains chilly in the evenings and mornings. The hot water bottles make sleeping comfortable, even though the heat is turned off. Good news is that the sun is meant to be with us for the entire day.

An early morning, due cappuccini and uno cornetto at Marco's. His business is picking up; perhaps it was the construction and barriers that made the entrance to his café difficult. We are pleased to see a steady stream of customers. As Em works out the bus schedule and stops, this will be a day dedicated to Donato Bramante, who introduced High Renaissance architecture style to Italy, in Trastevere: First, the Renaissance style Chiesa di' San Pietro in Montorioat Piazza di S. Pietro in Montorio; second, Bramante's Little Temple in the courtyard of the church. If a proper amount of time is with us, a final visit to San Francesco a Ripa, in Trastevere.

Bramante designed the monastery and cloister of Santa Maria della Pace, our favorite place to meditate and reflect. The late 15th century of the Church of San Pietro in Montorio hosts five chapels with important and beautiful frescoes by Sebastiano del Piombo, Giorgio Vasari's ceiling painting, and an altar piece attributed to G. Mazzini. The second chapel, Raimondi Chapel contains Gian Lorenzo Bernini's "St. Francis in Ecstasy," and has the last sculptures he completed when he was 75 years old. Included in the courtyard stands Bramante's Tempietto, the first Renaissance structure in Rome.

Bramante Tempietto (1502) is in the courtyard of the church. The temple is one of the most harmonious buildings of the Renaissance. It is circular in form, perfect proportions, and the earliest example of the Tuscan order (one of two classical orders developed by the Romans) during this period. This is an architectural marvel that should not be missed. As we sat inside the small temple, we reflected on how fortunate and over-joyed we were to be able to live in Rome on our fixed income. Some of the simpler pleasures of Rome are seeing the ancient buildings in the brilliant sunshine, illustrating the same watercolors that Em uses in her work: Indian yellow-red, cadmium red and orange, yellow-orange ochre and burnt sienna browns. We're peeking into the delightfully tidy courtyards, watching the artisans work in their ateliers, tucked in obscure back alleys, mostly hidden within those streets and alleys. We had to patiently search for them—but they are there to discover and appreciate.

It has been 55 days, over one-half of our time living in Rome. Everything is joyful (i.e., Marco seems to be enjoying the resurgence of his business, Em's knee is feeling much better after periodic resting, and my allergy symptoms are minimal at the present time). Buona fortune to Marco and family.

I have been looking forward to our revisit to the Basilica di San Pietro in Vincoli at Piazza di San Pietro in Vincoli, 4a. The Basilica San Pietro in Vincoli was built in the

Temple to commemorate a martyrdom, St. Peter's.

fifth century to house St. Peter's chains in the reliquary and houses the incredible statue of Moses by Michelangelo. After reading an insightful and detailed book by William E. Wallace, *Michelangelo: The Artist, the Man, and His Times*, we had to return for the third time to see the mausoleum of Pope Julius II, and the statue of Moses. We placed a euro in the slot, and Moses' carefully carved marble refinements, folds and details light up as if Moses were alive. Michelangelo's massive statue of Moses was unlike any other in the world. Moreover, there were seventh-century mosaics that console both heart and mind. In Wallace's book, we learned that Michelangelo carved his eight-foot sculpture from one piece of Carrara marble in three years, also while painting the Sistine Chapel in Saint Peter's, a tribute to his energy, devotion, creative and carving genius. He created a new world of art, and Moses was the high priest.

What we did notice during this visit to the church was there were only a few visitors, a photo shot extravaganza who were actually breezing by. They were having the captivating experience but perhaps not understanding the meaning of the artist's genius, time frame in art history, and Michelangelo's efforts to produce such a sculpture.

Lunch in the Jewish quarter at the Nonna Betta, an elegant Italian/Kosher restaurant at Via del Portico d'Ottavia, 16. On the outside window was an article from the *New York Times* by the great Anthony Bourdain, praising the restaurant's food, especially his favorite Roman specialty—fried artichokes. We split one and enjoyed a long (three-hour) leisurely meal. The long, leisurely meal was extended, as seated next to us was a perky and energized 30ish-year-old woman, a world-traveler from Vancouver and New York City. Needless to say, we had a lively and interesting conversation about how traveling defines who you are and the life choices one makes with respect to traveling. We talked about how we are retired, and we're redefining our enjoyment together through slow travel. Natsumi told how she gave up her Wall Street job to travel, as she so aptly indicated, "Travel is a journey into one's ignorance," and we can certainly know this firsthand. Incidentally, the artichokes were a tasty tapas treat; the pasta and anchovy pizza were even better, that's right!

Mid–March and the temperatures are normalizing at 41–59 degrees Fahrenheit. That means less use of heat, excellent walking and exploration weather.

We walked to the Villa Borghese, hopped on bus #116, one of 16 small (eight seats) electric buses that quietly dawdle through the very narrow streets within the historic center. The bus stopped at the Via Giulia, the only actual straight street in Rome. We stayed on bus #166 and rode

"Moses" by Michelangelo. The horns are a result of the Hebrew translation of "Rays of light coming from his head."

over the Tiber to Trastevere, bused up the Gianicolo Hill with a gorgeous view over-looking the city, and we could even point out many of the landscape buildings. As it is near Easter, as expected, the crowds are huge around the major piazzas. We really sym-pathize with the patience and tolerance of the staff in those shops, restaurants and cafés that must politely cater to the throngs of new tourists to their area. In Trastevere, you can never be bored walking the narrow medieval streets, as the sun's magic reflects the watercolor print of the burnt-orange and ochre-brown buildings. We took the same bus back to the Borghese, seeing everything from the other side. Honestly, the bus is never full as this route is used only by folks seemingly coming and going from point A to B, I suspect to work and back. A great way to see Rome's hidden treasures, in peaceful comfort.

Why do I have this alluring interest in, almost an obsession with churches? Lack-ing a devotional sense of mission, churches, for me, are fascinating rational physical objects that immediately tug one into their elegance, grace, harmonious proportions and ornate beauty. Rome boasts about 900 churches, and church architecture is exciting to observe and study. From the Pantheon of 113–125 CE to the Renaissance (1400–1600) and Baroque (1600–1830), churches are a marvel of structure and form, especially their domes, stained-glass windows, master builders marks, hidden misericords, devotional paintings, frescoes, facades and architectural harmony. I am also a committed tapho-phile, a cemetery lover, to discover the language of symbols.

The sense of geometric harmony is evident by the aesthetic principles of ideal pro-portion and ratios which result in their everlasting visual beauty. It appears that the inte-gration of technology, geometry, and engineering informs their beauty and function, a perfect union of science and of art. It was Georg W.F. Hegel who stated explicitly when asked to define beauty, "The perfect harmony of form and function is beauty." More-over, Leon Batista Alberti had his theory of beauty (1428), and he was a true Renaissance man—mathematician, humanistic, literature, theorist, and philosophy. For Alberti's the-ory of beauty: beauty is proportions; beauty is perceived; beauty is intuitive; beauty is nature; beauty is numbers; beauty is decorum, appropriateness for the setting.

There are also outbursts to the senses:

The smells of the woods, stones, stucco (moldy, damp, mildew); the sweet fragrances of frankincense, citrus and roses; the burning of candles along with the vaporized gas-eous wax; the essence of seasonal flowers; the aroma of the "heavenly" and biblical scents of the Garden of Eden.

The "merry" sounds of the pealing bells, like the rhythms of a waltz. The relationship between music, its architectural acoustics, and light (visual information) that is so com-mon in Roman Baroque churches. The voices from the mighty air vibrating organ that Mozart called the "king of instruments." Then there is the frozen music that is somehow there but not audible (e.g., heavenly performers like angels and saints). And the mono-phonic, unaccompanied, sacred Latin Gregorian chants. "As some to church repair, not for the doctrine, but the music there," Alexander Pope.

The touching of the intricate carved misericords under the folding choir seats, the "poppy-heads," those intricate wood carvings at the end of the pews, the silky smoothness of the limestone, marble and brass memorials that have been rubbed over centuries, the chiseled stone carvings around the flutes of the capitals, and the sometimes dramatic sepul-chral memorials—those reclining tomb effigies representing the past, present and future.

Sight light is a major interior factor as it projects diffused images, especially through the stained glass. Accordingly, as light passes through them, the walls of the church take on the qualities and glow of "heaven" itself. The sight of those exceptional wall paintings and devotional frescoes fosters an overwhelming visceral punch, the sensuous impact to the heart and to the limbic part of the brain. If you carefully observe around the church, in the tower, around the door and window jambs, you might find markings and designs for ritual protection (e.g., VV, or the master mason's graffiti marks).

You can, as I do, "taste" the sensation of being so close to perfection, proportions, craftsmanship and devotional love.

We stop off at Marco's, have our usual, and tell him that we are going to Bologna for a few days. He says, "Bologna e Bellissima, assicurati di vedere la cattedrale." I even understood what he said. We thanked him for his advice and bid him the Google translation of "ci vediamo tra pochi giorni," see you in a few days.

We had planned to take this little excursion from Rome before it got too warm, as the Emilia-Romagna region gets extremely hot. We set off early to Rome's Termini Station to Bologna. Our plans were to take the train from Bologna to Modena and from Modena to the Emilia-Romagna region of northern Italy and the city of Reggio Emilia (pop. 171,000). Some years ago, we spent six weeks during the summer living in a studio in the historic center of Reggio nell'Emilia while studying their Reggio approach to early childhood education. Most recently, as college instructors, we led two delegations of American educators to study and learn about their educational philosophy-psychology, which was borne out of the ashes of World War II.

Our plans are always tentative in that anything could change, and we must be up to any challenges. We planned some time to visit the Ferrari Museum in Modena before going to Reggio Emilia for three nights. Those plans were to spend Saturday exploring the many treasures of Reggio and on Sunday spend the day in Bologna, which also has amazing architectural and historical sights to discover.

We arrived in Modena at 11 a.m. from Rome. Em worked out which bus would take us near the Ferrari Museum. We enjoyed the two-hour tour of the modern and observed the original yellow color chosen by Enzo himself for his Prancing Horse Ferrari. The museum had about 50 autos from the beginning of Enzo's racing career, spanning 60 years. Back to the station for the train arriving at Reggio Emilia at 2:30, and immediately the hearts and minds start pumping. This is the most livable small city we have ever visited. No autos or buses in the center; pedestrians walk or ride bicycles everywhere. And the colors! Every organic color is present here. We had a small dinner at Amici del Rifugio Crucolo (food and service excellent) and a passeggiare around this gorgeous city center before returning to our hotel. Tomorrow we will explore the many interesting sights in the city of Reggio Emilia.

Reggio Emilia. Weather: 45–72 F. Sunny and beautiful ultramarine skies.

I had many return sights on my Reggio list, if I can remember any of them. As Em and I were singing "walking in rhythm," lyrics by the Blackbyrds, we paused and lingered at the Piazza Fontanesi where families and children played; adults were talking with parts of their extremities and generally enjoying the sunny day. At the entrance to Parc Alcide Cervi, the local park, children were playing, and dogs were running free as dogs! Inside the park was a beautiful sculpture dedicated to the Teacher of Italy. Strolling down Via Garibaldi, several blocks from the Hotel Posta, we unexpectedly found an exhibit of Andy Warhol's "Last Supper." We had a personal guide, Vea, that explained all about the painter and his two masterpieces: "Marilyn" and "Last Supper." We spent a considerable amount of time with our very knowledgeable guide and, always as students, learned a great deal about the artist and his life.

We spent the rest of the day in total bliss as this is a walking city. At the corner of Piazza Di Santa Giovanna was a tiled devotional mosaic embedded in a wall. I remembered that the mosaic was placed high, and we had to look up to appreciate its beauty. We definitely had to visit the Scala del Tricolore at Piazza Camillo Prampolini to further study all about the flag's origin in Reggio Emilia and its history of the tri-color Italian flag. The great puppeteer Otello Sarzi lived here; he passed away in 2001 and left a rich collection of puppets to the Reggio Emilia community, off to Otello Sarzi's Puppets House with its rich collection of puppets and marionettes. We didn't have a reservation, which was required to visit, but Paulo, the director of the House, let us in when we told him about our many visits to Reggio Emilia and our love for puppets. When we lived in Oxfordshire many years ago, Em and I took a marionette course, traveling from Bicester to London for nine weeks. The course was led by professionals, and we learned a great deal about the profession and the three types: string, rod and hand puppets. Nothing without joy. Reggio is a pedestrian and bicycle town; only taxis and residents' buses are permitted in the large pedestrian zone. We saw fewer folks smoking, walking dogs, or talking on their mobile phones as compared to Roma. The shops were a visual treat, exquisite, expensive, and the shop window displays were very well presented. The Max Mara enterprise was founded in Reggio. This is a very rich area of Italy. In the last decade or so there has been a steady increase in immigrants that makes the town-city more inclusive and organic. Reggio is famous for its production of Parmigiano Reggiano cheese and balsamic vinegar. It is the food and architecture and cultural-history that makes this a very special city in Italy.

The food is the best in Italy—fresh, seasonal, carefully prepared and professionally served. Reggio is not on the tourist trail, except for the hundreds of American-Canadian-Australian-Japanese educators that come here throughout the year to learn about the Reggio schools. When asked about adopting the Reggio approach to other countries, Howard Gardner, a developmental psychologist and a Harvard professor, indicated that we can only reinvent the Reggio Emilia approach when we understand the values and cultural beliefs of each culture. Furthermore, he maintains that we must then compare these with what Reggio Emilia has been capable of in creating its own unique context, with its own informed educators and designed resources. This is the dilemma of transporting one cultural set of beliefs and values to another culture or school system. It reminded me of the American dilemma regarding the British primary school movement in the '60s–'70s. Wish we had Gardner's advice then. However, we were amazed that there were a large number of folks from Germany, Holland and Belgium for the humongous motorcycle market—buying and selling of bikes—just outside the city in the burbs of Reggio Emilia. A visit to Reggio was not fully appreciated until we stopped to enjoy two Erbazzone Reggiano, the regional dish combining spinach, onions, garlic and parmigiano. While eating our Erbazzone, we had a lengthy chat with two buyers/sellers from Frankfurt, Germany, here to survey the huge array of cycling products. They were experts in their respective fields, one on the custom building of cycles and the other, rather large chap, the financial advisor, of sorts. They generously informed us about a subject (motorcycles—buying and selling for huge profits), a subject that we knew nothing about; now we know something more than before. It was Socrates who stated, "One thing I know is that I know nothing; this is the source of wisdom." Perhaps we are gaining wisdom during retirement. That's what slow travel is.

Parma, Italy. Weather: 39–67 degrees F. Cold, cloudy, rainy and partially sunny.

Itinerary: We had a change of plans for today. Since we are traveling out of Bologna station tomorrow, we shall save Bologna for tomorrow. Instead, we decided to visit the historic, founded in 183 BCE, and architecturally stunning tourist city of Parma (194,500), northwest of Reggio Emilia. The train ride is only 20 minutes, and the historical town center is very old and beautiful. Parma has its renowned Duomo, the Theater/Opera House, where Pavarotti first performed and where all the internationally known performing artists perform at some point in their careers. Again, a delightfully easy walking city, no cars, just people and bikes. Their bike paths wind all through the city, similar to Amsterdam. Any reliable guidebook would entice tourists to read about and visit the beautiful city of Parma. As it was Palm Sunday, all the churches were performing services, organ music playing and chorus singing; we merely sat, lingered, listened and reflected on how fortunate we were to be able to slow travel, as seniors, in Italy. The 12th-century Cathedral of Parma–Duomo—for 900 years is a place of art, history and devotion and an absolute masterpiece in architectural features. One highlight is the ceiling frescoes painted by Antonio da Correggio, born in Correggio, a town between Modena and Reggio Emilia, the foremost painter of the Parma School and a masterpiece of Renaissance fresco work.

Reflections: Parma, with its exporting gold mine of Parma ham/cheeses, Reggio Emilia, its cheese, and Modena, its balsamic vinegar, are very wealthy cities in the north of Italy. Their tax base allows for clean streets, sidewalks, and trash pickups daily. A difference that was notably the opposite of Rome and Naples. It seems that the further north in Italy, the more affluent. Having said that, Rome is very special, and Reggio Emilia is indescribably comfortable. We are off tomorrow morning via train from Reggio Emilia to Bologna. We have the best part of the day in Bologna and arrive back in Rome around 8:30 p.m. or 20:30 hours.

Weather today: 39–70 F. Itinerary: Reggio Emilia to Bologna to Rome.

Sights: Wow! Bologna is amazing: the culinary capital. There is enough in this city to make you want to slow travel for many months. Architecture included medieval, Romanesque, Renaissance palazzi, energy-filled university district, two leaning towers, cafés, shopping (if you're into expensive shopping), cultural, museums, arts and history. There is no other city in the world that has more porticoes (loggia) than Bologna, and within the city center, it's some 38 kilometers long, you don't have to let the rain or overbearing sun hinder your walking in Bologna.

We had been to Bologna several times, but long ago. We took the hop-on/off bus to get an orientation of this fantastic city. There are churches, parks, medieval buildings, history and beauty. We also did a walking tour in case we missed anything.

Reflections: The ten-minute walk from the train station to Piazza Maggiore places one in the historical center. The three main sights: Palazzo d'Enzo (Medieval); Palazzo del Podesta Duomo (Romanesque); Palazzo Communal—seat of the local government. The bronze statue of Neptune is located in the center. One outstanding feature in the Basilica di San Domenico, one of the major churches in Bologna, is an exquisite shrine and three statues by a very young Michelangelo. Within the three churches visited, there were paintings by such noted painting masters as Guido Rein and Filipino Lippi, Nicolo Pisano and Antonio da Correggio. Just outside of the center are the Piazza di Porta where the two leaning towers, Torre Garisenda and Torre degli Asinelli, stand and the beginning of the university district. Only a few of the more than 200 towers that once rose above Bologna, built by noble families, are still standing. The remaining two are barely standing as they are about ten feet off the perpendicular.

About the university: University of Bologna is Europe's oldest, founded in 1053. By the 12th century, more than 10,000 students from all over Europe attended the University of Bologna. Their scholarly alumni included Thomas Becket, Copernicus, Dante, Petrarch, and Federico Fellini. This forward-thinking university employed female professors, unheard of during the Middle Ages. This university began as student directed, as opposed to professor-driven curricula at the Sorbonne. Moreover, the political leanings of today's student body are displayed in leftist slogans that emblazon the 14th–18th-century buildings.

Lunch at Ristorante Alice at Via Massimo D'Azeglio, 65. Displaying white tablecloths and simple surroundings, Alice served up the ultra-Bolognese fare within a very local crowd. We let the waiter make suggestions, and we settled on an antipasti including Pecorino with balsamic, cured meats, chickpeas and sliced marinated eggplant. A wonderful lunch not far from the student quarter. Food and cafés in this quarter are very inexpensive and exceptionally good.

Transportation: Took the train from Reggio Emilia to Modena, changed trains to Bologna. Took bus #35 to the Piazza Maggiore and our regular walk to our apartment.

Sunday and Skype: All reported that everyone was well. The first time one of the grandchildren asked us when we were to come back; that saddened me! We had wash, cleaning and vacuuming to do.

Marco had his steady customers back as we recognized many of them. Marco asked us if we saw the Bologna cathedral and how about their food. Em did a fine job of responding in Italian, without Google translator, and Marco seemed to understand as he made several hand gestures along with a warm smile. Later, I mentioned to Em that Marco hasn't spoken to us anymore in English. Em commented that we need to speak more Italian; we are just visitors. She's absolutely right, as usual.

Later on, sunshine, and with the temperatures ranging from 53 to 70 degrees Fahrenheit, Em and I decided that we take a leisurely stroll to sit in a café and reflect on our past few days in Reggio, Parma, Modena and Bologna. We settled on Cigno Caffé Pasticceria at Viale Dei Parioli, 16A, to enjoy the fine weather, great coffee and people-watching.

We were silently interrupted by an American woman who evidently overheard our American voices and asked if she could join us. Her name was Sarah, and she indicated that she had lived in Rome for the past ten years. As the introductions were made, the inquiry-based question I asked her was, "What changes in Rome have you experienced during your time in Rome?" I took out my notepad and asked her if I might take notes while she framed her response to the question, "Yes, of course." Here are my rather random notes from our insightful conversation with Sarah.

She stated that she did not want to sound too cynical, but the reality was that she was not well prepared for it, and "Rome can be a very hard city to live in. Jobs were and are few, salaries are low, and just getting paid can be a task. Though Italians generally know how to live life to the fullest, times have changed measurably since I got here a decade ago." To the dismay of many of her friends and family back home, "the fantasy existence is gone. Virtually no one (including me) spends their days lounging around sipping cappuccinos in the middle of Piazza Navona." These days Italians toil just to get by. The dreamy days are over." Since she works in the tourism industry, her job is to peel away the layers of this gorgeous city one by one to give tourists the same awestruck sensation she felt when she first got here. That's the easy part. "The trouble comes after the vacation. What Hollywood doesn't show us is that most Italians' average salary is a measly $2,500–$2,700—that's U.S. dollars, she emphasized—a month (net after taxes) in take-home pay; and those are the lucky ones. Most 'young' Italians find their first real job in their late 20s, and if they're lucky can count on pulling in around €900 a month. Add utilities and other obligations, and younger workers rarely get to €20,000 a year."

Whoa! She sort of apologized for her rambling, but we assured her that we were eager to hear more about her coming to terms with living in Rome. We were certainly enlightened and surprised by Sarah's lengthy conversation. When we returned to our flat, I did some research on my own regarding some parts from our informed discussion with our American cohort.

According to statistics released recently by the finance ministry (2010), more than 20,000,000 Italians make less than €15,000 a year, with the Rome area averaging about 22,000 euros. But with salaries like these, can you blame young Italians for staying with their parents? The average cost for a decently sized Rome apartment (something around 50 to 60 square meters, or 600 to 650 square feet, actually the size of our studio apartment in the states) could set you back anywhere between €800 and €1,000 a month, not including the cost of utilities, where electricity and gas are extremely high. Want to talk about gas prices? I've noticed fewer cars, more mopeds and motorcycles on the road in recent weeks. Petrol in Italy costs about $5.95 per gallon. Filling it up in Rome at current exchange rates would cost you roughly $75–$80. Another good reason not to have a vehicle in Rome.

Reflections: The current heavy-duty austerity program is taking its toll. Food and household product prices seem to be increasing. The potholed sidewalks, street clean-ups and many buildings requiring repairs are minimum at best, at least in the non-tourist areas, such as ours. The tourist areas are clean and well maintained and are always very busy, as expected. We are not complaining as we are tourists-foreigners in an adopted city. We are fortunate enough to have this slow travel experience and will always cherish our three months in Rome. It isn't our business to pass judgment or complain.

After a few days off to rest Em's knee and for me to avoid the springtime pollen, as my allergies are taking a toll, we have about 20 days left in Rome. My list of sights grows every day. I checked the weather for today: 48–68 degrees Fahrenheit, perfect for discovering the past.

Marco wasn't in this morning. Benita served us, always with her attractive smile, our regular due cappuccini e uno cornetto. Em worked out the bus route and stops to revisit the Pyramide–Caio Cestio and the Protestant cemetery. The Pyramid was built as a tomb to Camus Cestius; its Carrara marble-covered structure gleams two thousand years later in one of Rome's busiest traffic circles; one must be extremely careful when crossing these circles of steel and rubber.

> "Lives of great men remind us we can make our lives sublime, and, departing, leave behind us footprints on the sands of time."—H.W. Longfellow

The Protestant cemetery is where many famous (Cimitero Acattolico) non–Catholic folks died in Rome and were interred. Shelley (only his heart), Keats and Goethe's son were found alive and well in this cemetery. The cemetery was well groomed, and spring flowers were spotted everywhere. There are directions and tables in Italian and English that lead you to the often-visited spots. The cemetery was located around the old

Aurelian Wall. Nowhere is the language of symbols more visual than in cemeteries, and if you want symbolism, try Cimitero dei Protestanti in the neighborhood of Testaccio.

"Buongiorno, Marco e malato." I know what "male" equals: bad. Marco is not well. Em sends our best, and "lo vedremo presto," we will see him soon.

"Weeping Angel" or "Angel of Grief" by W. Wetmore.

Em had the buses worked out. From the bus stop we walk to the Roma Lido and take the commuter train for a 30-minute train ride east of the Colosseum that will take us to the 620 BCE Roman commercial/military port of Ostia Antica.

We learned that at the mouth of the Tiber River, Romans set up this port town of some 60,000 people to protect the river and Rome. This might be considered the most underappreciated sight in all of Italy! We have seen Pompeii and Herculaneum, but this is very different. As we wander and pause among these ruins, one can see the remains of docks, apartment flats, amphitheaters, mansions, shopping malls, baths and potties—a firsthand peek of Roman lifestyles 2,000 years ago.

The significance of the salt flats as meat preservers and its naval base location were due to Ostia's strategic position at the mouth of the River Tiber. By 150 CE, when Rome controlled all the Mediterranean, Ostia served as its busy commercial port. With the fall of Rome, the port was abandoned. Over time the harbor silted up. Ironically, the mud, which eventually buried Ostia, protected it from the ravages of time and from stone-scavenging medieval peasants. There was a small museum with a number of found artifacts from the excavation, and offered for sale were many statuary figures. Also found were a few surviving frescoes, mosaic tiles and marble carvings, a historical and cultural view of Roman lifestyles. This is a sight not to be missed!

Another firsthand, concrete learning experience; now we must further study for more meaning of what we have experienced.

Marco is back. Our silent friend still looks ill; maybe it is something else? His business is steady, and we do see a few new customers but many only for takeout. Em rests her knee and works on her watercolors, I am trying to minimize my allergies by staying inside when the air quality is reported to be "Orange."

Em has us going to a very special exhibit of Jacopo Robust or Tintoretto (1519–1594)

A 2,200-year-old resting place.

at the Scuderie del Quirinale, which is on top of Rome's original Hills. I read up on Tintoretto, and this was the only major 16th-century Italian painter not to have had a major exhibition devoted to his work thus far. Jacopo Tintoretto (1518–94), one of the greatest Venetian Mannerist painters of the Renaissance, was influenced by Michelangelo. His bold brushstrokes and use of color that absorbs the direct light over each painting yielded new possibilities for subsequent art periods. Specific paintings that illustrated his mastery were "Saint George and the Dragon" and "Finding of the Body of Saint Mark."

Thanks to Em for sharing this exceptional exhibit. I have been fortunate enough to have seen and admired a few paintings at the Louvre, but to be able to view, linger and reflect on over 40 paintings from all over the art world was appreciated.

The presentation, room space, distance from the work and displays of museum paintings are significant to the viewer. We have been fortunate to be able to experience dozens of Rome's great museums. However, the manner and care in which the entire exhibit was presented, including walls of dark crimson, very well lit, and the masterful care of the production and installation task were the best we have seen.

The exhibition focused on three distinguishing themes: religion, mythology and portraiture. These were divided into sections comprising several carefully selected lauded masterpieces, beginning and ending with his two celebrated self-portraits: of himself as a young man, on loan from the Victoria & Albert Museum in London, and as an old man, on loan from the Louvre. Although he was in competition with Titian (another famous Venetian painter of the same era), Tintoretto was recognized among his contemporaries for his "utterly exquisite eye in portraiture." Another unforgettable painting in the collection was Em's favorite, "Miracle of the Slave," painted in 1548 for the Scuola Grande di San Marco, Venice, and with this painting, Tintoretto became known as one of the leaders of the Venetian art scene.

The rest was beneficial for Em, as she is all ready to spend our day with some chat time at our favorite cafe outside of our neighborhood, Caffè Bartaruga in Piazza Mattei. Only two seats were available. Lucky for us, with a perfect frontal view of the famous Four Turtle Fountain. We watched for hours the many tourists taking pictures and locals eating snacks and beverages on the two benches near the fountain. This magical fountain was at times so full of humanity that we could not see the fountain. We moved inside to listen to the café owner's marvelous CD selection of jazz, Italian classics and a variety of American rhythm and blues (including Tina Turner, Kool & The Gang, The Skyliners), doo-wop (Del-Vikings, Harptones, Flamingos, Lauryn Hill), pop-jazz-fusion vocals and our all-time favorite, "What a Difference a Day Makes," by Dinah Washington. We praised the owner with his music playlist, and we're told, in perfect English, that in the evenings at Caffè Bartaruga, "We have live jazz music. Come early as we have a small seating capacity."

All this in the center of historic Rome.

Whoa! Temperatures today range from 39 to 66 F. Cold, but sunny with bright skies.

Marco was not himself today. Em sensed there is something going on. He has been different since those barriers were removed. I remarked that his business actually picked up after the barriers were removed, and he was very upbeat. Perhaps there is something at home, or his father may be ill; who knows, but there has been a change in Marco. We hope all is well.

We're excited to take the one-hour and 45-minute train to Tivoli, outside of Rome.

The *Fontana delle Tartarughe* (The Turtle Fountain).

Tivoli sits on the lower slopes of the Apennines. This area has one of the most impressive ancient sites in all of Rome. The area was the richest building project in antiquity and was designed by Emperor Hadrian in 126 CE. These buildings are the beginnings of the Roman architecture that would continue for the next 1,000 years! A direct descendant from Greek architecture but with the addition of the first two (of five) Roman architectural styles. A few kilometers from Hadrian's Villa is Villa D'Este. The grand park was completed in 1550 and has hosted artists and writers such as Cellini, Liszt and cardinals of all sorts. The primary sites are the over 70 Renaissance fountains built against a dramatic hillside. This is a very special place to explore and wonder.

Reflections: First time taking the Metro. Our modes of travel included bus #84 to Termini train station, the Metro Blue Line to Rebibbia, and a bus to Tivoli. Overall travel time is about 1 hour, 45 minutes.

We quickly learned that in Italy, when you work on a day you typically have off, for example Monday, some national holiday, then you must have the next day off, which in our case today was Tuesday. The long story short, the Villas' doors were closed today. Not all was lost, however. The town was lovely, with impressive views and a magnificent setting.

Meals: Lunch at Artis Bar in Tivoli. Great fresh, multi-veggie salad, split a bowl of pasta, a few Sicilian sesame cookies, and we were good to go.

Bottom line: We shall return this week or next as this is definitely a sight to be seeing while in Rome.

We stayed in for a couple of days as my allergies were annoying enough to make me go to the pharmacy-farmacia. I asked the pharmacist if she could prescribe something for my allergies. She probably could tell I'm suffering due to my cough and a bit of tissue still hanging from my right nostril. How embarrassing, but I did receive from the pharmacist two different products: a eucalyptus nasal spray, twice a day in each nostril; Azelastine Hydrochloride, twice in the morning and twice at night. She said that I would be fine in a few days. She also advised me to check the seasonal pollutant index each day and stay in if the rating was orange/red. I thank her with my best Italian, "grazie, buona giornata."

I felt better already. While I was in the apartment, I researched what pollutants in Rome are contributing to my asthmatic symptoms. Found out that in Rome, desert dust particles are small enough to be inhaled into the deepest parts of the lungs, pollutant gases such as ozone levels, sulfur dioxide, nitrogen dioxide from motor vehicles, birch pollen, airborne allergens, plane trees, and grass pollen, etc. These city-life pollutants and seasonal allergens are the collateral effects of slow travel. I can either stay inside or continue to discover, explore and enjoy our retirement living in Rome. I immediately began to scrutinize my "see before our time is up" list and planned for tomorrow's revisit to the Tivoli. I checked; it will be open.

Return to Tivoli and view Villa d'Este, the 16th-century villa. This terraced hillside Renaissance garden boasted two UNESCO World Heritage Sites. This was a tad difficult to reach, hills, but not a problem. The return trip bus was extremely crowded as the tourists are out in force—good for them. This is a not-to-be-missed opportunity.

Reflections: The ultimate Renaissance fairyland of a hundred fountains included Neptune, Leda and Rometta, grottes—Grottos of Diana and Hercules, reflecting pools, gurgling rocks, and two diorama-like fountains built into the walls designed by Gian Lorenzo Bernini in the 1500s. Moreover, Travertine, one of the famous marbles, has been quarried in Tivoli for over 2,500 years.

The natural beauty of this setting was enhanced and influenced by the grace of the Mannerist style during that period. Many 18th-century French painters, for example, Charles Joseph Natoire and his students Hubert Robert and Jean Honore' Fragonard, spent their summers painting the dramatic vistas that featured the fountains, statues and lush foliage. Absolutely spectacular! And I love the paintings by Robert and Fragonard.

Marco was not working today. Benita and Marco's father were tending to the seven or so customers. We actually had to wait 17 minutes before our coffee and cornetto appeared. Time is irrelevant when we slow travel; I just kept time because we generally wait a few minutes. Em's knee is fine; my allergies are somewhat better, hopefully due to the medications.

One of the more unique opportunities we had planned from my "unique discovery" list was to scout out the new architecture in Rome. A few churches have developed new architecture in the past few years, and we set out to discover their uniqueness and beauty.

We bused south of Rome to a new neighborhood church. The design of Santo Volto di Santo Volto di Gesù would be described as minimal at best. However, the simpleness of the design and function made this particular church design interestingly unique from other relatively "modern" churches. After admiring the exterior, we walked to another nearby church when we met a couple of Rome University students. They explained in perfect English that they were working on a church architecture project and taking photos of the people who frequent these churches (I suspected that they first asked permission?) for their final grade. They explained what they were hoping to demonstrate through their research. I fell in love with the project's objectives. I envisioned a combination of interconnected disciplines including art-architecture-history-sociology! Moreover, they provided us with contextual information about the "fabulous" Santo Volto di Gesù and suggested a couple of other "unique" churches in the area.

Reflections: Santo Volto di Gesù Church was located at Portense quarter in the Magliana in the Malians neighborhood of south Rome. The church was completed in 2006, one of the most successful examples of modern religious architecture in Rome. The location was difficult to find, but Em is great at finding transport locations to unique places.

Here is the unique bit about this church and its neighborhood. This is a highly populated area with a history of social struggle, unauthorized building, and urban violence. The architects based their design and location on the relationship between public space and religious space and bring them both together. Alas, the open space in front of the church became a piazza, the public–social square the neighborhood never had. The project, we were told, was based on a direct relationship between art and architectural space, linking religious and artistic expression with ethics and aesthetics. The architects were Piero Sartogo and Nathalie Grenon.

Postscript Reflection: The church was geometrically beautiful, white-on-white exterior and a slanted concave dome-like area that allowed filtered natural light to enter the entire interior. The interior seats were all painted light baby blue and were set in uniform rows with high backs for easy sitting, a fabulous discovery while slow traveling outside central Rome. The two students, Rosa and Roberto, were most helpful and delighted to share their wealth of knowledge with us.

Temperatures are rising: 54–85. With the increases in temperature, humidity and tourists, this place is cool—Not! It seems as if within a couple of days, the whole climate has changed. We are not complaining as we don't have to use the electric for heating the apartment.

Sunday—a work day! Skyped the family and grandchildren. The report: Everyone was well, grandchildren were enjoying their spring school break, Ty playing with his Lego set, and Cole building with this Vermont company wooden blocks. Annika introduced us to her new stuffed owl.

The temperatures are in a reasonable range for layering if we venture outside today, 50–72 F, sunny for our clothes to dry in one day, hopefully.

In between the wash, vacuuming, dusting, ironing we lounged around our delightful neighborhood. On Sundays, many cafés and bars are closed as the major portion of their business occurs during their work week. However, one advantage of slow travel is that we have time to scout out new places or sights yet discovered in Rome. We found the Gran Caffé Sicilia at Piazza Acillia, 15–18, not far from our flat. This little café served fresh fruit, a Sicilian-style gelato and café a la Sicily (with chocolate topping). This was a chain café with several locations in Rome. The coffee was good and less expensive than Marco's, which is simply very hard to believe, but true. We prefer Marco's Illy coffee to Lavazza, just tastes better.

Reflections: Within the past few days we have found three new cafés, all with a different feature: easy to watch people pass, outdoors in the sun, self-service without the service fee, small and large capacities, and all with friendly and energetic service.

Marco's was closed this Monday. No vacation sign.

A rather dull day outside—cloudy, damp and on the cool side. A short bus ride to the Capitoline Museums at Piazza del Campidoglio, 1. Always a sensual pleasure to carefully observe the hill area around the Piazza del Campidoglio. Meeting visitors at the center of the piazza is a copy of the equestrian statue of Marcus Aurelius. Michelangelo designed and built the base for the statue, which is the symbol of the city's imperial glory and Renaissance energy and resurgence. The original is tucked neatly inside the Capitoline Museum. Capitoline Hill is the smallest but the most famous hill in Rome.

So many statues, why? During the Middle Ages, pagan Roman statuary (sculpture of statues) was seen as evil and disgusting by early Christians, so much of it was destroyed or simply discarded. However, by the time of the Renaissance, the ancient Roman sculptures were reborn and appreciated as art. Since Ancient times, Romans were not guaranteed freedom of expression, so these statues around the city become their "talking statues." People would gather around the statues to air their grievances; they were thinking of creative ways to communicate. By hiding behind their stone friends, they were able to avoid reprisals, which most times resulted in death.

Our focus today was the Capitoline Museums. The two museums are a massive collection of Classical art and the Pinacoteca-painting gallery.

The art is arranged according to the schools of art, for example, Ferrara, Venice, Emilia, Bologna and the Roman school. A fantastic collection, especially sculptures by

Piazza del Campidoglio on Capitoline Hill—Michelangelo's perfect design of Renaissance urban planning. His design was to take all components of a plan and make them have the same quality and quantity and be in unison in terms of style and proportions.

Equestrian statue of Marcus Aurelius in the Piazza del Campidoglio.

Bernini and Michelangelo, the Roman figures and statues, and, of course, the paintings by Reni, Rubens, Velazquez and Caravaggio's "Fortune Teller." A terrific museum day that we enjoyed very much. Walk around the corner and find another abstract, nonrepresentational art exhibit by a contemporary Italian artist. Love the blend of the various Mediterranean colors.

Sunday. Skype to everyone. The grandchildren only want to tell us about their playdates, their teachers, swimming lessons, climbing trees and reading. Their friends, school, and social time (recess) are developing appropriately. We enjoy their happiness. We are so pleased; surely they are finding our replacement?

Sundays in Rome are family day, and everything slows down, especially in our residential neighborhood. It is a wonderful time to stroll and be happy. Accordingly, more panhandlers are out on Sundays with their dogs—hybrids, terriers, sad-looking labs—taking advantage of the increased strollers, perhaps more money for their poor dogs lying helplessly on a dirty blanket. How very sad for both the humans and their dogs.

We entered from the south side Vatican wall to the modern entrance door with security guards and security checking all handbags, even purses. We headed upstairs to purchase two tickets and proceeded into the Pinacoteca, or painting gallery. Highlights: Here we viewed Giotto's "Stefaneschi Triptych"; Raphael's "Transformation," his last painting before he died at age 37; Leonardo di Vinci's "St. Jerome in the Wildness" (1480), his only painting in Rome. Also, Caravaggio's only painting in the Vatican is the dramatic "Deposition" in which it seems as if Christ's body is being passed on to you as you stand before it.

After what seemed to be endless hours and so many visitors, we needed to get some air and headed to the courtyard of the Pinecone. However, on the way to the courtyard we lingered while we passed through the Hall of Tapestries, beautiful 17th-century tapestries made from wool, silk, gold and silver threads. We continued through to the Hall of Maps, the walls covered with frescoes from the late 16th century. We detoured into a couple of rooms with modern art including several Braque, Dali and Botarro paintings. Moving cautiously, due to the extremely crowded corridors, we head to the Raphael Rooms. The four Raphael Rooms were intended to be Pope Julius II's private apartments. We left the Raphael Rooms for the Sistine Chapel, named after Pope Sixtus IV in 1471. New popes are elected here. Early Renaissance painters Botticelli and Perugino painted the walls in 1481–82. Michelangelo painted the ceiling between 1508 and 1512 and returned in 1536, at the age of 61, to paint "The Last Judgment" on the altar wall. The ceiling tells three stories from the Book of Genesis: Creation of the Universe, Creation of Man, and the Life of Noah in nine scenes. Most of the visitors were strapped to their audio guide, which required them to linger, pause and reflect without moving. "Must return at an earlier time," Em whispers. Learned that architect Bramante set the new cornerstone in 1506. Michelangelo designed the dome, and Bernini executed much of the bronze and marble sculpture. This is the largest Christian basilica in the world and the home of Michelangelo's "Pieta," his first work ever to be signed by him at the age of 24 in 1499. Finally, we reached the Fontana della Pigna with the pinecone sculpture crowning the fountain that represents the pagan symbol of fertility. We did not go into the church as the lines stretched all along the eastern protocols. A must-visit for sure. Learning every step of the way.

It was 3:02 sharp! I knew because the sound of sirens and the flashing of red lights woke us. Half asleep, I asked myself if these sounds were of an ambulance, police or fire sirens? The sounds were loud, angry and desperate. At first, we thought it was our building but quickly realized the fire alarm for the building is next to our front door, and it didn't sound. The sirens were very close by, and we smelled the smoke. I suspect everyone in our building, although I hadn't seen but one person from our building as yet, went outside to see the destructive inferno. All I could see from the back end of the hallway out the front door was a fire occurring across the street somewhere near Marco's Café. "Due machine in fiamme," was what they were saying. It was two cars on fire.

"What happened?" asked Em. I told her what I had seen and heard. Eventually, the piercing flashing red lights were extinguished, and the sirens went silent. However, the smell of smoke lingered until we both went back to a very light sleep.

I arose early the next morning. I hurried to see what had happened and realized that the two cars in front of Marco's were probably his and his father's, but I did not know for sure. I kind of recognized Marco's burned-up car but not the other one next to his.

Em dressed quickly and went across the street. Marco was in his café with two uniformed polizia and an authoritative-looking woman and man dressed in street clothes. Obviously, we did not enter. In fact, we left as soon as we could; for me, the uncertainty of the unknown was anxiety provoking. Hoping for the best, Marco.

Soon we found a little café on Via Regina Margherita, a great outdoor spot to watch the people wearing boots, winter coats, and alternative winter dress wear.

"Why are most Romans still in winter clothing?" I wondered aloud to Em.

"Because they don't like to be cold," she said, and Em pulled up her coat around her body.

We were curious about what had happened with the burned cars but decided to wait until we spoke with Marco. At 14:00 hours, the skies were covered with clouds, and it rapidly began to cool down so that all those winter clothes suddenly made chilling sense to me in my short-sleeved shirt.

Returning to Via Adige, we saw that Marco's café was open, but there was one customer sitting at the counter. The two burned-up vehicles were gone, the debris swept away as if nothing had happened. I hesitated. Should we ask him what happened?

"That's why we are going in to see Marco, isn't it?" said Em.

As we entered, Marco was staring out the glass door that led to the vacant two parking spaces.

Em, looking at the area where the cars were parked, asked, "Quello che e successo?"

Marco, looking dismissive, whispered "i miei padri e la mia macchina sono bruciati la scorsa notte!"

I got that his father's (padri) and his cars were burned last night. I wanted to ask how and why but restrained my sorrow and curiosity as Em had already programmed the question into the translator. Mario looked at us, his eyes blinking ever so rapidly, with his hands up as if to push the question away, and said slowly, "non lo so."

I knew what "non lo so" meant, because I used it every time a panhandler or beggar asked me a question or for money.

Too late for a coffee; we express our regrets and sorrows—"Ci dispiace molto," and slinked silently out the front door, passing the two vacant charred, incinerated, scorched black spaces.

At dinner, we hypothesized about the fire: How, what and why and came up with three possible conclusions:

- Old Mackie, the title character in Bobby Darin's "Mack the Knife," was back in town, and Marco would not give him any money (that's my addition);
- Marco's father owed someone else money, perhaps a gambling debt;
- Because Marco's business the last few weeks was booming, maybe the Mafia wanted more protection money and Marco refused?

We never knew why such a devastating thing like this was directed at Marco. The question remained, however, because there were five other cars parked along the four cramped spaces on Via Adige, but only Marco's and his father's vehicles were burned to a crisp.

Needing a pick-me-up, I began to deconstruct the famous quote by Loris Malaguzzi, the founder of the Reggio approach to early childhood education in Reggio Emilia, Italy. In "Meditations," Loris always ended his talks to visitors with "Nothing without Joy!" Marcus Aurelius said, "Joy was something you did, it was a process," as joy comes from human actions. For example, kindness to others, joy through observations and events in travels and in nature and with your partner. Nothing without joy, for me, was a compassionate sentiment connoting wisdom in whatever we do, especially when working alongside children, making sure to have fun. Mr. Malaguzzi reminded us that nothing in the school should happen without joy. Today, after rereading the works of Malaguzzi from a decade ago, I have a different meaning from those ten years. Specifically, for us, joy is being with our children, grandchildren, reading, researching, sketching, painting, learning and slow traveling together. Joy must lie in our actions and reactions and thinking of others. Proverb: "The body heals with play, the mind heals with laughter, and the spirit heals with joy": I feel so much better now.

Em suggested, "We should separate for a while from Marco's horrid situation."

"Like a diversion from the realities of a crime unsolved," I whispered.

We shall take the train to Frascati, which is in the Lazio region of central Italy. Whoa! The weather was perfect: 48–65 degrees Fahrenheit. This may have been one of the warmest and clearest days we had experienced so far. Great call by Em as we head to the town of Frascati (pop. 21,900). She noted that this town was famous for their white wine. It's a 35-minute train ride to the ancient settlement of Frascati. This bustling, but much quieter than Rome, town had many cafés, bars and restaurants. Half of the town was bombed during World War II; now the 15th–16th-century villas are beautifully restored. We enjoyed our two glasses of Frascati wine along with a delicious lunch at Ara Anua at Piazza Giuseppe Garibaldi, 1. The lunch experience was authentic: fresh ingredients and homemade. Everything from pasta to porchetta, if so inclined. We settled on splitting a ravioli di patate con salvia e tartufo—ravioli with potato, sage and truffle, mixed salad, side order of green beans, and a half liter of acqua. Service was friendly, and Adolfo, our server, was very patient and helpful in helping us make our choice.

From Adolfo, we learned that Frascati has many skilled employment opportunities, including the European Space Agency, the world-famous wine and archaeological digs that are ongoing with Sapienza University of Rome. Adolfo indicated that he was just finishing his master's degree in both archaeology and oenology. What I remember from our intermittent discussions was that the oldest-known winery was discovered in Armenia in 4100 BCE, and the first archaeological evidence of wine production was found at sites in Georgia and Iran in 4500 BCE. An open, positive mindset and attentive, listening ears equal factual knowledge.

Sunday: Skype time—washing—dusting—cleaning—vacuuming—nothing without joy! We watched a short video with our second-grade grandson playing Ladahlord, that mysterious man who makes magic things happen in "James and the Giant Peach." Funny, he missed a couple of lines (e.g., "book of smells," instead of "book of spells,") but made up for it with his angelic smile, his inherited fortitude from his mother and grandma. Everything else was fine, with some anticipating our return to the states in a couple of weeks.

Sunny and around 50–52 F today. We had a consolidation day. With only a couple of weeks to go, we worked on the budget, cash on hand, watered the few plants on the patio and generally tidied up around the apartment in the morning. We did not go to Marco's; don't know why, but we'll go tomorrow to see how our friend is doing.

My list of sites not to be missed included a visit to the Auditorium Parco della Musica (2002), north of the Villa Ada near the site of the Summer 1960 Olympic Games. This was an architectural venture to study the large public music complex, an outdoor theater in a park setting. There were three beetle, turtle or blob shaped concert halls designed by Piano Renso: Sala Santa Cecilia seats about 2,800; Sala Sinopoli seating 1,200; and Sala Petrassi with 700 seats.

We had coffee and surveyed the various music and live performances that took place all year long. We learned from the brochures that the facility is the second-most visited cultural music venue in the world, visited almost as often as the Lincoln Center in New York. Reflections: Wished we would have visited the Auditorium earlier, and the performance tickets were booked for the next four weeks, including such highlights as Crosby, Stills & Nash and the Roma Fiction Fest with *Midsomer Murders* star John Nettles. Damn, I was not on my game to have missed this!

Visited Marco's; however, only his wife, Benita, was serving a few customers. She nodded, said "buongiorno," and we reciprocated with forced smiles of sorrow in our hearts.

"Café lattes and uno cornetto, per favore." When I went to the counter I said, "grazie," and a soothing "prego" was pleasantly sent back. I wish we knew more about the car situation, but this is none of our business, and we decided to forget about it.

In *Wanted in Rome*, a monthly magazine in English for expatriates, I read about a "tea-chat" and contacted Annabel, an American who was organizing the tea at her home in the Prati neighborhood near Vatican City. As we are approaching April, it appears as if the temperatures are getting a bit warmer each day. The late 1990s' glorious-looking apartment building had the ubiquitous graffiti (I think it was political) on the ivory-colored, rusticated façade, and I found Annabel's name on the bell-board, and she let us in.

We attended the "Welcome to Rome 'tea-chat.'" A polite round of introductions from the expatriate women: Kirsten from Denmark, Charlotte from Australia, Ella from the United Kingdom and Annabel from Virginia. We chatted about special places to visit, food places, tours and things about Rome, as the women were very knowledgeable, caring and shared information that warmed everyone's hearts and minds. We learned that "Wanted in Rome" is an online source that provided news, events, jobs, and coming art exhibits. Another resource discussed was the biweekly publication, ItalianNotebook.com, a source of news in Rome in English.

Once again, I had blown an opportunity to learn more and gain knowledge about the Rome I wanted to discover. These women were in Rome for only intervals of one to two years before their government-sponsored husbands rotated to other cities or countries. They seek out and have the resources to do just about all there is to experience in Rome. We took several bits of useful information (e.g., the newsletter and online notebook of events) and indicated that we would try to visit next week.

We skipped Marco's. Very windy and pollen is everywhere. This is our last full week in Rome. We walked to Piazza Crati, another of our local cafés, chatted and jotted down on my "The Most of Rome" list to think about how we made the most of our slow travel stay in Rome.

Reflections: Living in Rome:

- Language: A nonissue, sometimes awkward to make conversation. Em did her best, and we did learn basic polite phrases and vocabulary. It pushes us to learn as much of the language as possible.
- Selecting a neighborhood: Got lucky to be able to walk to three major garden parks: The Villa Ada, Tortline Park and the Borghese, all within 20–25 minutes from our flat. One of our "must" criteria was to be near a park or garden.
- Advantages of our immediate walking neighborhood: seven markets within a ten-minute walk; three open produce markets within a ten-minute walk; ten cafés and 12 restaurants.
- Time of the year: Excellent choice as there were fewer tourists, and they were not out in full force until late February. However, it's colder, and utilities were expensive.
- With some creative budgeting, we managed for three months to stay within our initial budget. Our actual budget for the three months included: food, restaurants, bars-cafés, osteria, museum entrance fees, utilities (gas and electric), transportation (bus and trams), and the apartment for three months. We managed our budget by watching the daily euro exchange rate, bank card with no ATM fees (debit card works when the dollar is strong vs. euro). Also, made efficiencies to save money on utilities.

- Advantages of living in Rome: cafés, weather (April), museums, churches, parks, buildings, ancient and modern history, art and architecture.
- Cafés: We noticed the price differences in three contiguous neighborhoods, that was in Tresiste, Prati and Paroli—anywhere from three to five euros in coffee pricing.
- Frommer's *24 Walks in Rome,* Michelin's Green Guide, Moleskine Roma—best map we use as it is small and accurate.
- As a former school principal, I had a few blazers, sports coats and slacks that I brought along, and I was one of many well-dressed foreigners in Rome. Em always dresses well and looks super native.
- Accommodations were with wireless Internet, daily mail, and security in dealing with banking.
- Transportation: We only used the subways once. As slow travelers, we wanted to see everything above ground to get oriented. For us, buses and trams were easier, as Em made our transport within and outside of Rome very relaxing.
- Brilliant decision to join an informal "Welcome Neighbors" group of expatriates and other English-speaking folks who were working and living in Rome. The chat with tea morning was informative, and we learned about living in Rome and their attractions. Unfortunately, I should have made contact earlier in our stay.
- Slow travel "To Take the Time to Observe" list—simply our agreement to observe, study and reflect on every available exhibit, take part in the free museum week-savings, and not worry about getting lost. We believed that taking a detour fostered endless surprises and inspired many opportunities.
- Our fantastic landladies were extremely gracious and kind. Having the gas and electric meters within the building allowed us to monitor and manage our usage and ultimate costs.
- Italian TV: the game shows, mostly U.S./UK models, help us with vocabulary and understanding of Italian humor.
- Look past the bountiful graffiti, and observe the surprises in Rome.
- Marco and Benita, we will never forget their kindness and patience.
- I learned why most Roman residents walk with their heads looking down at the sidewalk. I originally thought that they simply did not want to look at one another. Not like in Paris, where everyone seemingly looks straight ahead, looking others in the eyes. The main reason is the dog poop! It is everywhere except in the tourist areas within the historic center. There seems to be no incentive to pick up.

Marco's was closed today. No sign. Skipped coffee and cornetto. From my list of "must return before we leave" we returned for the third time to the Basilica di Santa Maria sopra Minerva (1280–1370), the only Gothic church in Rome. Why the returns?

This is probably the only church in Christendom that has the following examples of works of art from master artists:

- Michelangelo.
- Bernini: church designs, sculptors both inside and outside the church.
- Fra Lippi: frescoes.
- Fra Angeleco: frescoes.
- Santa Maria sopra Minerva Basilica

Furthermore, it was in this church that Galileo (1564–1642) was tried by the Inquisition for teaching that the Earth revolved around the sun (Heliocentric model) in opposition to the church's geocentric view that the Earth was the center of the universe. He was sentenced to prison but cleared of the charges if he never publicly stated his belief that the Earth moved around the sun! Revisiting this particular scene rekindled my interest in rereading Galileo's *"Dialogues Concerning Two New Sciences."*

Em's knee is fine; my allergies are not. We expected one of the sisters to come over and read the meters, second to last time, I suspect. We waited until 10:45.

"Should I call Giuliana to see if and when she will arrive?"

Em hesitated and replied, "I'm sure she has other things to do; just relax and work on our reflections and summary of our slow travel."

We left with a note on the door indicating that we would be back at 16:00. "Sorry we missed you." I put the time we left: 12:30. Although we had a cool spell, 39–66 F, the slight rain was offset with a bit of sunshine in the afternoon.

Furthermore, the cooler weather had forced the Romans to pull on their scarves, gloves, fur coats and other types of winter coats. We found only one café open on Easter.

As we walked our neighborhood, we observed a few of the larger cafés were open and flourishing with business. Marco's was closed the entire week.

We returned to the apartment to see if Giuliana had come over; not sure, as the same note was still attached to our door. After lunch we took a stroll to the "high-cotton" area of Parioli. This area was considered a "zone of the affluent Romans." The most attractive parts of Parioli run alongside the Piazzale delle Muse and the Villa Borghese. It is fashionable, convenient, with plenty of shops and cafés and luxury apartment buildings, and most shops and cafés were open.

The last three entries from my "Sites outside of Rome" list were saved until the weather was a bit warmer: The Richard Meier and Partners' Jubilee Church, far from central Rome, the Moschea di Roma and Orvieto, after taking time to find and appreciate the Jubilee that Meier called the Jubilee Church, "The crown jewel of the Archdiocese of Rome." The Mosque of Rome is the largest mosque in the western world in terms of land area. The mosque, one of eight in Rome, located at the foot of the Monti Parioli, north of Rome, can accommodate 12,000 people. We took the train to Orvieto, Umbria, a region between Rome/Lazio and Tuscany. We were thinking ahead that perhaps Tuscany might be our next slow travel destination. From our multiple research sources, Orvieto was a must-see for archaeologists, art history majors, tourists, architects and slow travelers. This small hill town that is perched 1,000 feet high on volcanic rock has a history that dates back to the Etruscans (600 BCE). It seems that the longer we lived in Rome, the more prepared, historically, architecture and artistically, we were for the subsequent sites.

First on our site list, of course, was the famous Orvieto Duomo and painter Luca Signorelli, who painted the masterful frescoes in 1490. What made this so intriguing and, therefore, more interesting was that Michelangelo carefully observed, made sketches and studied Signorelli's frescoes at the Duomo before he painted the Sistine Chapel. In addition, Salvator Dali, the Spanish painter that Em really loves, was greatly influenced by studying the frescoes and paintings of Luca Signorelli. We also took the time to view the tufa-brick church of San Giovenale, one of the Orvieto's oldest, dating from 1004. One of the few solemn and brilliant examples of Romanesque-Gothic architecture we have seen. The marble 12th-century altar and inspiring 12th–15th-century frescoes topped off a quality art history lesson.

Reflections: On the 90-minute train ride back, I wrote a list of my reflections as Em was finishing her detailed sketch of the 12th-century altar.

Number one is to never miss this jewel of a hilltop 2,600-year-old town.

Second, the Duomo was magnificently detailed in tufa and travertine rock that proportionally represented the black and tan striped columns and façade, very similar to the churches in Pisa and Siena. Tufa rock is from volcanic leftovers. I learned that when mixed with concrete and travertine, tufa is an almost indestructible building material.

Third, the Signorelli frescoes, marvelously restored, were remarkable in their detail and representation of that period of Christian thought. The link, the connection, to Michelangelo and Dali from those frescoes was quite a valuable learning experience and lesson.

Fourth, a tourist town with a variety of attractions: travel here to experience the history, underground caves, Duomo and, of course, the famous Orvieto Classico wines. There were so many groups, especially American students, that we thought we were in Roma; good for them, as they will experience something extraordinary while in Italy.

Fifth, thanks to Em's masterful capacity to "read" directions, travel seems to get easier each day. Today, as she explained, "take the early morning bus to the main train station, Temini, catch the fast-train going toward Milan, with the second stop at Orvieto. From the train station take the funicular up 1,000 ft. to the summit, and from there, bus to the Duomo, and return." Em worked this out to perfection.

Meal: Caffé del Teatro Mancinelli at Corso Cavour, 122. We sat on the patio (bundled up) with a great latte and Italian small pastries. Inside is inviting with a friendly atmosphere. Super service. Later on during our lingering we did purchase a bottle of the Orvieto Classico.

Weather: Cloudy and partially sunny, 40–59 F. Definitely cooler than expected for April in Rome. Giuliana rang and explained that she was in Paris fixing an issue in her apartment; eventually, she must have another rental apartment in Paris. She will read the final meter the night before we leave for the states. I was not terribly pleased, as it had been over a month since our last utilities reading, and thankfully we were under our projected utilities budget. Nonetheless, another example where I cannot control something, so be it!

The last few days were rather anxious ones for me. I was worried that Em might reinjure her knee so badly that it would require hospitalization. I worry that crossing any street in Rome I, we, could easily become a fatality. In our neighborhood we have seen six accidents, two serious ones, involving motorcycles versus automobiles, and three where pedestrians were victims.

My allergies are out of control, notwithstanding the excellent pharmacist's recommendations; these seasonal allergies seem to get more chronic with each passing year. I'd just rather stay in the apartment and have a walk later in the evening around our neighborhood. Em, always the one to carefully assess a situation, agreed. She was concerned about my allergies and also plenty of watercolors to work on and finish up before we leave.

Visions are sometimes a memory, and memories can make a thing seem to have been much more than it was. This doesn't seem to be the case in Rome. I don't know what our memories would yield, but certainly living in Rome has helped actualize my motivation to fulfill my potential in life, although certainly not completely. I believe, given this experience, that my promises and purposes were partially satisfied, and I am ready to move to the next level of fulfillment, wherever that might be. I want to become the best version of myself. Rome's slow travel experience will foster more enlightenment experiences as we continue to slow travel together.

I wanted to make three composite lists of "Surprises," "Best of Rome," and "Could Be Improved." We made these lists over dozens and dozens of coffee chats, lengthy and lively discussions in the Borghese, Ada and Torlonia gardens, and working together when we stayed in the apartment and came up with our unbiased observations from our Rome experiences.

Surprises:

- Number of beggars, especially with sedated dogs, street sellers, and panhandlers increased dramatically from the first day until three months later.
- More immigrants from Romania, Albanian and Morocco are settling in, and many are selling goods on the streets.
- Everyday dressing for females and males seemed more casual except for older groups. The casual dress resembles the American look, but generally their casual clothes quality is not the same as ours. Examples: more jeans, white and black Adidas and Nike sneakers.
- Frequent changes in the bus routes and times required more double-checking before planning bus routes.
- Winter clothing was still being worn in April. However, the temperatures in the past week or two have been in the high 60s–70s.
- Graffiti, mostly political—perhaps more neighborhood defined—but very little in tourist areas.
- The sign posting in Rome needs work. Also, very few English explanations in the art galleries but excellent most of the time with the special exhibits.

Best of Rome:

- Food: Gluten-free, vegetarian and low-carbohydrate cuisine are readily available and tasty.
- Bus drivers are incredible skilled drivers. I really can appreciate their skills as we have ridden on many buses. The parking is atrocious; coupled with the bicycles, motorbikes, motorcycles, and cars, these professionals do a super job.
- Art exhibits and staging are the best anywhere. The presentations are always perfectly matched to the exhibit. Let's face it, all of Rome is a museum!
- Cafés: There are many, many inexpensive and expensive cafés to choose from at any time. The coffee is always good and the presentation excellent. Ironically, the smaller cups make for a longer-lasting sit, as opposed to our 12-ounce version.
- Intercity trains are on time and quick to reach their destinations.
- More new museums have been exploring and exhibiting more contemporary and modern art scenes.
- Italy has the third-highest number of foreign residents in the European Union. Even with the increase (690,000 since 2010) in migrants, the Italians are still the most tolerant and generous of any group we have seen in our slow travels. To see their compassion is to feel it!

- There was clear evidence of a dramatic increase of newer and more accessible opportunities for people with disabilities. This was one area that I was particularly focused on during our stay. There are more accesses and transport services available now for folks with disabilities. This is one great improvement for the general population of Rome and for tourists. We were also impressed with the accesses available in the city of Milan, the smaller cities of Reggio Emilia, Parma, Modena.

What Could Be Improved:

- Three serious accidents in three weeks at our corner due to poor parking arrangements and random illegal parking. No police present to monitor or investigate.
- Parking is random to the point of endangering pedestrians.
- Neighborhood (ours) sidewalks and streets are in disrepair to a point of testing their national health system; very dangerous for young and old people.
- Still too many young folks are smoking. A large upper secondary school (Scuola Superiroe) is down the street where we pick up our bus in the morning; more than half the students waiting for classes to begin were smoking.
- Dog poop is on the rise. Few picker-uppers but many leavers.

Weather: 50–69 F. Sunny, bright and humid. Wanted to say goodbye to Marco and Benita, but the café was closed. No reason for their closure was noted. We will miss our very kind and patient friends. Em wrote a note, in Italian, and taped it to the door. "Vi ringraziamo e auguriamo il meglio a Bonita e Marco e alia loro famiglia." We thanked them and wished Benita, Marco and their family the best. A sad day in what has been almost 90 days of happiness and joy.

Reflections: In summarizing our three months of slow travel in Rome, we did explore more than Rome and its neighborhoods. For example, some of our visits took us to large cities (e.g., Naples)—which was diametrically opposite to smaller, touristy cities like Bologna, Reggio Emilia, Modena and Parma. All places visited were very special with a reputation for fine food, architecture, and art.

Ostia Antica and Tivoli were authentic Roman antiquity—visualizing their past helps to understand their present.

Orvieto and Frascati were pleasant train trips to fabulous wine areas. We did more exploration via train travel; no need to rent a vehicle. In addition, we visited almost every art exhibit that came to Rome. We repeated visits to most of our favorite churches, and added a few extras, and all of our favorite museums. Café hopping was extensive and enjoyable, as people-watching was still the least expensive activity in Rome. We were very fortunate to have engaged in conversations with travelers and locals (most of whom spoke some English) and fellow train travelers. These kind and caring people provided us with new insights and information, which were appreciated.

Day 90. Weather: 55–66 F. Perfect! Sunny and beautiful cerulean skies: I see blue skies, and they are smiling at us. Skype to family: "We are coming home!"

Reflections: Ready for travel day. Merely picking up the pieces and replacing objects that collected dust that I put away while we were here. Airline e-tickets were a bit of a hassle—someone double-booked our reservations that were subsequently cancelled. A number of calls back and forth to Alitalia and Delta took two hours. Em sorted it out. Giuliana and Simona came at 9:30 to collect our final month's utilities payment. We thanked them, and said we shall return—Soon! The cost for this month's utilities was $95, somewhat less than the two previous months. We averaged out to $115 per month. Our focused effort to conserve electricity and gas turned out to be the best method to save on expenses. We leave Rome more confident and appreciate our good fortune to slow travel in Rome, as seniors.

A few suggestions on making the best of living in Rome:

- Leave your ego at home. Mistakes and embarrassing situations are made in language, entrances and exit points, ordering, and getting attention at the open markets and bakeries. These are meaningful learning opportunities.
- To reduce the confounding problem with the language, you must learn a few words and phrases, for example: good morning, good afternoon, thank you, please, sorry, tickets, exits, close, open and lunch. A polite thumb point is fine as long as it is not a direct or an attitude point. I learned that when I held up my pointer figure to signal uno, I received a not-so-friendly look.
- There are many folks who speak English well enough to understand what you want or need. That has not been a problem even in the locations far away from the tourists, like our neighborhood. Respect and honor their bilingualism; wish we were better with languages.
- Public transport is relatively easy if you have an Emily in charge. She is a master at bus station locations, bus routes and approximate bus times. Because we use the buses more than twice a day, by the mid-month, we have already paid for the monthly pass, and the rest of the bus rides are basically free.
- Food. Easy to purchase at many supermercados, marcatos and little specialty shops around Rome. If you have shopped at Whole Foods or Erewhon markets, you expect to pay fair money for quality food. The costs are less for milk, bread, butter, cereal, fruits, vegetables, wine and cheese. However, laundry soaps and house-cleaning products, packaged and prepared foods are rather expensive. Packages are smaller, and there is not as much variety or selection; that's just fine with us.
- Money. This is an open question and an important issue since many reference guides provide different attitudes and methods about money and foreign exchange. We simply purchased an appropriate amount of euros—watch the rates—during our stay. I simply placed my euros in my neck pouch, tucked it under my shirt, and placed it in my underpants, safe and sound until I arrived at our flat. Once at the flat I merely placed the euros in a safe spot. When we leave for the day, we bring a set amount for that day. Mastercard and Visa cards work all over Rome. We use the credit card (we receive the exchange rate of the day) for museum entrance fees, monthly bus passes and groceries. Cash for coffee and snacks. When we need more cash, we use a debit card to withdraw euros. There are many credit card companies that provide free withdrawals and waive transaction fees. The money situation is such an individual issue, especially if you are on a tight or fixed budget the entire slow travel time in Rome.
- Rent and utilities. Once the rent rate has been established, before you leave home and if utilities are not included (which they very rarely are, as gas and electricity are high), one has to use caution as these valuable resources run high. We expect our first month's utility bill will be probably over $150. It has been cold, sometimes

damp in the apartment. We chose to live in Rome in the winter; there were both positive and negative consequences. The pros for winter: less tourists, few visitors at museums and churches, cheaper flights. The cons: after we made the appropriate adjustments, we kept the utilities cost to a reasonable amount.

As I finished off this three-month slow travel daily journal, I have kept an account of almost exactly how much this adventure cost. I wrote down every euro spent and credit card purchases. The total spending for the 90 days, inclusive of all expenses incurred, was $2,500 less than we had budgeted. The total budget for the 90 days, including airfare, rent, utilities, museum passes and guides, bus passes, food, books, coffee and incidentals (e.g., pharmacy) was $155 per day for 90 days. In summary: we stayed well within our budget.

PART FOUR

Tuscany and Florence

Five fast months have passed since we lived in Rome. The grandchildren had an active summer with vacation time, golf and reading. All three are ready to move up to the next grade at school. The only thing different in our lives was that the boys, Cole and Ty, had to move to Maine where their father Jim is employed, and this will save him the two-hour-plus commute from New Hampshire. We were very happy that Jim now would be able to spend more time with the boys since their new home would be only ten minutes from his workplace. They moved and were settled into their new house before the new school year began; the boys were extremely happy to have their own bedrooms. We spent less time with the boys but did commute many weekends from New Hampshire to Maine to be with them. Our other granddaughter, Annika, was still a six-hour drive to Connecticut, but we tried to see her a few times this summer. We think that she is getting to know us a little better each time we visit her.

Since the Sunday Skype catchup calls worked well for all whilst in Rome, we happily agreed that in Florence we would call each Sunday at 12 our time and 6 their time.

Em attended a couple of quilting workshops and remained an active participant in the local library book club discussions. She has also been busy studying Italian and preparing for our next two months of slow travel in October and November to Florence and Tuscany. Seriously, we have both been planning this adventure ever since we arrived back from Rome.

I enrolled in two exciting online courses this summer: "The Meaning of Rome: The Renaissance and Baroque City," and "Architectural Imagination." Both brought significant background information and connectivity to my investigation into architecture. "The Renaissance and Baroque City" was well matched to my experiences in Rome. It enabled me to better "read" Rome, its rebirth in the 15th century and subsequent reshaping in the following three centuries. The city that resulted emboldened a deep cultural and social values system, which was expressed in art and architecture through its use of ideas, materials, and aesthetic forms.

The other course, "Architectural Imagination," led me to better understand architecture as a cultural expression as well as a technical achievement. We studied and analyzed exemplary buildings from a wide range of social and historical contexts that were behind major architectural works from past to present. Coupled with hands-on exercises in drawing and modeling all together brought me a little closer to the work of an actual architect. Both courses served me well in allowing me to become a bit more knowledgeable heading to Florence. However, I am still only an enthusiast, not a serious student of architecture.

Between the two courses, my extensive notes, and Em's input and reflections, I summarized what was learned about art, art history and architecture during our Rome "term," which were our initial purposes in rediscovering the joys of travel and learning during our junior year abroad.

First, we certainly did rediscover the joys of retirement travel, as evidenced by our confidence to return to Italy and Florence to study more deeply about Italian Renaissance art and architecture. As slow travelers, we redefined retirement by active learning through discovery, exploration, research and reflections.

I learned in education that there is nothing educative in an activity or event that does not lead the mind into new fields of endeavor. Joyfully, our relationship has grown deeper as partners, collaborators and slow travelers, and our love and affection for each other is as steadfast as ever.

I begin with the notion that memories can make things seem much more than they actually were, meaning I can only recall and restate my memories of the art and architecture experienced in Rome in a sort of a linear sequence. My level of understanding is not mature enough to be able to describe art and architecture in terms of their inextricable relationship to other things, like culture, social values and historical underpinnings. Furthermore, the courses I took this summer did inform me that I still know very little about architecture.

I very broadly begin with Ancient Roman Classical architecture and my favorite building in all of Rome, the Pantheon. The Classical referred to the style of buildings in Ancient Greece and Rome (450 BCE–475 CE) which were the building blocks that shaped the subsequent approaches to buildings in Western architecture. The Pantheon was the perfect example of Classical construction using the elements of precise rules of ratios, symmetry, proportions, and the Classical Roman Doric and Ionic columns. Their circular plan represented the sphere of the world in Classical terms. Rules of construction were observed and recognized, evidenced by the concrete dome, the elegant use of Egyptian purple porphyry, that hard volcanic stone in the center of the floor, and the white Carrara marble used on the Corinthian capitals.

The Column of Trajan, completed in 113 CE, was a constant site-reminder during our walking tours of Rome. Other prime examples were "The Altar of Augustan Peace" and the "Column of Marcus Aurelius," in the Piazza Colonna. In terms of Ancient Greek and Roman sculpture: At the Borghese Museum, in particular, two copied sculptures from the first and second century, the "Figure of a seated scholar with unrelated portrait-head," and the "Boy with a Duck," are both inspired by the Hellenistic models. The Vatican's enormous displays of Ancient Greek and their Roman formal statues were completely overwhelming and had me constantly reading and researching everything that I did not know, which was plenty. The ultimate, the oldest highlight in the Vatican, and one of particular interest to me, was the marble statue of "Laocoon and His Sons," depicting the Trojan priest Laocoon and his sons being attacked by sea serpents; I could never forget this image and the legend.

My evidence of the Romanesque architecture in Rome (800–1200) was best represented by the many churches that displayed the intricately patterned Cosmati pavements and floors. The two best examples that I remember were the Church of Santa Maria in Aracoeli and Santo Quattro Coronati. The Romanesque period's relationship to art and architecture was especially evident in churches. This was a period affected by shifting politics following the Carolingian period and the Crusades. I recalled one superb example which was in another one of our favorite churches, the Church of Santi Quattro Coronati.

I can remember the Cosmatesque marble floors that were laid out in an intricate tapestry of white Carrara marble, glass and precious stones swirling in patterns of serpentines, circles and squares from the 12th and 13th centuries. The two most memorable visual treasures were the frescoes that decorated the walls of the oratory in the Chapel of Saint Sylvester and the 13th-century frescoes in the Great Hall. That was as closely as I can represent the Romanesque period in Rome; I'm still learning.

The lone medieval representation of Roman architecture within the Gothic (1150–1500) period, inside the ancient walls, was the Church of Santa Maria sopra Minerva, which was defined by its high ceilings, pointed arches and stained glass. Gothic art in Rome was once again represented in the Vatican with the incredible work of Giotto. Giotto designed the double-sided altarpiece of St. Peter's in the Vatican's Pinacoteca. We'll definitely see more of Giotto's work in Florence. Somewhere I read that Giotto was the first Renaissance painter.

On to the Italian Renaissance (1420–1550) and the rise of the wealthy patrons of the arts and the city states, one being our next slow travel landing in Florence. What stood out when observing and studying these structures was the rebirth of their passion for and devotion to the classics, also in terms of art and literature. My examples of the Renaissance development were seen in the Palazzo Farnese, Bramati's Tempietto, St. Peter's Basilica and, my favorite, the Church of Santa Maria della Pace. Moreover, if the Renaissance architecture could be summed up in a single building, I would have to say St. Peter's Basilica best represents it. Italian Renaissance, the rebirth of Classical values, lasted almost 500 years. The most important elements of Renaissance art were its perfectionism, humanism, and perspective drawings. These were realized from the early Renaissance examples from the frescoes of Fra Angelico and Luca Signorelli. Fra Angelico's frescoes were in the Niccoline Chapel at the Vatican and Luca Signorelli's in the New Chapel on Orvieto Cathedral. High Renaissance, there are so many, such as Raphael, Leonardo da Vinci and Michelangelo. I could go on and on. More of these masters' works of art will be found when we live in Florence and visit the surrounding towns in Tuscany.

The last major Roman architectural style that still held the ideals of the Renaissance but went for elegance instead of balance and symmetry was the flamboyant and highly cinematic Baroque (1600–1725) period. There were many compelling examples for me, not only in architecture but in art as well. Architecturally, Borromini's San Carlo alle Quattro Fontana and Bernini's St. Andrea al Qurnale were my teachers. Em's all-time favorite sculpture was Bernini's "Apollo and Daphne" in the Borghese Museum. Not to be forgotten was his "Ecstasy of Saint Teresa" in the Church of Santa Maria della Vittoria. The utmost lasting memory I have for this period was studying the genius of Michelangelo's "Moses."

I could not complete my limited knowledge and study of Rome without mentioning the fascist-era style. This style intrigued me when I first saw such a fascist building, coming in from the airport, when I asked the sisters, "What is that large white building over there?" as I awkwardly pointed to it as we were whizzing by. The response from one of them, not sure which one, was, "The area is called the EUR, or Esposizione Universale Roma." I knew that I had to follow up on this area. Later I learned that EUR was a design inspired by a Roman Imperial town planning, using limestone, tuff and marble, traditional materials associated with Roman Empire architecture. The iconic symbol of this era was the Colosseo Quadrato building, the large building I saw from far away. We visited this area several times; I might add, it's a wonderful oasis from the historic city of Rome.

I assimilated most of the architecture periods and styles by memorizing the specific elements of each style; then I gathered some grasp of the art within each architectural period. In that way, this method assisted me in at least having some awareness of which art goes with what architectural period. No matter how carefully I observed, and regardless of the lengthy research-study, architecture and art history is definitely a long-term learning commitment. Even knowing that I lacked the background knowledge to be an "expert," I'm still enthusiastic for both art forms. I am semi-satisfied that my attempts to connect what were the most interesting and intriguing pieces of art, that is, paintings and sculpture, with the architectural periods, will motivate me to continue to learn as we move on to Florence and Tuscany for our second term abroad.

An orientation: Tuscany is a region of Italy with a population of 3,900,000 inhabitants. Renowned for its wealth of vineyards, idyllic landscapes, wealth of artistic heritage, earthy food, red wine and incredible beauty, it was ruled by the Etruscans and the Romans for centuries. Tuscany is surrounded by the Apennine Mountains, the Apuan Alps and the Tyrrhenian Sea. There are ten provinces of Tuscany: Arezzo, Grosseto, Livorno, Luca, Massa-Carrara, Pisa, Pistoria, Prato, Siena, and Florence (Firenze).

Although Florence was the city where Renaissance in art and architecture began, Rome supplied the classical models.

With Tuscany being the region, it is Florence, the Renaissance city, that is our slow travel road trip location for the next 60 days.

As with our apartment search for Rome, I used the same agency to narrow our choices to three, with Em making the final selection. The selection criteria were: budget limitations, parking and location in or near Florence.

Em selected number three on my list. The other two were located in the center of the city of Florence. The only issue with both of them was they were far more expensive for our fixed-income budget, and there's no assigned parking space in the city. Em's choice was a prudent one. The apartment was 14–16 kilometers, or 8–11 miles, to the historic city center, depending on which part of Florence. The owner's information paper indicated that the apartment was located in Bisticci in an 11th-century building with two recently updated apartments; this information interested me.

We accidentally found the building and eventually the apartment. As it happened, as we were slowly looking for a sign for Bisticci, Em saw at the bottom of a hill, under a cypress tree, on a narrow path, several sheep, one with a black face, grazing on grass alongside the ancient olive trees. I was tired. I turned into that small, narrow lane that led to the grazers, pulled over, and watched those sheep as Em took photos of these innocent, lovely creatures to send to the grandchildren.

Because the lane was too narrow to turn around, the only way out was to continue up the hill, and after several twists and turns, we came to a small, battered, black-and-white sign that indicated Bisticci, but where was the building and apartment? We continued up the steep hill leading to the apartment building, pulled into the gravel drive, and found a woman outside raking some stones onto the driveway, presumably to fill up the holes. She introduced herself as "Cid," and she was the owner along with her husband. Cid invited us to look at the apartment we rented online. We anxiously moved up the 14 medieval concrete steps, no railing on either side, to the apartment. Cid cried out, "I'll talk to you after you have a look around." The apartment seemed so much larger than we read about, and we certainly did not require such a big place for the two of us. I said to

The black Massese sheep is raised throughout Tuscany.

Em, "This is not the apartment we selected, is it?" "No, Cid might have thought we were the people renting this large apartment; let's speak to her about this." Semi-hurrying, no side rails down the 14 steps, we found Cid sitting on one of the two benches in the huge fruit tree garden. When asked about the apparent mistake, she nicely indicated that "the smaller original apt you were supposed to rent suddenly became unavailable; anyway, this one is bigger, and for the same price as the other." "Fine," I said, and "thank you," not with any feelings. Sure enough, after we sorted the arrangement out, Em did choose correctly. The three bedroom apartment with one mold-free bathroom with a tiny shower was fine. The apartment was clean and had tile floors (no carpets, thank goodness), a fine open-planned, decently equipped kitchen, unusual for Italian apartments, and a kind owner who spoke perfect English. Furthermore, Em admired the fruit trees and garden, and the apartment was situated on a rather high hill that provided a marvelous expansive view of the surrounding hills, forests of Italian cypress, ash and umbrella pines, and peek-a-boo views of the Apennine Mountain chain. After we schlepped up the 14 wide concrete steps with our two bags, we hugged each other, knowing that this would be a very enjoyable second term abroad. We unpacked and went down the 14 steps to have a more formal orientation chat with Cid.

The owners, we learned, were Cid from Brighton, England, and Francisco, her husband, from Florence. They gave us a simple orientation of the apartment, but more importantly, Cid warned us that it would be cold at night in October and November. To me, that means heat; what kind of heat are we dealing with, I asked myself. Another rookie mistake by me; I did not inquire about the heating and gas situation beforehand.

The description for this apartment on Sabbatical Homes indicated that "some" utilities would be included in the rent. I should have known from our Rome experience. Dammit. When I sheepishly asked, "What is the heating method?" Cid said, "You heat with electricity." I grumbled to myself, "We can expect these two months to be very expensive in Tuscany." Em very politely asked if she would read the meters every week in order for us to budget accordingly. Cid replied, "We usually do the meter reading at the end of the stay." Em's smooth comeback was, "Let's do it every other week, OK?" Cid agreed. Cid looked English but behaved Italian, with lots of hand gestures and spoke rather fast. Her English look could be described best as lovely, smooth, white skin, thin brownish-red hair and no makeup. "She obviously does not partake in the Tuscan sunshine, or perhaps it is too cold to go outside," I snarked to myself. Francisco was very much Italian, darkish skin, handsome face, grayish black hair and shorter than Cid. I thought, because Em always reminds me to stand up straight, if Francisco had better posture (as his shoulders and head were bent forward), he would have been much taller than Cid or me. Francisco would have been someone I would want to share a glass of Chianti with, as he must have a wealth of knowledge about Florence, past and present. But language limitations worked against my picking his Florentine memory. He spoke only a few words in English to us, "hello," "from where are you?" You could tell by the way both of them were dressed— boots, one with gloves, scarves, and both handsomely outfitted, with Cid in a dark green Barbour quilted jacket and Francisco in a dark blue Barbour vest over a flannel, collared shirt—that they were ready for winter, I thought. As this was the first day of October, it was going to be colder than we had expected. I did a temperature check on Florence before we left, and we expected temperatures in October to between 51 and 70 degrees Fahrenheit. I couldn't take my mind off heating this three-bedroom apartment with large kitchen and two sitting rooms only by electricity. I began whining, "I wish we would have received the small apartment we originally requested." Em, as always, said, "Never mind, this is going to be a wonderful time in our lives." Em, the big picture visionary, and her reassuring refrain, "Everything will work out just fine." Thank goodness for her, and I felt at ease.

Nevertheless, we needed to shore up some food for a day or so and asked Cid where we should go. She directed us to the closest COOP supermarket ten kilometers away. The drive from Rome to Bisticci to our village was mostly on the autostrada. In Tuscany, this ten-kilometer drive to the COOP was on narrow and curvy two-lane roads. I drove very slowly through several small villages and around, up and down a couple of hills. Twenty-five minutes later we reached the COOP. Cid's directions were a little sketchy, as we couldn't find, or missed, the glowing green "farmacia" sign two blocks on the left before the COOP. One problem was that I saw two glowing green farmacia signs on the way. The consumers' cooperatives is the largest supermarket chain in Italy. We were extremely happy with the quality and varieties of their food products and purchased enough food for the day and tomorrow morning. "This will be our go-to market for sure," I reassured Em. We were anxious to sort out the apartment arrangements and possibly how we might be able to turn off the electricity in some of the rooms. Our sweet little Fiat Panda, with the assistance of the manual transmission, made negotiating the narrow streets, steep hills, and zigzag curves easy, and was small enough in order to park easily into those sometimes even smaller parking spaces. "It was a wise choice," I said, and Em agreed.

Our first full day we took Cid's advice and ventured to an open fresh market in the village of Incisa. The small village sort of reminded us of an English/Italian village setting in the Cotswolds-Tuscany area in a picturesque way. The village was tidy, flowers hanging from the street lamps, and the shops and cafés attached to the rows of small houses. The October Tuscan seasonal market was replete with fresh produce that included: aubergine, beans, broccoli, carrots, fennel, arugula, walnuts, pumpkins, Gala apples, blackberries, grapes, pears, dates and many types of cheeses—goat (Caprino), cow's milk (Pecorino Pisano) and sheep (Pecorino). A large selection of wines were labeled to indicate which of three regions the Chianti wine came from.

An early exit this chilly and windy morning, and a 50-minute slow drive through Tuscany's many hills, with marvelous landscape views of the umbrella pines and cypress trees. We arrived in Greve (pop. 14,000), considered the front door to the Chianti area. We absolutely enjoyed a slow and observant walk around this lovely medieval town. We lingered long enough to partake in a late lunch at Ristorante La Castellana on Via. Di Montefioralle, #2. We had a salad of arugula, walnuts, fresh pears and Reggiano Parmigiano, homemade fresh baked bread, a small plate of prosciutto slices, melted Pecorino cheese and honey, a shared plate of penne con porri pancetta (or leeks and bacon), and a liter of water, and sat for a couple of hours. We took this restaurant to be a local favorite, as we heard no other language but Italian. Excellent service, well presented and tasty food. We sat outside and admired the well-behaved canines sitting with their companions on the terrace. Since it was 78 degrees Fahrenheit at 4 p.m., we decided that was a full first day in Tuscany.

Our procedure went like this: we decide what each day will bring us. I had already researched and listed selected towns, villages, churches and museums that we should visit, with Em adding those sites she wanted to include. These tentative sites were listed in the order of distances from Bisticci, so I could link the travel time and distance from Bisticci. I recorded the distances from our apartment to all the sites on the list. Our combined list included churches, museums, villages and towns and possible detours and diversions. After dinner we sat down and planned the next day. I always email a brief overview of our day to our families, whereas Em takes care of any photos. We also check the weather for that day. Weather, especially fog and heavy rain, most times will determine where or if we venture out. From our combined list, we determine how we feel about the follow-up site visit, how much walking, taking a train, or where and what to discover and explore. We never had a conflict regarding where to go or what to see as we were both excited to see everything we could during these slow travel two months in Tuscany.

In deciding the next day's excursion, our conversation usually goes like this. "Em, what do you want to see tomorrow?" Her reply, "Anything on our list; we will enjoy anything and everything!" This makes every day exciting and fun.

We repeated the 45-minute drive to Greve-in-Chianti to experience their open market on the Piazza Matteotti. Our Michelin Tuscany Guidebook was invaluable for providing details we sought about the villages in Tuscany. We purposely did not go to Florence; we were anticipating it eagerly but not ready just yet. As usual, our focus was mostly on historical/architectural structures and art history of the area. I was hoping that the little bit of information I learned over the summer might be of some value to me in Florence. Our quest for self-learning is what makes our slow traveling so exhilarating and enjoyable. We scheduled only one site at this small and active town of 14,000, and that was the Church of Santa Croce. In front of the main piazza (Piazza Giacometti Matteotti) there were numerous medieval aged buildings, including the original 11th-century Chiesa Santa Croce, rebuilt in 1325. The church housed several paintings from the school of Fra Angelico. We were introduced to Fra Angelico's masterful devotional frescoes in Rome. This was a "working" church, as we observed a handful of local residents preparing for their daily inspiration.

Slow travel allows us to veer off any pre-planned schedule; I've always said, "A detour is always a surprising opportunity to discover something new." We had the time, no hurrying necessary. Ten kilometers from Greve, with spectacular views of the corrugated hills that seemed to follow us along the way, we arrived at the small village of Radda (pop. 1,200). As we approached Radda, high on a hill, I could appreciate its high defensive position, and most of the town's thick, medieval walls were intact. From the Michelin Green Guide, I read that Radda, during the Middle Ages, was one of the three original members of the Chianti League and became the main town in the League in 1415. The League was a political and military institution to protect the Chianti territory.

To find free parking space outside the 600-year-old medieval walls that surrounded this tiny hamlet was quite a pleasant gift, this being touristy—Tuscany! We followed the narrow streets inside the walls that lead to the central square and the Romanesque church of San Niccolo. Around the corner we happened upon the white marble façade of the Palazzo Pretoria, then opposite it was the imposing Palazzo del Podesta, with its original 15th-century portico. I made note of another sight, the Museum of Sacred Art, while meandering, to definitely put on my "Will Visit Another Time" list.

As it happened, we attended a wonderful art exhibit in a former 12th-century prison, with paintings included in the cells and the dungeon. The well-known and award-winning Italian artist Angela Crucitti was alone with us for the entire two hours. Her work was an integration of Tuscany meets abstraction with a flair for color and resonating textures. As the light reflects on the paintings, the colors and textures change. Em remembered seeing her work at a gallery in Reggio Emilia. Signora Crucitti mentioned that a Naples, Florida, gallery had commissioned her paintings and said proudly, "and they are very popular." I made a note to look her work up at the Antinori-Arsenault Gallery in Naples, Florida.

We finished off the long day with a stop at the COOP. A strategic mistake:

Today was Saturday, and it was 3:30 p.m. Trouble finding a parking space in the rather small lot in front of the market intuitively meant it was going to be very busy. Inside it was initially quite baffling. For example, it appeared that some of the customers operated their carts as they drove their vehicles—hushing and switching lanes from one side to the other—no lines were followed straight; folks stopped abruptly at the end of aisles and read every ingredient in each item before choosing. Also observed were fathers pushing their children in strollers, in and out and around other folks' carts, as if they were on the autostrada. Delightfully reassuring, older folks, some with canes, walkers and wheelchairs, were inching their way confidently around all the confusion; it was inspiring. We shall make subsequent and appropriate adjustments, I made a note, to avoid shopping at COOP on Saturdays from 2:30 to 4:30 in the future. It is just better for our health.

Sunday, our first in Tuscany, was warm and sunny. Our only plan, since traffic might be less on a Sunday, was to drive 10–14 kilometers from Bisticci to Florence. With the assistance of Cecilia, our GPS guide, and Emily's fine navigation skills, we made it to the train station parking garage in about 45 minutes. As imagined, Florence was very busy even in the midmorning. The object today was to get an orientation of this fabulous city—stroll around, linger, pause, stare at the monuments (e.g., Neptune in the Piazza Vecchia), locate the museums and churches that we will be spending much of our time visiting. I was anxious, as I remembered that Sunday was Skype day. We had plenty of time to better explore this city in more detail and purchase museum tickets. We Skyped everyone; the boys were finishing their dinner. When asked about school, they said, "School was good." Our granddaughter, on the other hand, revealed more about her teacher, how he misspelled the word "potatoe" on the blackboard, and she and her class-mates laughed. Flashbacks, I can remember doing a similar misspelling of "tomateos." Never again.

Our first diesel fill up. I was anxious about running out of petrol or not finding a station somewhere in a village far out in the hilly Tuscan hinterland. Although the fuel gauge registered three-quarters full, I thought it best to try and top off the tank. It had been a long time since I purchased petrol in Italy, so for a first-time adventure I had a go. First, I read the small sign on the pump that read "nessun cambiamento" and asked Em to look up what "nessun cambiamento" means. She looked up the translation: "no change." If I tried to place my 50-euro banknote, the only cash I brought, into the pump slot, I realized that I would receive no change back. Looking perplexed, Em pointed to a cam-biamento machine near the last pump that would hopefully change my 50 euros into tens and twenties. I was a bit hesitant to put the 50-euro note into the well-worn slot but care-fully smoothed out the edges and slid the note into the opening. "Ecco!" Right, this time. I received two 20s and one ten-euro banknote. Next, I moved over to one of three pumps: Benzina and Gasolio. I looked on the top of the petrol cap, and in red letters was the word "Gasolio." I assumed Benzina was unleaded. Deciding which banknote to use, the 20 or a ten, I chose ten euros, and at the ten-euro point on the machine, the pump shut down. Surprisingly, I thought ten euros would be too much, but it almost filled up the dash-board's fuel gauge; petrol is expensive, I snickered to myself. Later I researched that if I want to use a credit card, it is best to use the more popular stations such as Esso or Mobil.

We are finding that the weather is important each day, unlike when we lived in Rome, because with the car, it rather dictates where we go and what we do that day. I'm not ready to drive any distances in the pouring rain or thick fog—not yet. However, today's conditions were ideal for our drive to the large hilltop city of Arezzo, 70 kilome-ters from Bisticci. We decided not to use the autostrada; it would have been 15–20 min-utes quicker, but then we would have missed the idyllic landscapes of Tuscany. Arezzo (pop. 99,500) had many reasons to visit:

- It's a beautiful medieval town. I recall the movie, *La vita e bella* or *Life Is Beautiful*, with Roberto Benigni, who received an Academy Award for Best Actor in a leading role in 1997, was filmed here in Arezzo.
- The painter and art history author Giorgio Vasari (1512–74) lived here and it is the home of his museum.
- The incredible frescoes by Piero della Francesca.
- The poet Petrarch (1304–74) was born in Arezzo.

Once again, with time on our side, we tried to orient ourselves to the marvels of this town, knowing that we shall return in time. Of course, Arezzo was placed on my "Must Return" list.

As the day was growing short, on the return drive from Arezzo we planned a stop at the medieval village of Gropina to visit one of the best examples of a Romanesque church in Tuscany, the Parish Church of San Pietro in Gropina. The church was built around 1000, characterized by the use of heavy, large blocks of ashlar stone and two lancet windows. We found Pope Leo X's (the first of the Medici popes) House of Medici coat of arms (1522) positioned above the architrave (door frame with a mounding). From my readings, the eighth-century stone circular pulpit, which was supported by two knotted columns, was another Romanesque design element. The "knots" express a mystery of faith (i.e., Trinity, knotted by the "Holy Spirit.") The bell tower, built in 1233, and the semicircular apse were two further important representations of Romanesque church construction. We didn't see many Romanesque churches in Rome, but the Romanesque period relied on sturdy purity and respectable human scale, lending to pleasing proportions and steadfast grace. I truly love these churches.

Another diversion, just two kilometers from Gropina, was the medieval village of Loro Ciuffenna (pop. 5,900). Loro Ciuffenna was a town of Etruscan origin and hosted many important medieval historical and architectural sights. It is rated as one of the "most beautiful villages in Italy." We lingered long enough for cappuccini at the busy Café Gallo. We knew that we would be back at some point—much too idyllic and peaceful not to spend more time. I placed Lora Ciuffenna on my growing "return to" list.

Another bright, warm and a foggy Tuscany morning. Off early for the 55-kilometer drive from Bisticci to the medieval town of Bibbiena (pop. 12,300), which was nuzzled between the Falterona mountain and the Arezzo plains. Bibbiena was another town of Etruscan origin (an advanced civilization that preceded the Roman) and the home to the tenth-century bishops of Arezzo. Our planned experience in Bibbiena was the 14th-century Church of San Lorenzo. As we were admiring and lingered in front of the church, we were approached by a middle-age Italian gentleman who spoke to us in Italian, "bellissimo." I politely said, "Si e bellissimo," and he quickly realized he would be better understood if he spoke English. He told us his name was John and that he was a church volunteer. His background as an architect for over 45 years interested us a great deal. Since our focus today was church architecture, we thought how fortunate we were to have an expert to inform us. John had the keys to his original tenth-century wine cellar below his architecture studio and also to the private chapels of a former noble family. I have to admit, I was skeptical. I thought, keys to the dungeon, no way! Nonetheless, Em trusted him. Inside the church, John pointed out two porcelain-glass terra-cotta plaques by the famous Renaissance sculptor Andrea della Robbia. Walking toward the ornate Oratorio of San Francesco (1580), John mentioned that this next room was closed to visitors, but we were allowed to view the elaborate ornamentation and pastel color palette of the Rococo-style (1730–1760s) interior of the mid–1700s. John walked with us to the Palazzo Dovizi and explained that it was a perfect example of Renaissance rustic architecture. Onward to the Chapel of St. Ippolito and Donato, which John pointed out once was a part of a castle of which two towers still existed. The chapel itself was the home of some fine frescoes and paintings dating back to the Renaissance period.

What an amazing, knowledgeable and kind man. Emily did a nice job with the translations and was able to comprehend most of what John explained in Italian. Reflections: We would have never been able to experience these unique historical and architectural treasures without "Gentleman John." We expressed our sincere appreciation and thanked him for his time with us. During our travels abroad, we have not been surprised by the kindness and thoughtfulness of the local people we have encountered along the way, and today was another example of kindness.

Today is cleaning, washing (sheets hanging in the warm Tuscan sun), relaxing and recharging. We have been out ten straight days. We popped early into the COOP and had coffee in a café near the River Arno overlooking a medieval tower that was attached to a villa. Towers in medieval times were a symbol of wealth and power: the more and higher the towers, the more wealth was exhibited.

Recharged, with the apartment cleaned, fresh sheets, we are off on this foggy, wet morning. Mind you, we had researched and cross-checked all the sites—opening and closing times—we planned to visit within the towns and villages before we arrived in Tuscany. What I didn't account for was the drive time and distance ratio: The distances were all researched (both country roads and autostrada) for each town and village; however, the time was something I could not factor in. Even when I used the distance-time calculations, the time assigned was never accurate for us. I guess that I drove more slowly than the suggested distances and times forecast. Nevertheless, we are slow travelers on a road trip to one of the most organically beautiful areas in Europe—what difference does a few extra hours make?

After much deft down-shifting as a result of the sharp curves and hills, we found the Badia (Abbey) a Passignano in the small hamlet of Travarnelle. The imposing religious complex and abbey were founded in the 11th century. The complex's renovations were near completion, and we leisurely strolled to admire this 11th-century campus. The opening times were different than those I noted from their website, but it didn't matter as we will come back another time. I wrote the abbey on my "Must Return" list. This detour provided us with an opportunity to experience the surprises that await us deep into Chianti valley.

Trying to keep all eyes on the road, I was so tempted to look at what Em was excitedly pointing out along the way through the Chianti hills and the medieval village of Castellina in Chianti. As keen observers, we saw a sign marker indicating an Etruscan site two kilometers away at the next right turn. One annoying proclivity I have is my adroit capacity to suddenly veer into small lanes or pasture paths when I see a shadow of a tower, an Etruscan sight, a castle or a church. That's exactly what happened here—the sixth-century graveyard and tomb were in remarkably great shape. It's a short drive from the Etruscan tomb to the hidden Chianti landmark of Castellina in Chianti (pop. 2,800). This, too, was an Etruscan settlement, then Roman, as were all the medieval villages that bordered these territories of Florence and Siena. We didn't take the underground tunnel that circled the historic center, but the humongous fortress, now the town hall, and huge 14th tower did pique my interest enough to trek up to take in the magnificent views of the town and surrounding hillside. The ultimate highlight was the Church of San Salvatore, sitting high up on the village square. Inside was an important 14th-century fresco of the enthroned Madonna, attributed to Bicci di Lorenzo, and a wooden Renaissance statue of the town's patron saint, St. Barnabas. The church, we learned, was damaged during the Second World War but rebuilt in inspiring Neo-Romanesque style. We enjoyed a traditional lunch at Ristorante Albergaccio di Castellina, a rustic but stylish building. We read that they highlight their culinary approach as the "territory on the table!" I would say it's imaginative without forgetting the regional flavors and seasonal produce; super lunch, excellent service, and value-for-money experience. Our final stop is at one of the local enoteca to sample the local wines.

Reviewing the highlights:

- The massive castle (La Rocca) and the restored 14th-century tower that houses a small Etruscan Museum.

- The Church of San Salvatore, rebuilt after its destruction during World War II, in new-Romanesque style but with a marvelous 15th-century fresco and 14th-century wooden statue.
- Surprising number of noble palaces.
- A small archaeological museum and tempting Chianti wine shops nearby.
- Via delle Volte. The entire street was underground and vaulted with many shops, artisans' workshops and restaurants.

After the long drive-day yesterday into the Chianti Hills and at the Tuscan village of Castellina in Chianti, we decided to stay home today; it was very foggy, cloudy, chilly and wet. Rain was forecast for the entire day. After 14 days, we asked Cid if she would please read the electricity meter and let us know how much we used and the cost of this electricity to heat the apartment. On the second day, I tried to find the heating valves in each of the rooms we never would use in an effort to minimize the electric usage. However, there were no zone controls for the heat! The meters were in Cid's basement or storage area, and she did not invite me to check the meters with her, so I anxiously waited for her return. Cid indicated that the kilowatt meter reading and the rate cost per kWh worked out to 1.17210 euros per kWh. In our case we used 59 kWh over 14 days for a total of 70 euros. Whoa, at this rate we will either go without heat or find some efficiencies therein, as we did in Rome. Cid acted as surprised as we were at the usage and 14-day cost. I had to kick myself for not identifying what, specifically, were those "some utilities" included. I did inquire about which utilities were included, and Cid kindly indicated that the gas for the stove, garbage pickup and water were included in the monthly rent. "Oh," and I thanked her for all the utilities included. Cid, being a kind English woman, and Em, a clever Italian-American woman, together worked out a new method of insuring less costly heat for the duration of our stay. Em suggested, and Cid agreed, to switch our electric hot water heater to gas with the understanding that the hot water will only be on for four–six hours rather than 24 hours with electricity. With this arrangement, we would only be paying for the electricity used in the sitting room.

Em soothed my anxiety by saying, "This should help; plus just using the gas fireplace in the sitting room would be more efficient than heating the entire apartment." "Another challenge, well done, and thanks," I said.

The other budget concern while sequestered in the apartment that day was the cost of operating the little Fiat. Diesel fuel, being cheaper than unleaded petrol, was a known factor before arriving in Italy. The cost for a liter of gasolio fuel in Tuscany was 1.193 euros per liter or about $5.10 per gallon. With the constantly shifting hairpin turns, the Chianti hills, and probably my less-than-effective driving skills, we'll no doubt rack up a decent size petrol bill at the end of our road trip. I wrote a reminder on my "Think Next Time" list:

To inquire what are the "some utilities" included and to think about them when planning future slow travel road trips, to prepare for the petrol costs of slow travel versus public transport while living in the city without a car. For Italy, I researched that petrol would be expensive, and we knew from living in Rome that the electricity would be expensive. Em skillfully accounted for these expenses when she formed our fixed budget for Florence. One pleasant surprise for us was that so far our food costs were lower than expected.

Sundays are a great day to travel as the trucks are not out on the roads. Also, the Italians tend to get out a little later in the mornings on Sundays. Our destination was to Cortona (pop. 23,000), an hour and a half drive. "But Em, we have our Skype call at 12," I snipped. "Fine, we will call everyone now, before we leave." It was 9 a.m. our time when she proclaimed the Skype solution: "That's 3 p.m. their time; will anybody be home?" Sure enough, the boys were outside playing with their dog, Hanna, and Annika was out collecting chestnuts and climbing a tree in their yard; not at the same time, mind you. We explained our earlier-than-usual time, and the respective parents said that they would send our love to them and tell them how sorry we were to have missed speaking with them. Our daughter, sensing that I was disappointed, said she would try and call us tomorrow when the boys returned from school. On the road again, we passed a sign indicating that we were entering Chiusi (pop. 8,700), which I later found out was recognized as one of the sovereign towns of the Etruscan Confederation during the 6–1st centuries BCE. A delightfully inspiring Renaissance town with two highlights: The Etruscan Museum—with artifacts and written history about the Etruscans to the Romans and for many centuries an unbroken pathway of knowledge and civilization. The Cattedrale di San Secondiano was built over the ruins of a sixth-century medieval church. The interior walls were of marble and travertine, along with the marble capitals, looking more Greek (e.g., Doric and Ionic) than Roman. I reckoned that they were recycled or reclaimed from older buildings.

When we returned for the day, we excitedly told Cid what we had found in Chiusi. Cid, we learned, was trained as an archaeologist at the University of Durham (Durham's Norman cathedral) and said, "You just visited one of the few Early Christian churches in Tuscany." We asked her for more information about other Early Christian churches in the area, and she said she had some documents in her house and would leave them on the doorstep of our apartment in the morning. Are we in a time warp? I questioned myself. Is the flow of time speeding up or running more slowly? Does it really matter?

After an absolutely engaging time in Chiusi, we drove through the enchanting Chianti Valley to Cortona. Little has changed since Renaissance times: the medieval town's thick walls and the commanding citadel that replaced the Etruscan building. Our focus was to observe the magnificent art of Cortona's own, Fra Angelico, and to view his major work "Annunciations" in the Chiesa del Gesù. A complete rest stop at the Museo dell'Accademia Etruscan exhibit, which is reported to be the best Etruscan museum in all of Italy. One final stop on our way back to Bisticci was the town of Castiglion Fiorentino (pop. 13,000) just 15 kilometers from Cortona. We paused, looked, lingered and strolled through the Porta Fiorentina to the main entrance to the town's historical center. The beautiful Romanesque church of Sant'Angelo that once served as a hospital and wine cellar is now used as the Municipal Art Gallery. The recent excavations found an Etruscan wall said to be from the fourth century BCE. A delightful compact town center to meander around the steep lanes, narrow streets, as we found only the "locals" taking their leisurely stroll.

The Etruscans were people from the Etruian region between the Tiber and Arno rivers west and south of the Apennine Mountains. They reached their height in Italy from the eighth to the fifth century BCE. Many cultural and societal features were adapted by the Romans, such as their alphabet, techniques about engineering, the hydraulic system, temple design and religious rituals. The Roman Kingdom finally conquered the Etruscan League in 396 BCE.

We exited very early to enjoy the quiet town of Greve (pop. 14,000) and the fine people-watching café on the town square (Piazza G. Matteotti). We noticed that there were no other cars parked in the free parking area of the square where we had parked in the past. "How fortunate to have free parking this morning," I proudly mumbled. We noticed that some vendors were beginning to set up their tables in the square; how nice, a market day. After caffè latte and cornetti, we did a run-in to the COOP around the corner from the square; upon our return to the car, a pink ticket was attached to the windscreen. "Nessun giorno di Mercato del parcheggio." Rough translation: "cannot park in square the day of the open market." They had begun to set up their stalls around the car. A hefty fine—another learning experience—read the parking signs, translate their restrictions, and, if not sure, park somewhere else where it is legal to park. The fine of 30 euros was paid at the police station in town.

The boys did call; it must have been 9 their time. Called to say, "Hello, how are you?" Our younger grandson mentioned that Hanna, their black lab, "had to go to the vet's because of an earache or something." He added, "She is better now." We mentioned that we are having a wonderful time discovering Tuscan towns and exploring the old churches. Our daughter asked if we had spent much time in Florence. "Yes, a couple of times," I replied, "but we'll start to pick up our time in Florence very soon." Actually, Em reminded me that we have been to Florence four times and are only waiting for our museum passes to arrive. I'm not sure why we are waiting almost two weeks to return to Florence. It is getting colder each day, it seems; more heat is required. Today we bought two water bottles at the pharmacy in Rignano sull' Arno.

Tuscany is synonymous with Chianti wines as expressed by A. Dias Blue: "The geography of wine is as much an emotional landscape as it is a physical terrain." With wine in mind, we were up early and off to a pretty little town situated on the edge of Chianti Classico wine-growing region. Impruneta (pop. 15,000) is also noted for its high-quality bricks, tiles and decorative terra-cotta ware. A little unknown fact about Impruneta was that Brunelleschi's Dome on the Florence Cathedral was made of Impruneta tiles. We admired the Basilica of Saint Mary. We learned that although it had been destroyed after the war, they carefully restored the church to its original Gothic-Renaissance style. Loved the undestroyed 14th-century cloister with a fine 1300s central fountain. There was a very informative and well-organized, six-room Museum of the Treasure of Impruneta located next to the church. Impruneta was heavily damaged after the war, and the present-day architecture was not one from the Middle Ages. This was a great find, and we decided that we should return.

We are finding that over time the drive to and parking in Florence is questionable use of our time and energy. It takes 45–55 minutes (depending on day and time of day) to drive; however, it was quite easy to park at the train station garage, but expensive, then we had the 50-minute drive back to Bisticci. We are less than ten or so miles from Bisticci to the train station, but traffic moves slowly.

We have tried to adjust our drive time to avoid morning commuters, but there is still local traffic, school vans, local buses and slow-moving trucks.

Cid is a wealth of knowledge about Tuscany, but particularly of Florence, as is Francisco. She does offer detailed information and welcomes our questions when we see her around the property. It seems that she and Francisco have day jobs and rent their two apartments as extra income. I asked Cid where the closest train station is located. She kindly drew a rough map to the town of Rignano sull' Arno (pop. 8,700), just a 10–15 minute drive from Bisticci. "Parking is wherever you find a space—just takes some patience." I didn't mention that I am still learning to be more patient. After a nine-minute drive we were in Rignano sull' Arno. As we drove around the town center, it seemed like tourists did not dominate the streets, only the locals. A few shops, two cafés, and many structures from the 14th-16th centuries are now used as shops and flats for the residences. Our lucky day, as a parking space became available near the train station, we located the tobaccoria-café nearby that sold tickets for the train. The attendant didn't speak English, but I knew enough to say, "due ritorni, grazie." She countered, "Dove? Santa Maria Novella Stazione, per favore." I noted that there were two advantages to using the train: It's only a 30-minute train ride to the station and is the same price for two that we paid when we parked at the station in Florence. This eventually becomes our twice-a-week routine to Florence: Rignano sull' Arno to Florence.

I am avoiding going to any details regarding all the sights we eventually experienced in Florence, as there are so many excellent guidebooks that provide the essential highlights of the enormous treasures on offer in Florence. However, the major attraction that brought us to Florence today was the museum of Santa Maria Novella—13th Century.

We purchased tickets for the museum: that includes the cloister of the Dead, Green Cloister and the cemetery. Santa Maria Novella is the first great basilica and one of the most important Gothic churches in Florence. Architecturally, the exterior was the work of Leon Batista Alberti and Fra Jacopo Talenti. The interior: decidedly Gothic, as the multicolored light was pouring through the blue, red and yellow stained-glass windows and is supposed to be the work of Brunelleschi. The church holds extraordinary works of art including Masaccio's magnificent "Holy Trinity." What Em mentioned to me, after her long observation of the fresco, was "Masaccio placed both the sacred characters and his contemporaries on the same level, in the same space, in a Renaissance chapel." I said, "All the characters are seen as they would be in a photograph, not larger or smaller depending on their importance!" Em replied, "And this was painted in 1427!" I read, with amazement, that Tommaso di Ser Giovanni di Simone was the first great Italian painter of the Quattrocento period of the Italian Renaissance; I had mistakenly thought it was Masaccio. Overwhelmed, not yet, below the splendid stained-glass window was a fresco cycle by Dominico Ghirlandaio, telling the "Stories of the Madonna and St. John the Baptist." At the Sassetti Chapel was another fresco by Ghirlandaio called "Approbation of the Rule of St. Francis." Interestingly, the fresco was to illustrate the life of St. Francis, but who shows up in the fresco but Lorenzo the Magnificent, the patron art saint of Florence, in the Medicis parish, with a bunch of children and teachers in the fresco. We sat down at the end of the last pew to take a break. I said to Em, "This is why we came to Florence. Florence in the early 15th century took an idea that changed art and society forever." "Profound, where did you learn about that?" she whispered. "I read it somewhere, but I also read that the Florentines rejected the Gothic style and adopted a new set of principles to create what we are experiencing in Florence today." "And for the next six weeks," she replied. One last masterpiece, in the center of the nave, raised high like God and masterfully restored ten years ago was Giotto's "Crucifix," 1288. The Christian spirituality was evident by the theme of love, with the black, white and red colors representing the passion. For me, the extraordinary beauty lies in the realism of the figure, not the idealized form of the former two-dimensional and abstract Byzantine art. So much, too much, must return, I recorded on my growing list; so many chapels, artwork, sculptures, and frescoes to embrace and appreciate. As we are slow travelers, we made time for the Grand Cloister, our favorite today, especially those 56 arcades built around 1340. The museum was more than an art museum; it is more like a mini-church with multicolored marble and a Latin Cross form. Artworks by Pisano, Ghiberti, Brunelleschi, Ghirlandaio, Robbia, and Giotto were alive and well in the Church of Santa Maria Novella. We returned on the 5:05 train back to Rignano sull' Arno and reached the apartment at 5:55, exhausted with excitement and love.

A full day of rest. Em worked on her cypress landscape sketches and watercolors. I needed to research more about Masaccio, Ghirlandaio, Robbia, Pisano, Brunelleschi, and Tommaso di Ser Giovanni di Simone, whom I knew nothing about.

We are here in Florence this "term" to learn about the art and architecture in Renaissance Florence. Love the train ride, quiet, slow moving, and we have the opportunity to see the concealed-compromised side of Florence along the way. Three minutes from the train station, smack in the city center, and we are at the Duomo–Santa Maria del Fiore.

The ultimate feature for us was the Brunelleschi Dome. We both read Ross King's "Brunelleschi's Dome: How the Renaissance Genius Reinvented Architecture," which was definitely an insightful and informative good read. Ross's book tells the story of how a Renaissance genius bent men, materials, and the forces of nature to build an architectural wonder we observed today. The book weaved drama amid a background of plagues, wars, political feuds and intellectual challenges of Renaissance Florence.

The "Dome" took Brunelleschi 15 years and was the first dome ever to be constructed over a roof over such a vast building. The multicolored geometrically decorated structure required a hoist to move the blocks of stone weighing over three tons. The man,

The Basilica of Santa Maria Novella, one of the most important pieces of Gothic architecture in Tuscany.

Brunelleschi, designed a hoist capable of moving the blocks to their present location. I did manage to climb the 463 steps to the top of the dome, noting the following: the steps were three feet wide, no stopping, very crowded, as folks must enter and exit the same narrow stairs. The highlights of this interesting workout were the fantastic view of Florence and the ingenious drums that Brunelleschi developed to withstand the weight of the roof. What a trove of valuable, interesting and delightful mastery and craftsmanship.

We took a rest-at-home day. The temperatures were in the 60s, and we decided to take some time sitting outside in the yard under a cluster of apple trees. I developed a few inconclusive comments about driving and life in general in Tuscany.

Here are a few I came up with:

- Autostrada–We have used this speedway only once. A lot of construction and detours, making it a little difficult to get on from an exit or to pass the large semi-trucks, especially if a lane was closed.
- Driving in small towns and villages one must be constantly aware of bikes, motorbikes, walkers, cars, buses, scooters, speed bumps, children and tourists.
- Having enough small bills for petrol fill-ups.
- Having correct change at checkouts.
- Using a glove when touching produce—oftentimes you are not permitted to touch the produce, as I learned in Rome.
- Be prepared to wait longer periods in lines at the markets as the checkout folks know many of the local customers and like to inquire about how they are doing, and the children have the same interpersonal politeness as in Rome.
- Get used to shops, cafés, petrol stations, churches, and restaurants closed from 1 to 4 p.m.
- Always be humble and courteous to all people—we are merely foreigners in their country. We are having such a marvelous time in Tuscany!

A brilliant sunny morning, off early for an expected two-hour drive to arrive at the Abbazia di Sant'Antimo when it opens to visitors. The abbey is located deep in that gorgeous serene Tuscan landscape: the silvery olive groves, fields of sunflowers, vineyards, stone farms, medieval castles, harmonious villages and towns, and the cypress tree-lined avenues. We stopped to take in this precious scenery and to be thankful for being able to experience this year abroad, as seniors. Since the Etruscans, little has changed here since the tenth century BCE. As usual, we were slightly diverted on our way to a nearby village, near the Abbey of Castelnuovo (pop. 6,000). We spent almost two hours in this village, which we later learned was founded in the eighth century. Highlights: the 12th-century castle, home to an archaeological museum, the 16th-century Renaissance façade of Duomo of Sts. Peter and Paul, while the interior is dramatic Baroque. There was one brilliant canvas by Domenico Ghirlandaio depicting the "Madonna with Saints."

After a few kilometers, we arrived at the majestic abbey; the church, built with travertine stone, was an exceptional example of Romanesque 11th-century architecture: massive, sturdy and dark. The rib-vaulted roof supported the columns crowned with superb alabaster carved capitals with floral and animal motifs. Just spectacular! It was here that the abbey hosts spiritual retreats and prayer meetings run by the Augustinian monks. We were extremely fortunate to be able to stay for 30 minutes and listen to the free-flowing, melodic, nonrhythmic, harmonizing Gregorian chant: brilliant and exhilarating.

Twenty minutes away lies another famous abbey nestled among the cypress trees in a landscape of eroded hills. Monte Oliveto was founded in 1313 by Benedictine monks. The cloisters were decorated with a superb series of 36 frescoes recounting the life of St. Benedict. They were painted by Luca Signorelli from 1498 and finished off by Sodoma (Giovanni Antonio Bazzi) in 1502 (Frescoes seen in San Brizio Chapel-Orvieto).

We finished off the exciting day with a stop in the hilltop town of Montalcino (pop. 5,000). This was an exquisite Renaissance village, with the 12th-century walls around the town well preserved. We planned to return to take full advantage of the town's hospitality and historic sites and learn more about the famous Brunello wine that is grown in this restricted growing area.

Another 40-degree morning. With the car heater on, we drive to Fiesole (pop. 14,000), a little city founded by the Etruscans in the sixth century BCE. The purpose of the trek to Fiesole was to experience firsthand the Etruscan tombs, Roman Theater, the Duomo-Cathedral dated from the 11th century and the villas of the Medici, who owned all of this area for centuries. This was also the birthplace of Fra Angelica and Giotto di Bondone, exemplary master painters of the 1400s. Lying brilliantly in the center of the town was the Duomo and, as expected, a stark interior; however, the spectacular capitals date from ancient times. It's a steep walk up to the Piazza San Francesco for stunning views of the City of Florence, the Dome and the countryside. A ten-minute walk from the Piazza San Francesco to the Convento di San Francesco, a modest convent, with a small, well-attended cloister, where monks have lived continuously since the 14th century. I think about why we will have a cold apartment when we return, as I had turned off the radiator heat.

A very crisp morning—but sunny and temperatures around 38 degrees Fahrenheit. We are beginning to notice the dramatic decrease in both hours of sunshine and temperatures as we head into the late Tuscan autumn. It's a 20-minute drive to a small town called Antella (pop. 2,900), not a tourist town but a residence town with plenty of accommodations to rent as it is close to Florence. At the center was a Pieve di Santa Maria all' Antella, a solid Romanesque (1100) church, with modifications completed in 1700. Inside Pieve di Santa Maria all'Antella was a restored 14th-century fresco and a terra-cotta painting outlined with a semicircular green and white marble border. Nearby was the Oratorio di Santa Catarina dated 14th century. We were told that they hold sacred music here occasionally.

Since it was not raining, we planned to head to the UNESCO World Heritage Site and the medieval town of San Gimignano (pop. 7,800), adorned with its amazing remaining 13 towers (out of the original 70 towers). It is one of the most inspiring and relaxing medieval towns we have seen. So much packed into this small town: several 13th–15th century churches (e.g., Collegiata di Santa Maria Assunta and Sant' Agostino Basilica, both with remarkable frescoes; the large Piazza del Populous, Piazza Luigi Pecori and; Piazza della Cisterna, paved in medieval bricks forming herringbone patterns). I placed San Gimignano on my "Must Return" list.

With rain forecast today, we take the train to Florence. One focus today was on an interesting exhibit, "Inganni ad Arte (Art and Illusions)" at the Palazzo Strozzi. The theme, we gathered, was of how illusion was contrasted between make-believe and reality as a source of enjoyment in all the arts. Over 150 works of art from the 15th century to the present time were exhibited. More questions than answers followed this experience. For example, what is the relationship between painted space and real space in the art of illusion? Is it a pleasure to be deceived by art; is it intended to manipulate reality? The essential question might be this: Did perception precede illusion or vice versa? We had interesting conversations about these questions. We had time for one more slow travel accounting procedure (i.e., to purchase a year-round pass that would allow us unlimited entrance to all the museums and the Uffizi and no waiting in lines). We worked out that after three visits each to galleries and museums the pass pays for itself. This was a wonderful deal if you have the time and inclination to visit many of the treasures in Florence: slow travel fosters these kinds of excitements and savings. Spending as much time to linger, study and reflect as possible in Florence was one major factor in our selection to live in Bisticci.

At the Uffizi, temptation beckons us to see everything; however, we knew that we would be back many times, so we satisfied our craving and visited only the Botticelli and Caravaggio rooms. We added four more Caravaggio paintings to our Rome list: The paintings seen today were: "Boy Peeling Fruit," "Bacchus," "Medusa," and "Sacrifice of Isaac." Excited and thankful for the opportunity to view these two masters: Botticelli from the Early Renaissance and Caravaggio in the late Mannerist period; now, more than ever, our two favorite painters.

It's raining and foggy, a stay-at-home day with us bundled in the sitting room with the radiator on full blast. A brief chat with the family, and "How's it going?" with the grandchildren. Summation: Everybody was fine and asking with the cold weather if we are still enjoying our living in Tuscany? Of course, I email everybody every day with a brief summary of where we went, weather, and sometimes I mention a special lunch or meeting a knowledgeable person like John. I do keep everybody up to date but rarely complain to them about the heat, or lack of it, expenses, the hair-raising driving on "S" curves or the slow-ups and rapid down pace driving on the Tuscan hills or the dense fog that makes driving dangerous. No complaints or regrets. We are very happy, and our living in Tuscany has allowed us to meet any challenge that may come our way! We shall continue to discover, explore, enjoy, and learn as much of Florence and Tuscany as we possibly can in the remaining eight weeks.

Yesterday, by procuring the museum yearly passes, which were rather pricey, budget-wise we will have the experiences and save euros as well. This morning, we received our two-week heating bill that was tucked under our door. After a quick review of the cost, we made a couple of practical decisions: When we are in the apartment, we wear an extra sweater; be sensible and conservative with the electricity; and just pay the bills, and spend less euros for a few days to make up for the utilities. Em doesn't like the chill and will use the small electric heater that Cid provided us. For seniors engaged in long-term slow travel road trips, we must stay within the pre-planned budget and make whatever adjustments are sensible.

I had other books and articles to read, but I'm sure that I missed something in Ross King's *Brunelleschi's Dome: How a Renaissance Genius Reinvented Architecture*. So I read about the mystery of the competition for this commission. He had to solve the problem of how to roof the vast sanctuary. He solved this by designing two flattened domes linked together by a network of internal arches and buttresses. The genius managed (in 1420) to design the dome without external buttresses or apparent support. When I climbed those 463 steps in Santa Maria del Fiore, I didn't have an understanding of his support design. Now, it is clearer to me just how amazing this engineering feat was almost 600 years ago.

A refreshingly warmer sunny day was ready for us to explore the Giardino di Boboli,

The largest masonry dome in the world, the Santa Maria del Fiore designed by Filippo Brunelleschi, which took 16 years to complete.

the gardens that Cosimo Medici began in 1549. The park was a fine example of an Italian Renaissance terraced garden, dotted with fountains, playful statues, and the Neptune Pool. Before the garden visit, we saw a stupendous panoramic view of Florence from the Piazzale Michelangelo, just south of the historic center. This squared Florence terrace was designed in typical 19th-century style and dedicated to Michelangelo, as his masterpieces are housed throughout the city. A large bronze cast of "David," one of the two copies, faced towards Florence from the center of the square. We walked to the highest point in the city to admire the Basilica di San Miniato al Monte, one of the finest Roman-esque buildings (11th century) in all of Tuscany. The façade featured multicolored marble with geometric patterns similar to those we had found on the facades of Santa Croce and Santa Maria Novella. Inside was another special discovery: zodiac symbols and marble inlaid within the patterned floors. All around the nave are patterned floors, sixteen fresco scenes from the Life of St. Benedict. There was so much to explore and admire, and I placed this magnificent building on my "Return List."

Parking near the historical center is expensive, but if we arrived early in the morning, we always found a space if we drove around until one became vacant. Entering through the Porta Romana, we walked past the grottos, the large fountains, until we reached the Pitti Palace. The Pitti will be explored at another time as we have the time. Our immediate impression of this vast, green expansion was the way it was layered out, like a real outdoor museum. We spent much of the delightful day just reflecting on the beauty of our surroundings and being grateful for our good fortune and to be able to enjoy slow travel in Florence. We eventually returned a number of times to the Boboli and Pitti Palace.

The weather, sunny and bright skies, was with us once again as we planned an extensive travel day to Montepulciano and Pienza. We hesitated to take the autostrada, but due to the distance, we did so in order to have more time exploring those towns. The drive time was about one hour and a half to Montepulciano (pop. 14,000), which claimed to be "a perfect example of a Renaissance town planning," set high—2,000 feet—in the Val d' Orcia, one of Tuscany's most celebrated landscapes. Even before we entered the town, far in the distance the Torre di Pulcinella's clock tower dominated the historical center.

An "ideal Renaissance town" concept was developed by Leon Batista Alberti in the 15th century and was to have these features to claim such a title:

- After choosing the location, the town was to be set up according to size, direction of streets, location of bridges and gates, and finally a building pattern of perfect symmetry.
- The town square would be flanked by the main monumental buildings to reflect the balance between the civil and religious authorities through architectural harmony and beauty.
- A cathedral would be opposite a communal palazzo, with an open loggia for people to have a covered walkway on the grouping floor.
- The other sections of the town would be designed for aristocratic mansions, and a well for all the town's people.

Reaction: Montepulciano has met most of these criteria: symmetry and harmony explain the serenity and peacefulness.

Although this ancient town is of Etruscan origin, it's the violet-scented ruby wine, Vino Nobile di Montepulciano, that is as famous as the town itself. We learned that Montepulciano was also a major producer of pork, "pici" pasta, and honey. We spent considerable time learning about the Vino Nobile di Montepulciano at the Gattavecchi Winery, specifically, the Sangiovese grape varieties (at least 70 percent of the final wine), its history, manner in which the wine was aged, and modern technologies. The aroma had a strong scent of oregano and pepper, and the flavor profiles included the tastes of plums, smoky tobacco and sour cherries. We enjoyed the insightful and relaxing experience at the Gattavecchi Winery, where the staff, and specifically Maurice, a vigneron, spent so much of his time and expertise with us.

A 20-minute drive through the classic and iconic Tuscan rolling hills, umbrella pines and cypresses lined the roads from Montepulciano to the small enchanting town of Pienza (pop. 2,100), which was a summer retreat for Pope Pius II. The Piazza Pio II was framed by a few 15th-century Renaissance buildings (e.g., Pienza Cathedral, Museo Diocesano Di Pienza, and the Piccolomini Palace). UNESCO has declared the town a World Heritage Site and for very good reasons. The famous local Pecorino sheep's milk cheese is a well-established product of Pienza. Some of the most vivid pleasures and memories of Tuscany are the simple ones.

Still plenty of time for one more stop at another hilltop town of Monte San Savino (pop. 8,800). We read somewhere that this town was the birthplace of the high Renaissance sculptor Andrea Sansovino (1460–1529). It's a classic Tuscan town, dotted with medieval and Renaissance palazzi, beautiful churches and the Logge dei Mercanti, with their impressive Corinthian columns, designed by Sansovino. Somehow this extraordinary town has managed to avoid the perils and riches of commercial mass tourism. This town is what I called a "Betcha-by-Golly, wow," direct from the Stylistics playlist.

What is going on here in Tuscany? Here we are nearing the beginning of November, and we have another perfect day for exploring more Tuscan treasures—no complaints! We planned only one sight visit today, especially after the very long drive and informed discoveries yesterday. Slow drive to the peaceful and entirely enclosed medieval wall town of Monteriggioni, which lies on top of the graceful hill north of Siena. This fortress (11 towers) was an outpost built by the Sienese in the early 13th century. Monteriggioni was described by Dante in his "Divine Comedy" verses from the 31st canto of the "Inferno."

It is here that the Italian poet writes "on the circular parapets—Monteriggioni crowns itself with towers." With our Illy espresso, we just sat in the brilliant sunshine looking out at the ninth-century Church of S. Maria Assunta-Monteriggioni. This was such a romantic time together.

November, and another beautiful day; we could not resist and headed to another Tuscan discovery: the town of Volterra (pop. 10,500). An hour of winding "Z" curves, and I'm being extra careful not to look at the glorious autumn colors: gold, greens, yellows, oranges and copper of the landscape. Coming down from the crest of another steep hill, we were somewhat shocked to see a huge, red circle sculpture smack in a field as we approached Volterra.

We found a car park and walked around to relish the silent beauty of the rather austere and sober Renaissance villas, with their twin bay windows, massive crenellated roofs, and travertine tiles located off the Piazza dei Priori. When we returned to the apartment, I found out who the sculptor of the huge, red circle was: Mauro Staccioli, born in Volterra. He has permanent collections of his sculptures in Rome, Seoul, San Diego and Portugal. I am glad to have found out more about this sculptor, as his art, I learned, had a strong relationship with the places where he worked.

After two long driving days, we take the train to Florence. Our focus was the Bargello National Museum, free on our yearly pass. The large Gothic-style palazzo was built in the 13th century; today it houses a valuable insight into Italian Renaissance sculpture.

We focused on viewing the Renaissance masters: Michelangelo, Donatello, and the marble reliefs of Donatello's most famous student, Desiderio da Settignano (1430–1464). Too many treasures to mention, except our favorites: Michelangelo's "Drunken Bacchus" and the unfinished "David-Apollo."

Reflections:

Not knowing much about sculpting, I imagine that marble must have been a difficult material with which to achieve perfection, requiring a genius's touch and feel (both in heart and hands). Not to downplay the exquisite bronze sculptures by Donatello, which were aesthetically very pleasing as well.

After a couple of days of recharging, cleaning, washing, dusting and Skype chats, we saved some euros by hanging around the apartment. Today, despite the foggy, hazy morning, we head 85 kilometers to Siena, known to all for the "Palio," the biannual horse race (over 800 years old) or "corsa al Palio," around the Piazza del Campo. The "Palio" banner was awarded to one of the ten "contrade," or neighborhoods, that compete. What was unique about the Piazza del Campo was the architecture that surrounded the square. The harmony that exists between the Romanesque-Gothic-Renaissance buildings was something to admire. You could see the 14th-century Torre del Mangia from everywhere in town, as it dominated the square. The architectural periods were once again evident with the examination of the Cathedral of Santa Maria Assunta–Duomo. Beginning in the 12th century, it dramatically demonstrates the architecture of the times: Romanesque (1075–1125) and Italian Gothic (1228–1290). A hands-on architectural history lesson, I might add.

The leaves are changing rapidly to golden browns, yellows and oranges. The Virginia creeper was now bright red and looks marvelous against the dark green cypress and umbrella pine trees. The autumn blue skies in Tuscany represent the blueness of the skies and sea and with temperatures in the 60s F. Our goal today, as we continue our slow travel road trip, was to visit an interesting geological area, less touristy, more organic in nature. The Valdarno region is located in a valley through which the River Arnolfini flows. We point the Fiat in the direction of Castelfranco di Sopra (pop. 9,600), settled in 300 BCE. Castelfranco di Sopra is one of "The Most Beautiful Villages of Italy." It has been said that Hannibal passes through this village during the Punic Wars. The main entrance, of the three gates to the town, is through the splendid 14th-century tower, Torre di Arnolfo.

While enjoying our slow drive through the yellow-copper Tuscan countryside, we came across an interesting geological formation called the "Le Balze." I read about this unique phenomenon, evidently created by soil erosion, which draws a yellowish-copper landscape interspersed with the villas, farms and small towns around the rock formations. We enjoyed our slow travel road trip to the inspiring, interesting, and beautiful Castelfranco di Sopra.

We gathered our enormous energies for our fourth trip back to the Boboli Gardens. I am not keen on driving in Florence, especially on a weekday, but the gardens were located on the south side of the River Arno or on the other side of the city center and the train station. Our faithful GPS managed to get it wrong, and we eventually arrived smack in the city center. Somehow we managed, thanks to Em's navigation skills, to avoid the bike riders, fruit carts, people with tourist credentials displayed all over themselves, and locals who knew exactly where they were going—all, mind you, on the very narrow medieval streets of the city center of Florence. Love the Boboli for its many attractions aside from the gardens, fountains and statues. For example, the huge Palazzo Pitti Museum, where the modern art and porcelain museums are inside the gardens. With the weather so conducive to staying outside, we merely took a slow stroll around the garden walls. We did come across the Grotta Grande, a cave built in the 1500s with sculptures captured in theatrical Rococo style—1800's.

Since we had to choose either one, two, three or five hours on the parking meter, we selected the five-hour option, so indeed we had time left on our meter to walk to the little corner in the center to find Chiesa di Santo Spirito. The restoration was beautiful. Admiring the stark Romanesque exterior designed in perfect proportion, integrating light, shadows and space by Brunelleschi, we were dumbfounded with admiration for the creative genius of such a structure by Brunelleschi. The interior was classic Brunelleschi design: a huge but harmonious space, symmetric architecture, emphasizing white walls and gray stonework. For us, the simplicity of the interior empowered the treasures of the statues, relics and the artwork. The natural light Brunelleschi designed made it easy to appreciate the beauty of symmetry and proportions. One final piece of artistic craftsmanship we surely did not want to miss, and that was the painted window by Pietro Perugino; his most famous pupil was Raphael.

November weather has been pleasantly mild—less electricity being used—euros saved. Since the weather has been so favorable, we journey to southern Tuscany to Sansepolcro (pop. 16,000). The entire center was enclosed within medieval walls and numerous houses dating from the Middle Ages. We were surprised by the few tourists in circulation, only joyful folks of Sansepolcro, it seemed. We easily park in a blue zone space, pay the few euros in the meter and walk directly into the Piazza Torre di Berta, the very heart of the old town. Stunning honey stone city atmosphere: medieval tower flanked with Gothic, Renaissance, and Mannerist (1530–1590) mansions; flat streets; the stunning Romanesque Duomo of San Giovanni Evangelista, with frescoes by Perugino and hometown hero Piero della Francesca, who painted the "Legend of the True Cross" in the Cappella Maggiore of San Francesco in Arezzo.

One cannot overstate the harmonious beauty of this city. This is an open museum of architectural styles.

With time (that is the core of slow travel) on our hands, and excitement in our hearts (you ingest that emotion during slow travel), we drive eight kilometers to the village of Anghiari (pop. 5,700), which has a deep history of battles with its rival, Sansepolcro. An authentic medieval town: massive 13th-century walls, stone houses with small windows, wooden shutters and doors, sometimes needing paint and repairs but nonetheless still characteristically charming. A marvelous place to relax and just absorb the colors and beauty of the chrysanthemums, jasmine and roses on the balconies and entrances. What a wonderful place to reflect and be grateful for being able to experience Tuscany and all its glories. This is a town that takes outdoor living dramatically—bars, cafés with umbrellas, flowers in pots, folks strolling with joy in their hearts.

November, so far, has been good to us with respect to the weather. A sunny and warm day is waiting for us as we head north to the midsize town of Lucca (pop. 88,500). We notice instantly that the topography in the northern area of Tuscany has fewer olive trees and vineyards, no cypress trees, not even hills! As a result of its flatness, there are many farms of all varieties. We were told most of the area's farmers were deeply committed to the land and to organic and biodynamic agriculture, "the old-fashioned techniques." We also learned that there are more biodynamic farms in Lucca than anywhere else in Italy. Further research indicated that the stringent standards for biodynamic certification were all based on the guidelines originally set out by Austrian-born Rudolf Steiner (founder of the Waldorf Schools—a pedagogy that emphasizes the development of students' intellectual, artistic, and practical skills in an integrated and holistic approach). Biodynamicism was created as an alternative approach to using chemicals for crop control. It is regarded as the first modern system of agriculture that is truly sustainable.

We stopped in at a biodynamic farm-guest house, San Martino, and chatted with the owner Giuseppe Ferrua. He talked about his certified organic wine and his extra virgin olive oil, which he pointed out was in the renowned Lucca tradition. We gained a number of important insights as we chatted with Mr. Ferrua. I asked politely if I could record his lecture, and he agreed. He explained to us the difference between organic and biodynamic: "For one, biodynamic farming uses all the methods used in organic farming, plus other substances such as fermented manure, and plant and mineral based preparations, which are added to the soil and crops." Giuseppe slowly and passionately continued to explain to us, "Biodynamic farming has at its core philosophy the importance of the creation of a farm that functions holistically (i.e., with its soil, animals, humans, and plants are projected as diverse 'organs of one living organism')." At the end of his inspiring talk, Giuseppe handed us an informative booklet about his guest farm and biodynamic methods and said, "This might help in your research."

We literally count a day lost if we don't learn something new!

Lucca's center was not congested with vehicles but with bicycle riders, as the flatness is an incentive to ride. A majestic historical center square, Piazza dell'Anfiteatro has a unique shape akin to a Roman amphitheater, which it was in Roman times, and now is the landmark of the old town, replete with impressively restored medieval buildings; we knew that we would return, and I placed Lucca on my "Return" list.

On the way back to Bisticci, Cid had written down to stop in Pescia when we were talking about Byzantine churches in Tuscany. We found this old parish church in the heart of the village of Pescia (pop. 19,500) that dated back to the Middle Byzantine period in 857 CE—rebuilt in 1281 after a fire destroyed the city. Today it's called the Cathedral of Santa Maria Assunta. As we carefully observed the exterior, we saw traces of the pre–Romanesque stonework and the chiseled graffiti doubled "V V" symbol near the bell tower by the master builder, which referred to the "Marian mark" associated with the Virgin Mary. The Pescia is known as one of the most important areas of flower cultivation in Italy. The entire town square of the village had buildings attached to each other that circle all around the large rectangle square; certainly a different medieval architectural arrangement for us, anyway. A neat and tidy square completes the village. Nearby, we passed through the small village of Collodi, famous for the fairytale "Pinocchio."

As mentioned before, weather dictates, or at least seriously determines, what we're about to do or not able to do for the day. I absolutely limit my driving around these hills and winding country roads, especially when the heavy fog lingers over the grassy wet roads. These conditions, however, do make the discussion regarding what we might explore a bit easier.

Peering out the top floor window, hoping that the day wouldn't be as harsh outside as yesterday we were surprised to find a pleasant autumn Tuscan day. We drove to Piazza Michelangelo—the tourist balcony over the city—found a parking space and walked over to the Basilica San Miniato al Monte, dated 11th century. This is the third visit to this basilica, a true Florentine Romanesque architecture with its white and blue/green inlay marble façade sparkling brilliantly in the morning sun's rays. We had to revisit the interior frescoes by

Taddeo Gaddi (14th century) and Pietro Aretino (16th century) and examine more closely those glazed terracotta decorations by Luca della Robbia and the 12th-century gold mosaics. Such a remarkable structure, and almost equally peaceful are the great views of Florence.

The parking garage near the train station always seems to have a few spaces available if we are willing to drive to the fifth floor, although a couple of times the elevator was not in operation. We walk to Ponte Vecchio (1345), the oldest bridge in Florence and the only bridge not destroyed by the German withdrawal from the U.S. forces in World War II. The arcade along the bridge was lined with jewelry and gold shops. In the middle of the bridge was a bronze statue of the most famous Renaissance goldsmith of all, Benvenuto Cellini (1500–1571).

Basilica of Santa Maria Novella, completed by Leon Battista Alberti in the Gothic-Renaissance style.

One more famous site while we still had a couple hours on the parking ticket was to trek over to the rather plain exterior of Santa Maria del Carmine. To our delight, we found a cycle of frescoes, masterpieces of Renaissance painting, reported to be a collaboration by Masolino da Panicale and Masaccio (born Tommaso di Ser Giovanni di Simone), who was the painter of the "Madonna and Child, St. Anne and the Angels" (1424) in the Brancacci Chapel. The frescoes were kept in the dark to protect them from light. We signed up for time for a viewing, deposited a euro in a slot, and viewed them for 45 seconds in the filtered light. Six hundred plus years—absolutely brilliant! This is why we spend every possible hour exploring the immense treasures of Florence.

Forecast: Cold and rainy all day. Too cold to stay in the apartment as it does take time to heat the sitting room. Right, off to the train station to Florence. Our yearly pass had already paid off, so we made good use of the passes and headed to the Galleria dell' Accademia. For anyone who wishes to observe and study the precious sculptures of Michelangelo, this is the museum of choice. We were further treated by viewing the exquisite paintings by Domenico Ghirlandaio, Filippo Lippi and Pietro Perugino. We found "Mels," a bookshop-cum-café nearby, a fortunate place to relax, reflect and appreciate our great opportunities in Florence. The lattes were excellent, and the variety and organization of the English and Italian books were ever so appreciated.

Cloudy, fog, rain and sunshine? Yes, by midmorning the fog and rain were suspended for the day, and we headed east toward Arezzo to continue our quest for new learnings and firsthand experiences. On the way, we see a small, white, rectangular sign, and painted in black letters is the name of the town, Poppi (pop. 6,500). We had to stop, as that is what our grandchildren affectionately call me, "Poppi, do this..." We had to visit the 11th-century Parish Church of San Pietro in Romena, where Dante stayed as a guest in the early 14th century. Unfortunately, we could not enter, but the sublime Romanesque exterior was certainly worth the stop to linger and wonder about such an architectural gem!

Continuing another six kilometers, immediately an imposing Castello di Poppi pops into view. Parking was a charm, as we took the first vacant space we found, paid the meter, and walked to the historical center of Poppi. A few marvelous 12th-century churches and an abbey were at the center. However, our focus was the castle. Normally, we would be reluctant to spend $24 to visit a castle, yet there was something very special about this one. High on a hill, this 13th-century Gothic-style castle had many of the Gothic architectural features that make such a structure so interesting: trefoiled window bays, merlons (those solid, upright sections of a battlement), a keep, a tower, and for an impression of extra height they added a roof with wooden balconies and an outside staircase. Whoa, the interior was smack out of a movie set.

- A library with over 20,000 books.
- First editions of Galileo's books.
- Exhibit, a tondo by the Botticelli School painters.
- A Luca della Robbia glazed terracotta plaque.
- Frescoes by Taddeo Gaddi, Giotto's student.
- Add the massive staircase made of sandstone, with tessellated cut-glass windows.

There you have it, an entertaining and educational experience. We did not just have the experience; we felt the meaning of that experience deep in our minds and hearts, and I began to see the connections for further study.

A brilliantly foggy, cold and cloudy November morning. We planned a rather ambitious day. The months of research prior to any of our slow travel road trips significantly pays time benefits and cost dividends; that's what slow travel offers.

First, straight to the Orsanmichele Church and Museum (1290), which was an unusually shaped church, probably because previously it was a grain storage structure in 1240. The exterior was as impressive as the interior. The niches around the church were occupied by very large statues of the patron saints of the various guilds; for example, bronze works by Lorenzo Ghiberti and marbles by Donatello. The interior was a simple rectangular hall. However, it contained a splendid Gothic tabernacle with polychrome marble, mosaics, bronze and gold. A fantastic experience: architecturally, historically, culturally and artistically.

Our last destination was back to the Piazza della Signoria and the magnificent (Medici) Palazzo Vecchio with the Uffizi Gallery. Significant works of art from Michelangelo, Benvenuto Cellini, Donatello, Giorgio Vasari, Agnolo Bronzino and the sculptor Andrea del Verrocchio: all supreme masters of the Renaissance era. We had another hour and a half before our 16:40 train and stopped once again at Mel's bookshop-cum-café. We took the opportunity to further read and research more about the Tuscany region and what others had to say about Tuscany and Italians. One quote by Mary McCarthy in *The Stones of Florence* was somewhat apropos to our slow travel road trip: "The Florentines, in fact, invented the Renaissance, which is the same as saying that they invented the modern world."

We are getting very used to the early morning fogs that are eventually dissipated by the sun's rays. We make the 40-minute drive to Boboli Gardens, circle around for 20 minutes to find a parking space, slide seven euros into the meter, and we are good to go to the Palazzo Pitti, the massive sandstone structure built in 1457 by the Medici family (their motto, "Hurry Slowly"). Of course, today it is the home of the Medici's art treasures. There are so many attractions for all kinds of interests: the 20 royal apartments, decorated period furnishings, a costume galleria and a precious stone museum. We spent the time in the Palatine Gallery hosting the masterpieces of Guido Reni, Perugino (Raphael's teacher), Raphael, Tiziano Vecelli (Titian), Botticelli, Caravaggio's "Portrait of Fra A. Martelli" and the Flemish and Dutch masters Peter Paul Rubens, Rembrandt, Fran Hals, and Jan van Eyck. This was the most unbelievable collection of Renaissance masterpieces ever experienced in our lives. This kind of "quality experience" promoted further interest in and appreciation for art and art history. Autumn in the Boboli Gardens is just another special treat for us. Meaningful experiences for us were having a lasting social–emotional value and a significant connection to future inquiry and learning.

Late November coldness—the occasional Avanti winds were sometimes fierce—was becoming an interesting challenge. Accordingly, we were up to that challenge by using the "hot water bottles" and turning up the heat in the one room; easy solutions.

Today, notwithstanding the raining, foggy and cold weather, we planned two visits in Florence: Cappella dei Medici and the Church of San Lorenzo.

We entered the Cappella dei Medici chapel through the crypt, to the funeral chapel, where the Medici Dukes are buried. Michelangelo designed the chapel and produced all the sculptures on the tombs. The architectural features were straight out of the Classical Architecture playbook: bright white walls, contrasted with gray decorations and pale-colored marble and multicolored marble cornices, niches, pediments and windows. One reflective and recurring feeling was observing Michelangelo's artistic power when viewing his allegorical figures, "Day and Night." What a genius!

The Church of San Lorenzo, consecrated in 393, was rebuilt in the 11th century, completely redesigned and restructured in 1418 by Filippo Brunelleschi. The rather harsh façade utilized no marble and could be seen as unattractive. Not for me. When Brunelleschi died in 1446, Michelangelo was commissioned to complete the Florentine Renaissance basilica. The Church of San Lorenzo had works of art by Donatello, Francesco Lippi, Desiderio da Settignano and Bronzino (Agnolo di Cosimo). Michelangelo's tomb of Lorenzo the Magnificent was viewed through the Chapel of the Princes. From the inside of the 15th-century cloister were super views of the Duomo and Giotto's tower. A perfect place to contemplate what a valuable architectural and artistic sight was and how fortunate we are to be able to live in Tuscany, very close to Florence.

No rain or fog today! We took the train to the Palazzo Pitti to see the other areas of the Galleria d' Arte Moderna and the Galleria del Costume. The Moderna hosted a grand collection of mainly Tuscan work from the 18th–20th centuries. Sadly, we did not recognize many of the Tuscan painters; made a note on my growing "Learn More About" list. A fascinating insight into the history of fashion from the 18th century to the 1980s awaited us in the Galleria. I actually enjoyed the displays of shoes, dresses, and a line of accessories that we saw today, evidence of the artistry and vision of the past correlated to the trends. I'm reminded of what Coco Chanel referred to when she spoke of fashion simply as a trend, whereas style was inside the person; it resonated with me today. "Everything about Florence pleases me, its name, its sky, its river, its timber beams, its palaces, its air, the grace and elegance of its inhabitants, its setting and surroundings–I love it all," Hector Berlioz said in *Berlioz in Italy*; well said, our sentiments exactly.

Next morning we are off to the train into Florence. Our plan today was a return trip to the Museo e Chiostri Monumentali di Santa Maria Novella (1229), which attracts novice art history enthusiasts like us to the frescoes by the masters of the time: Paolo Uccello, Francesco Lippi, and Domenico Ghirlandaio. Dating back to the 13th century, these Renaissance masters all depicted the lives, times and scenes of biblical characters in remarkable detail and color. We continued our stroll until we found the Church of Ognissanti—I should mention here that we rely more on our downloaded maps than using phone GPS—just a matter of choice, and perhaps it might take longer to find our location. Also, I always carry a copy of Mario Erasmo's book *Strolling through Florence* with me at times. In this beautiful 13th-century building lies a bounty of attractive frescoes by Domenico Ghirlandaio (1448–1494) and Sandro Botticelli (1445–1510). No expert, but when we observed carefully (only three people here with us), we both commented on the beginnings of softer, more delicate facial features. "Halos," not just a light bulb overhead, like in the past, but now light gently and ever so sensitively illuminating the heads and faces. I begin to see color and movement in the clothing, more realistic than previous periods. These two Renaissance masters, and their new painting style, were far ahead of their time, ultimately influencing the next 200 years of Western painting. Absolutely remarkable, and the learning continues.

As we walked back, Em found a niche in a wall of an old wine door, with the wooden door still intact. Further research indicated that the "buchette del vino" was for "on demand" wine during the 1500s; evidently, only a few of them still exist in Florence.

Having our base very near Florence was the absolute key element in our planning and learning about the Renaissance, where it happened, in order to make return visits to Florence.

Today we are off—via train—to the Duomo, Santa Maria del Fiore, one of the largest

Christian buildings in the world. Although we have admired the Duomo many times, it is the Museo dell'Opera del Duomo that we come to see once again. Upon entering the museum you feel the profound importance the cathedral had on the people of Florence as illustrated by the names of thousands of people who contributed to its building, growth, expansion, decorations and preservation. In 1891, the museum was founded to house the works of art previously removed from the Duomo and Baptistery. The building's 6,000 square meters, or 1.5 acres, is conveniently laid out for great works of devotional art and sculpture: 25 rooms with a floor plan on three levels and over 750 works of art.

Highlights:

- Lorenzo Ghiberti's original "Gates of Paradise" brass doors from the Baptistery—restored and cleaned to perfection.
- Michelangelo's "Pieta" when he was in his 80th year.
- Luca della Robbia and Donatello, side by side, the two choir lofts that once stood in the Duomo.
- The Galleria della Cupola, centering on the architectural masterpiece of

The Cathedral of Florence, designed by Arnolfo di Cambio in Gothic style.

Brunelleschi, the Cupola. The room connects the construction and inventive tools used for the purpose of reaching extreme heights, designs of the decorations and windows. By far the most inspiring and impressive experience so far in Florence!

What could come next after such an exhilarating two and a half hours?

A stroll several blocks from the museum to the "prettiest square" in Florence and its beloved church of Santissima Annunziata (1250). Next to the church was the Ospedale degli Innocenti, designed by the one and only Brunelleschi. The Luca della Robbia glazed terra-cotta medallions, beautiful decorated arches and elegant porticos are of special consideration and appeal. It was here at this hospital that abandoned children were left during the Middle Ages.

Off to the Sinagoga, built in the 1800s and based on the Byzantine Hagia Sophia in Istanbul. The interior was designed in rich Moorish frescoes and mosaics. The Jews of

The *Tempio Maggiore Israelitico* in Moorish style.

Florence lived in a ghetto between 1571 and its abolishment in the 19th century. From our excellent guide, Roberto, we received a brief history and a visit through the Jewish Museum. Another important learning experience to add to the hundreds of others during this slow travel road trip.

Our focus today is on two major attractions in Florence. First, the Church of San Marco (1434). The importance of the Dominican order was noted by two members: the famous painter Fra Angelico and the other infamous Girolamo Savonarola and his "Bonfire of the Vanities" (the burning of books, wigs, musical instruments and poetry as a protest against the ruling papacy of Pope Alexander VI). The monks were housed in individual cells as they studied and rested. Fra Angelico, the ultimate master during this time (1400s), marvelously frescoes each of these 44 cells. There are other works of art from the master as well. The most impressive fresco was Angelico's "Annunciation," restored to perfection.

"I had the urge to examine my life in another culture and move beyond what I knew," Frances Mayers said in *Under the Tuscan Sun*.

We returned to both of Brunelleschi's designs—the Church of Santo Spirito, in the Oltrarno quarter, and the courtyards of the Palazzo Pitti. Fortunately, Santo Spirito was open only for the second time in seven previous tries—the interior was magnificent; especially the rounded, high arches and vaulted ceiling were architectural and engineering marvels. The exterior was an exquisitely proportioned Renaissance structure. As expected, there are numerous works of art and carved corbels.

A 20-minute walk and we are at the Museo La Specola, the Natural History Museum. On exhibit was an extensive zoological collection consisting of 600 amazingly lifelike anatomical waxworks—ostensibly used by students several hundreds of years ago. Interestingly, today there were a number of students making drawings of both the vertebrates and the human organisms.

Our last stop: the Palazzo Pitti and the courtyard. A special treat to again view the masterpieces by the masters of their time that garnished our attention, including Raphael, Peter Paul Rubens, Jan van Eyck, Giorgione, and two Caravaggios: "Tooth Puller," and "Portrait of Fra Antonio Martelli." Off to the courtyard to admire once again the mathematically ruled, proportioned, marble arches by Brunelleschi. Mysteriously, the stone relief donkey was only one of three monuments in the whole of Florence dedicated to animals. We found the bull on the right side of Santa Maria del Fiore, but we are still looking for the third, a horse head near the River Arno.

"From the Tuscan bellosguardo [west hill overlooking the Arno] where Galileo stood at night to take in the vision of the stars, we found it hard, gazing upon the earth and heaven to make a choice of beauty," wrote Elizabeth Barrett Browning, *Poetical Works of Elizabeth Barrett Browning and Robert Browning*.

Whoa, a gorgeous morning of sun and warmth in late November! If we were ever fortunate to return to Tuscany, we would settle in Arezzo, our favorite city with a population of 99,500. However, the historic center is somewhat difficult to walk as it has some steep inclines and narrow side lanes but has plenty of cafés, small trattorias and bars along the way. They tell us that this is the best time to visit Arezzo because it is not during the tourist season. Our aims are a couple of museums: the Giorgio Vasari Museo, the Museum of Medieval and Modern Art, and the Roman amphitheater. G. Vasari was a true Renaissance man—painter, sculptor, architect, and art history writer. Although his paintings and frescoes were extraordinary in quality and beauty, he is probably more famous for his architecture and biographical books on the famous artists during the Renaissance. We have both volumes of his "The Lives of the Artists," and they are very informative and a delight to read. The visit to his Casa del Vasari was a thrill to view his frescoes, paintings, architectural plans, and drawing of the Church of Santa Maria della Pieve with the façade made up of 40 double bays. Moving slowly and with focus, we are at the Palazzo Bruno-Ciocchi (15th century) and the Museum of Medieval and Modern Art to spend as much time as we wish to examine the huge collection of Renaissance magnolia ware, paintings, silverware, ceramics and glassware ranging from the Middle Ages to the 19th century.

On the way to the amphitheater, we stopped to admire the large collection of rare paintings and frescoes in the 11th-century Church of Badia Sante Lucilla—impressive beyond belief. A brief look around the Roman amphitheater (117–138, the Hadrian era) at the southern end of the walled city, considered the most important Roman monument of Arezzo. The ruins are enough to give a clear idea about the importance Arezzo had for the "Eternal City," evidenced by the elliptical area harmoniously sharing space for the food and storage stalls, covered corridors, and the human-scale movement access people had within and throughout the structure. One of the very best preserved Roman amphitheaters we have ever experienced, right here in Arezzo.

With only a few days left on our slow travel road trip, it was time to drive north to the large city of Prato—fourth largest city in central Italy. I'm not always comfortable driving into big cities, but there were exceptional sights to visit. There certainly was the appearance of a peaceful and provincial old town. The shops, cafés, bars and the best-selling gelato, Rivas, were in full swing. The 12th-century Duomo was the main attraction. The exterior corner was a rather unique circular pulpit with a fan-shaped canopy and the frieze decorated by none other than Donatello. We walked around to view the exterior of two Romanesque and one Gothic church also within the historical center of Prato.

Time was right for the couple of days for us to discover the many hidden treasures of legends and popular beliefs in Florence—today we are expected to find the following:

- The small church of Santa Margherita where Durante di Alighiero degli Alighieri, Dante fell in love with Beatrice. The small church, called Dante's Church, has the remains of his dear Beatrice.
- The Tower of the Castagna (chestnuts) in Piazzetta San Martino was famous not only because of its extremely ancient contraction and elegant beauty but also because all the Prior of the Guilds (guilds made major policy decisions during the Middle Ages) used to meet here to confer about difficult cases concerning their respective trade unions. Interestingly, the name of the tower is derived from the habit the Priors had of voting. They compared the number of chestnuts in the bag with the number of voters present. In Florentine dialect chestnuts are known as "ballotte," or ballots, hence the origin of our present name for the voting between two candidates.
- Not far from the Piazza della Signoria we found a small church, the Oratorio dei Buonomini di San Martino; there during the Middle Ages, there was a sandstone box underneath a tabernacle where the alms were collected for the poor. The poor, reticent about having their miserable conditions made public, were not willing to go to the church to collect charity. When the brothers of the

Confraternity found the sandstone box empty, they had a habit of lighting a large candle in front of the large painting of San Martino in order to advise the "ashamed poor" that assistance was waiting, and they could come anytime to pick up their alms. A phrase today, "to be down to the candle," originated with this practice. Note: We enjoyed this treasure hunt very much!

Our third last day in Florence, and we are off to find the remaining hidden legends and stories. First, to find a marker at the Piazza Santa Croce, which was the setting for a historical football match in MDLXVI (1566). The marker was the halfway point on the piazza where the ball was placed to start the match. Twice a year, there is a match in the piazza, and the marker indicates the midpoint of the start of play. Em found this one rather quickly! The second find was a profile carved by Leonardo da Vinci engraved into the corner of the Palazzo della Signoria. The legend has it that it's the profile of a man who owed Leonardo money, so he carved the man's profile into stone so everyone would remember what this man looked like. Evidently, this pleased old Leonardo very much. One more, for good luck, was to find the marzocco, the Florentine lion with a red lily symbolizing the Republic of Florence. This particular lion was "lionized" and purportedly spared a young child's life; Via dei Leoni is the street name. Found it!

Today, Tuscany weather met us with a beautiful sunny day—off for our second to last day and headed for a tour of the Chianti Hills. With the autumn still showing its golden yellows, reds, browns, burnt oranges, and emerald greens, we did a slow drive through the western and central part of the Chianti's wine route. Two stops: Gaiole in Chianti—a small wine town, no tourists—and Radda in Chianti, no tourists, surprising? Today was simply the slow travel drive among the chestnut trees, an abbey or two, gently sloping hills, elegant estates, mansions and vineyards. These marvelous landscape scenes were to be a wonderful, lasting memory of autumn in Tuscany. Em loves to capture these landscapes in sketches and watercolors.

Our final day, and we are ready to really swing, metaphorically. We head for the Piazza Santa Trinita and pop into the 11th-century Holy Trinita Church, a Baroque façade (14th century), and what we found were exceptional fine Gothic altarpieces and devotional paintings by Domenico Ghirlandaio (1483). A pleasant respite, we enjoyed the Gregorian chants as well. Em noted that the Ferragamo Museum near the Piazza should be a stop. A wise move, as the museum narrated the entire history of Ferragamo's rise to fame and fortune and how the shoes made him his fame and fortune. The final, really final, visit was to the Bargello National Museum, which provided us with a valuable insight into Italian Renaissance sculptures and decorative arts. The gallery has devoted specific rooms to master artists and sculptures: Michelangelo, Antonia da Sangallo, Benvenuto Cellini, Donatello and Luca della Robbia.

Just another, of so many, Florence syndrome or Stendhal moments. In our case, the psychosomatic conditions involved were rapid heartbeat, confusion (the starting point of thought), and hallucinations, all induced by being overwhelmed upon being exposed to such objects of such great beauty.

This slow travel road trip was an academic complement to our four months living in Rome. We wanted to rediscover the joys of travel and learning after our retirement, and those joys have re-emerged as a result from those experiences and learnings in Rome and now in Florence. The road trip was necessary in order to experience, learn and appreciate Tuscany, especially Florence, and we were delighted and motivated to get out almost every day. The renting of a small car was a wise choice for parking in the small spaces, excellent on petrol (more than we budgeted), and performed well for those hilly and sharp corner turns that seemed to follow us wherever we drove. After Em worked out with Cid the electric to gas arrangements, our two-month total for utilities was much lower than we had budgeted for and more than made up for the extra cost for petrol. We bid fond farewells to Cid and Francisco. Our purpose was to establish a more comprehensive base of knowledge about and appreciation for art and architecture of the Renaissance, particularly in Florence.

The progressive evolution of Florentine art and architecture was depicted as recapitulating the processes that led to the glories of ancient Greeks and Roman art and architecture.

Upon reflection, only a brief survey of our eight-week road trip can be expressed at this time; I, we, need time to let these experiences settle in and find the connections so we can further our efforts to extract meaning from it all.

In addition, Em has informed me that we need to begin to learn French: some polite phrases, vocabulary and sentences. Our final term abroad will be four months living in Paris.

One off-the-cuff comment I will offer once again after making this enlightening and inspiring road trip. I still maintain that those devotional paintings and relics that were really meant to be for sacred and religious purposes, and in their own original setting, might be better appreciated in the churches from where they came and belong.

I leave you once again with my favorite "philosopher" T.S. Eliot, in *Little Gidding*, "We shall not cease from exploration, and the end of all exploring will be to arrive where we started and know the place for the first time."

Total of different villages-towns-cities visited = 36
Total slow travel days = 61
33% of our time spent in Florence
57% spent road-tripping
10% spent in short drives from our apartment

Odometer 5,800 kilometers = 3,500 miles or 58 miles per day.

We managed to visit 36 different villages-towns-cities. A slow travel visit required at least three of the following: a full stop, park, a stroll, visit a sight(s), and/or coffee/lunch. Included in these 36 visits were 11 of the 18 towns designated and referenced in James Bentley's *The Most Beautiful Country Towns in Tuscany*: Bibbiena, Fiesole, Impruneta, Pescia, Sansepolco, Castiglion Fiorentino, Colle di Val d' Elsa, Monteriggioni, Montepulciano, Volterra and Chiusi.

The few wine-tasting experiences we had the privilege to partake of in Tuscany included: Rosso di Montepulciano, Vino Nobile di Montepulciano, Chianti Classico DOGG, Brunelleschi di Montalcino, and Chianti.

Certainly, we agree with Benjamin Franklin when he said, "Travel (slow) is one way of lengthening life." It has been a journey of a lifetime.

Thank you to my loving partner, Emily, without whom there would not be such a slow travel road trip.

List of 36+ villages-towns-cities:

- 3x to Greve in Chianti
- 2x to Radda in Chianti
- Castellina in Chianti

- 20x to Florence
- 4x to Arezzo
- 2x to Loro Ciuffenni
- Bibbiena
- Cortina
- Chiusi
- Castiglion Fiorentino
- 2x to Impruneta
- Castelnuovo dell Abate
- Abbazia di Monte Oliveto Maggiore
- Montalcino
- Fiesole
- 3x to Antella
- 2x to San Gimignano
- 2x to Montepulciano
- Pienza
- Monteriggioni
- Monte San Savino
- Volterra
- Siena
- Castelfranco di Sopra
- 5x to Incisia
- 2x to Sansepolcro
- Anghiari
- Lucca
- Pescia
- Colle di Val d' Elsa
- Poppi
- 5x to Rignana
- 8x to Figlini
- Prato
- 9x to Bagno a Ripoli
- San Donato in Poggio
- 2x to Gaiole in Chianti

PART FIVE

Third Term: Living in Paris

We had two months between our two months in Florence and our final preparations for our time in Paris. We remain steadfastly curious, thirsty for knowledge, attempting to comprehend and expand our joys of retirement.

Although we had been seriously preparing for France, Tuscany and Florence were still very fresh in our minds and hearts. Florence opened a new horizon to see the interplay and interconnections of art, architecture, culture and society. The fortunate opportunities we had to observe and study better informed me about who those artists and architects were and their periods of genius. However, emotions allowed me to re-engage with many of the situations on new terms: of endearment, behavioral reactions, but mostly new eyes—becoming more aware of the context of the visual arts and the culture. Most importantly, my admiration for and inspiration to learn from my partner and lover grow exponentially. We have never been so closely allied to our collective purposes of joy in retirement, joy in travel, and joy for each other. I'm truly blessed.

This fifth part of the book is in the style of a travelogue. According to various travel experts, a travelogue should be interesting, enjoyable, and should include the following:

- Extensive research about the place
- Highlight various attractions
- Ways and means to reach destinations
- Name a few excellent cafés and eateries
- Mention some non-tourist attractions
- Provide some cultural–historical background
- Address some do's and don'ts of travel

Our final semester is presented as a chronological narrative: a memoir of learning to live, studying, enjoying, and sharing our life as we redefine retirement on our own terms.

Paris would complete our nine months abroad as seniors. Having spent the first three months in Rome and returned to the states, after our second semester in Florence, we returned and then saved from our fixed budget in order to spend four months in Paris. Although Paris would be the location to complete our living and studying abroad, we expected it to be more challenging as we did not speak French. In Italy, we managed as Emily had some background in the language, and we accumulated vocabulary and added to the necessary polite phrases but not enough to converse intelligently. Although, to some relief, we had visited France many times during our previous travels and always found the French people to be respectful, polite and ever so patient. Our overly ambitious purposes for this time in Paris would be to discover, explore and learn firsthand the evolution from the Renaissance, Baroque,

Romanticism, Realism, Impressionism, Art Nouveau periods to the Post-Impressionist and Abstract-Expressionist painters, sculptors, and the architecture of French Gothic, Baroque to Baron Haussmann's 19th-century style.

We reckoned that focusing on two or three areas would be a practical and manageable beginning in providing exposure to other humanities such as music and literature, therefore, bonding connections about critical periods in history and knowing how those timeline experiences influenced the future times. We also knew that the focus would be ambitious and time consuming, which is why we decided on taking four months. Concomitantly, because of slow traveling, we had the time to observe, orient and reflect on our redefined retirement enjoyment.

We began planning for Paris in 2009, just before we set off to live in Rome and found out that there would be a small issue that we did not have to contend with in Rome or Florence, that being the requirements for a long-term visa to stay in France for more than 90 days.

Once again, we would pay the distant relationship price of leaving our three grandchildren for four months, not three months as before. Skype to the rescue once again. All three grandchildren would be in elementary school, so I rationalized that they would be in school for most of the time we were away, minimizing that feeling of betrayal. As promised, we would continuously talk and remain connected to them via Skype; it seemed to me a kind of virtual substitute, but acceptable. Nonetheless, we set off to complete our full year of study and discovery.

Subsequent research informed us that to live in France for more than 90 days, the Schengen bilateral agreement allows a United States citizen to apply for a long-term visa. To acquire this long-term visa requires that we complete the extensive paperwork and apply in advance. We started to gather the required documents several months before making an appointment with the French Consulate in Boston. The entire procedure takes months depending on when you can secure an appointment at the consulate. You must apply in person. The carte de sejour, or residency card, is the ultimate goal for us.

Here were the requirements to obtain our French residency card:

- Passport must be valid for a minimum period of six months from the date of arrival in France. Must have two copies of the pages containing birth date, photo and expiration date.
- Long-stay application forms to be printed and signed and completely filled out in black. Long-stay application forms are in French; we used Google Translate to complete the forms.
- Photographs—six photos and must be passport size.
- A proof of U.S. resident status in the U.S.—three copies.
- Financial guarantee—two copies. We used a letter from our bank stating that we have sufficient means of support to live in France, plus submitted our last bank statement—three copies.
- Authorization statement of our retirement pension—three copies.
- A notarized declaration from our sponsor stating that he/she will be responsible for all our expenses and proof of his/her assets.
- A document notarized, dated and signed by the applicant, stating that he/she does not intend to have any paid professional activity which requires a work permit, two copies.

- Proof of medical travel insurance with full coverage valid in France. A letter from our physicians and insurance company, four copies.
- A noncriminal record check that must be certified by the police station in our city of residence, two copies.
- Notarized deed of our apartment's ownership in France, three copies.
- Processing fee: payment by credit card (Visa, Mastercard) or cash per person.
- The Consular services have full authority to request more documents than those submitted by the applicant. The latter is hereby informed that submitting the aforementioned documents does not ensure automatic issuance of the visa.

At the same time we were preparing for the long-term visa, we searched the Sabbatical Homes website to find an affordable apartment in the Marais district located in the 3rd and 4th arrondissement. As in selecting locations in Rome and Florence, the hopeful criteria were: affordable, parks nearby, walkable to shops, lively neighbors, access to public transportation.

From our extensive research and speaking with colleagues who had personal knowledge of the Marais district, these were the reasons we wanted to reside in the Marais:

Le Marais is a unique and lively district in Paris. The district is hip with quirky boutiques, galleries, cafés, restaurants, design shops, tea shops, colorful stalls, cobblestone streets, museums, Gothic churches, historic and architectural buildings, and a hub of LGBT life in Paris. The Marais spreads across parts of the 3rd and 4th arrondissements in Paris (on the Rive Droite, or Right Bank, of the Seine).

I found several attractive apartments in my search. Em selected a flat in the Marais area, affordable and exactly where she wanted to live. I wrote to and began lengthy phone conversations with the owner of the flat, C. Swenson. Upon further referencing who Madame Swenson was, we learned that she was a renowned poet, university professor, and noted translator of French manuscripts and poetry and was living in the USA.

We agreed on the rent fee of 1,800 euros per month for four months, including utilities and free Wi-Fi. Madame Swenson was kind, considerate and very accommodating regarding our leasing the apartment. Looking at Google Maps, we located the street and parks nearby and were excited that the lovely Place des Vosges was a five-minute walk.

Our flat was located on rue des Rosiers, in the very heart of the Jewish community. The Jewish community had lived on rue des Rosiers since the Middle Ages and is still a major center of the Paris Jewish community. The walls around the center feature announcements of Jewish events. There are bookshops specializing in Jewish books, also numerous kosher restaurants and other outlets selling kosher food. The synagogue on 10 rue Pavée, two steps from rue des Rosiers, is an established religious center and serves as a strong base for the Jewish followers of both the Chabad and Ashkenazi communities. It was originally designed in 1913 by Art Nouveau architect Hector Guimard, famous for having designed several Paris Métro stations.

As per our instructions, we were to pick up the keys to the apartment from Ms. Lexie Giles at #14 rue Pavée. Lexie is a friend of Ms. Swenson and a Harvard student in her junior year.

The directions to arrive at rue des Rosiers were rather explicit: take the taxi to #14 rue Pavée and have the driver drop you off at that address. Alternatively, she mentioned we could take the RER line and the Métro to St. Paul metro station. We took the taxi. Em

A storefront advertising Jewish food. During the past 100 years, an influx of Jewish immigrants came to the Marais from all over the world.

stayed with our two bags at #14 rue Pavée. All Parisian apartment buildings have codes to get into them. The code for #14 rue Pavée was 2351. When I put the code into the little box, the door will click; I push it open, hit the light on the left, and walk to the end of the corridor where there is a set of names next to the buzzers. The names Riggs and Berrada I was to find. I pushed the buzzer, and Lexie came to answer. Earlier in the day we had notified Ms. Giles that we would be there around 11 a.m. Long story short, it all worked to perfection. A total of two and a half hours from the airport we reached Lexie. She handed over the code for our door, two keys and a black fob for our fourth-floor apartment at #4. The keys, she explained, included a large main key to the apartment door, a black fob, and a small mailbox key. The black fob opens both the street door to the building and the inner door of the building. After many questions from me, Lexie kindly and patiently explained the directions to the apartment: Walk up to the next corner, which is rue des Rosiers, turn left and walk to the middle of that block. The door you want, #3 ter, is between the two Adidas stores and directly across the street from the Ecole de Travail; we brought our bags to #3 ter. Now, you can either use the black fob to open this door by putting it against the black disk at the bottom of the keypad or use the code number 36A78, which I did. As we entered the small hall, at the end on the right was a glass door with a plaque of names and buzzers on it. At the top of that plaque was another black disk. If you place the black fob against it, it will click open. At that point of entrance we saw the stairway and the elevator. The two-person elevator wasn't big enough to hold two people and two carry-on bags and required two very slow trips.

This chap is enjoying the Jewish neighborhood in the Marais known as the Pletzl. In the background is the famous L'As du Fallafel, which serves simple and delicious Middle Eastern foods and tasty falafel.

It was easy to find #4 as there was only one other apartment (4a) on the fourth floor. The key was relatively easy to use by facing the name "Fichet" up, pushing the key in slightly and giving it a triple turn to the right. I entered the flat with some suspicion but was very pleasantly surprised by what we found. Em had a careful look around the flat and was exhilarated to show me where we are to live for the next four months. Tall floor-to-ceiling windows, parquet herringbone-patterned floors, two small sitting rooms, a desk, rather large kitchen area, a separate room with a toilet and small marble sink, and another bathroom with a small shower, toilet, small washer and bidet, and a small bedroom with two wardrobes for our clothes. Ms. Swenson left us detailed operating instructions for the tiny washer machine, fuse box, etc. She also provided helpful operating hints on post-its regarding kitchen appliances and shower use. Ms. Swenson's major concerns, it seemed, were the keys, cost of replacement, and the locking of the doors every time. The door locks automatically when it closes, meaning to always make sure you have the keys in your hand before you walk out the door and triple-lock the apartment whenever you leave. Ms. Swenson also provided us with another set of keys left in the gray marble mantelpiece in the right sitting room. To make sure that we never left the apartment without the keys, I always attached one set in my neck pouch under my shirt. This concealed flat pouch was where I also carried my debit and one credit card and a copy of our passports.

Since I am paranoid about being accosted or pick-pocketed, as I had been once before, I always carry a "fake wallet" containing a few expired credit cards, Visa or Mastercard gift cards, five euro bills and some euro coins. I know this sounds rather ominous, but I feel more comfortable with such a "fake" sense of security. If the opportunity ever arises, I'm prepared to give my "wallet" to whoever insists on having it and hope they do not stand around to verify the dates on the invalid credit cards.

After we unpacked and had a longer look around the apartment, we had these reactions: The apartment was airy, bright and clean, larger than we expected; how cool, in a typical French 19th-century building, toilet in closet (WC); tiny shower in a rather new bathroom; and we're completely surprised to find a rather new large, open kitchen with a long table. The small bedroom off the kitchen was equipped with a couple of wardrobes with adequate drawer space to accommodate our two carry-on bags of clothes and toiletries. We learned in Rome and Florence to always travel light.

Emily connected her computer up to the security password, but my computer would not take to another hookup. We will decide later if we need two online computers as we would have to hire someone to hook my computer up to a secure line. I placed our belongings in the two wardrobes in the bedroom closets. The apartment will make a fine base for our four months of slow travel in Paris. But first we must find a supermarket to purchase some start-up groceries for the kitchen. We made sure that we triple locked the door before we set off in excited spirits. I placed the key in my neck pouch, and we went out to find a supermarket. Several blocks from the flat we found three markets: Monoprix on rue Saint-Antoine, G20 Supermarché on rue Saint-Gilles and Carrefour City on 53 rue de Turigo.

We selected the G20 on rue Saint-Gilles. Smaller, compared to our states' supermarkets, but just fine for our requirements. Purchased some fruit, some cookies, tea, eggs, cereal, milk, Gruyere and Manchego cheeses, Wasa crackers, butter, Dijon mustard, salad stuff, a half kilo of boiled ham (found out that a half kilo of ham is too much—will adjust next time) and a jar of Bonne Maman apricot-raspberry preserves. Took out my credit card from my neck pouch before reaching la caissiere. I watched the people in front of me to see how the cash-out operations worked. While waiting in line, I selected two G20 bags to place my purchase in because I observed that you bag our own groceries, so we could use the canvas bags whenever we shopped. Once the total was shown on the screen, I placed my Visa credit card in the machine provided, and voila, our first of many super-marché purchases. The 33-euro purchase was equal to $47.

We thought we might get a better handle on the food costs by comparing them with the other two markets over time. We desired a fresh baguette for our dinner, and just a block from our flat at 29 rue des Rosiers was Korcarz's Jewish bakery. I needed some small change for the bread; however, I did not yet have any coins. I felt embarrassed to use a 20-euro bill to pay for a two-euro purchase, so I wound up purchasing two apple strudels and two crème brûlées. That made the transaction a bit more comfortable for me and the person serving me. I had hoped that the strudels and brûlées would last a couple of days.

A note about obtaining euros. Euro coins are absolutely required for small purchases such as coffee, bakeries, street food shacks, etc. Also, merchants love customers to have the correct change when making small cash purchases. We now have a change purse of coins for any occasion. For paper euros, we used a bank debit card at the French abbreviation DAB, or ATM machine. Every time make sure the ATM machine will accept Visa or Mastercard (the symbols are on the machine), and always withdraw money with a partner to make sure nobody is around to see you punch in your code. Merely select English for the directions and the amount to be withdrawn and presto, the euros will appear at the slot opening either at the top or bottom of the machine. Carefully place the cash in a very secure place on your body (e.g., money belt or neck pouch). Make sure the "transaction terminee," before you leave.

Later in the day Ms. Swenson called us to make sure everything was satisfactory and to ask if we had any questions. We certainly appreciated her concern, but so far, we were fine. In the evening we received a gentle knock on our apartment door. There were no peek-holes to see who might be wanting to greet us. After deepening my voice, I stated, "Yes, who is it?" and a friendly sweet sounding professional voice echoed back, "It's your next-door neighbor, and my name is Claudette." As I fumbled to turn the key in the lock, three times this way or was it three times that way, anyhow it opened. Evidently, Ms. Swenson notified Claudette that we would become her new neighbors from the United States and to let us know she would be there to be a good neighbor; I think that is what happened. We exchanged kindly introductions, "Do you require anything? If so, I'm next door," and Claudette left. We certainly were glad to know that our next-door neighbor was thoughtful and kind and spoke perfect English.

We had a neighborhood walk after our grilled cheese and salad dinner, and five minutes later we're at the Place de Vosges, so beautiful, so exhausted! Our first day in Paris, but we stayed up until 9 p.m. and went straight to sleep. For some good reason if we stay on the time schedule of the place we are in, walk around as we did upon arriving, don't nap, even though we're exhausted, and rise the next morning at our regular wake-up time, we will not have the annoying "jet lag."

Tomorrow and the next few days will be neighborhood orientation days as this particular neighborhood is larger than the neighborhood we stayed at in Rome. Much more tomorrow, day two of Paris living.

Interesting observation: The skies are dark until almost 9 a.m. It wasn't until after 10 a.m. that the day was light. This is not because it was foggy or particularly cloudy, it is just the shorter daylight time during this period of the winter. We went for our first "real" walk, from rue Rosiers to rue Rivoli. On rue Rivoli we found a giant department store called BHV Rivoli with the official government-sponsored sale: "Solders," in French. The schedule for these solders is controlled by the government and strictly enforced. We purchased a sheet for our bed since we prefer to sleep with a sheet inside the divan. We were looking at the art supplies, books on art, towels and pens. We headed further down rue Rivoli until we found Brioche Doree, a franchise cafeteria establishment. A large selection of sandwiches, quiches, salads, drinks, desserts and café/tea for a fixed price at 7.80 euros per person. That total of 15.60 euros was equal to $22 or $11 for such a tasty lunch and a real value for the money. However, given the size of the portions, next time we will just order one fixed meal for two. We shall return as the food was very fresh, and many tables were available as long as we arrived before 12:30. After this enjoyable lunch, we headed across the River Seine at the Pont d'Arcole, down rue Arcole to Notre Dame Cathedral. Cathédrale Notre-Dame de Paris: This medieval church is a symbol of Paris; building began in 1163 and took 70 years to build on the site of an old Roman temple. We shall visit often, as Notre Dame is only a 15-minute walk, or less than one kilometer, from 3 rue Rosiers.

On the return we stopped off at an ATM machine and withdrew 200 euro to last for some time. Each time we use the debit card we pay a bank fee, so instead of taking out a small withdrawal and paying the bank fee each time, we take out a larger sum with one bank fee. We happened upon a lovely shop, called A L' Olivier Paris, at 23 rue de Rivoli, that sold extra virgin olive oil and Balsamique de Modene. We purchased small bottles of extra virgin olive oil, balsamique and shower gel. We started out at 11:20 and arrived home at 3:10. Upon our return Em and I worked on our budget to calculate how much cash and credit card expenses we are allotted each day. She indicated, "It will take a week or so to work out costs." We did a slow nighttime walk around the neighborhood: Paris is something else, hard to explain perfection—day or night.

Note: We located tons of specialty shops of every variety imaginable. We found more expensive shops selling wine, chocolate, tea, coffee, pastries, olive oil, boots, kitchen supplies, cheese, clothes, paper, art supplies, books and more. These shops are only a number of blocks from our flat. Accordingly, once we get out further we might have a more flexible budget to deal with as opposed to Rome and Tuscany. Of course, we don't have the expense of the car, but still, this is Paris!

It was certainly strange to wake up at 8 a.m. and find it completely dark and raining outside. Not until almost 10 a.m. was there any appreciable light source. We stayed inside most of the day reading, researching and map reading. Em's knees were bothering her; rest was the best treatment. She twisted her knee in Rome, and the issue presents itself when she walks too much without resting. I went to the Supermarché (Monoprix) to procure food for today and the next day. Sundays most shops will be closed. The food items and produce were of a better variety than G20 but a tad more expensive.

Later I ventured out for the next couple of hours scouting out our neighborhood. The first stop:

Place des Vosges, a five-minute walk from our flat. The Place des Vosges is Paris' oldest square (1407). The name was derived from the Vosges department, the first to pay its taxes in 1800. A neat park with 36 identical townhouses (1604) surrounding the park. Only the two at opposite ends are slightly different. One has to look very carefully to see the little difference.

Place des Vosges, the oldest planned square in Paris. It was built by Henry IV in 1605, and is a true square: 140 meters by 140.

Next up was the Église Saint–Paul–Saint–Louis, built in 1627 and modeled after the Gesù Church in Rome. In 1802 the church was renamed Saint Paul–Saint Louis. The façade is Italian but with French Gothic verticality and Dutch ornamentation. Moreover, there was an exquisite painting by Eugene Delacroix, "Christ in agony on the Mount of Olives," around 1825. The interior has a single aisle and barrel vaulted chapels and tall Corinthian pilasters lining the walls. The church was spacious and had ornate decorations and marble sculptures. Previous experiences visiting and studying many churches and cathedrals in Rome and Florence had given me a cosmetic familiarity with church architecture; I am better able to "read" churches (i.e., to interpret the images, symbols and architectural styles).

My final stop was a visit to the Place de la Bastille, which remains a symbolic rallying point for demonstrations, marches and public celebrations. This was the scene of historic revolutions and revolts of 1789, 1830, 1832 and 1848. The Colonne de Juillet, a bronze column over 200 feet high, rests proudly on top of Le Génie la Bastille. This crowned figure of Liberty was a memorial for the Parisians killed during the uprisings of July 1830 and 1848. There was quite a history within this area, and a great many symbolic references were attached as well.

My walk this early foggy and snowy morning was to the heart of Paris and the Cathedral Notre Dame. This magnificent religious edifice is one of the supreme masterpieces of French art and has been a source of visual and literary inspiration over the centuries. The construction began in 1163 during the reign of Louis VII and was completed in 1300. Notre Dame was to be the first church to be supported by flying buttresses. The soaring height and sheer size marked the important turning point in the development of Gothic architecture and building techniques on a grand scale. The remarkably massive stained-glass windows are a testimony to the technical skill of the medieval masons. Inside, this majestic church was very busy with tourists from many parts of the world.

Our first Skype call to the families, all is well, and brief chats with the grandchildren. All three mentioned how much they liked school and their teachers. Wonderful news—what else could former teachers ask for?

Later, we strolled around Le Marais 4th arrondissement, which accommodates both the well-established Jewish community in rue des Rosiers and the younger gay set around rue Ste-Croix-de-la Bretonnerie. Moreover, we observed many trendy bars, coffee shops, sheltered antique shops, art galleries, jewelry shops and off-beat fashion designers ateliers. Of course, there were more traditional shops, mostly clothing, around rue St. Antoine and rue Rivoli. We stopped for café cremes under the loggia surrounding Place des Vosges at Café Nectarine. The coffee was delicious but pricey at nine euros, approximately $13. However, we are paying for the location, which perfectly overlooks the park of Vosges, and watching the children playing in the slight accumulation of snow. One is also paying for the privilege of sitting for over an hour outside with our heater as the temperature was around 30 degrees Fahrenheit. No complaints, enjoyment has no cost; that was the value of the experience.

We took a slow stroll past the Jewish bakery and stopped at the pharmacy for Em's Advil and returned to our flat. It was astonishing how beautiful Paris is in the wintertime. The city's streets were livelier with more families out and about than Rome's. The people, Parisians, tourists and travelers, were well bundled up, many young people, few smokers

For over 850 years, the most famous of the Gothic cathedrals of the Middle Ages: Notre Dame.

or cell phone users. Sadly, we saw a few homeless, some with pathetic-looking dogs, and a few adults with small children sitting on an old blanket or cardboard waiting for a hand-out. We are on the quiet end of rue Rosiers, very few cars, with pedestrians only except for delivery mini-trucks or motorcycles. The neighborhood was super for walking to the Place des Vosges. A terrific choice, and we are very fortunate to be at this location in Paris and to be a guest in Paris.

We decided that we must get up earlier than we have been. Behold, the alarm went off at 7:31, and I jumped with anticipation and excitement for the new day. It is pitch dark outside! Emily got up at 7:40, tea was made, and she asked, "What is on our agenda to explore today?" I yelled from the sitting room, "Everything!" Em's brilliant, always relevant and practical response was to find the tourist information center on 29 rue de Rivoli. Oh, closed until 10:30. Fine, we continued to walk northwest to the Forum Des Halles, which contained various shops and a museum; a little further north we came to the French Gothic St. Eustache church, reminiscent of Notre Dame, completed in 1632 having taken 100 years to build. We walked back to the rue du Louvre and to the Musée du Louvre, walked around the great old fortress, now the art center of Paris. "We will visit this museum dozens of times before our four months are up," I commented. We strolled across the Pont Neuf and were awestruck looking at the Île de la Cité, the first settlement of Paris, which was located at this exact point. After the two-hour walk, we took the foot-path along the Seine to Pont d'Arcole, the bridge near the Hotel de Ville, and back home down rue de Rivoli.

Notes: I discovered that the walk to the Louvre Museum took me about 16–20 minutes straight down the rue de Rivoli. At 9:15 in the morning I suspected that most people on rue de Rivoli's wide sidewalks were walking to work and adroitly allowing people to seemingly slide by each other without missing a step. I was impressed. After our apartment lunch, a rest for Em's knee, we ventured out to look for cafés in our immediate neighborhood. We selected a small, two tables and five stools, café (The Broken Arm), just south of the Picasso Museum and in the hippest and trendiest part of the 4th arrondissement. Of the six customers that came in, three were American, two Canadian and one Australian. A lovely intimate place, coffee was excellent, but the price for two café lattes was dear at nine euros or about $13. We surmised that specialized, fresh roasted coffee would be rather expensive in Paris, and it was. We decided that for the immediate future we should give up coffee at cafés until the warmer weather when we can sit outside for hours for nine or ten euros. The next big adventure: for our first time living in Paris we head to the nearest Metro Station at Saint-Paul-Saint-Louis church and purchase a set of ten tickets for 11 euros, and two stops later we are at the Louvre. Because of her knees, Em avoids the steep narrow steps and people rushing up and down, but she indicated that the Metro to the Louvre was fine and only two stops away. We decided to seek out the best museum pass available from the Louvre and what other museums allow free entry with the Louvre passes. After working out the cost per single visit as opposed to a year pass, we decided to purchase the one-year Louvre pass. The cost for a one-year pass for the two of us was 90 euros or about $130. Since it cost 18 euros for two each time we entered the Louvre, we only needed to visit eight times to make up the initial cost. We knew that we would surely use the passes more than eight times within the four months. We bought three postcards, ten airmail envelopes with stamps (11 euros), to send letters to our grandchildren. On our return, we did not take the subway but walked to Le BHV department store on 52 rue de Rivoli to purchase two hot water bottles for our feet at night when we turned down the heat. One last stop to the Monoprix for some groceries for dinner. A big spending day for us, but the yearly Louvre pass will be a constant motivation to explore the museum as often as we want; plus we will save money in the long run.

The French gray and sunless skies continue to hang over us once again. We have not seen the sun since we arrived six days ago. It was cold, and winter gear was appropriate. We were following the first two tours available in the book called *A Guide to Impressionists: Paris*, by Patty Lurie. It was obvious in reading this book that the Impressionists did not restrict themselves to village scenes, as several chose to investigate the "modern" City of Paris as a prime painting motif. Drawing inspiration from the 17th-century Dutch masters and other artists, these young French artists re-explored an older painting tradition that was made popular again by the depiction of contemporary people in an urban sitting. These painters included Childe Hassan (American), Camille Pissarro, and Claude Monet. It was so cold that my hands were numb, and I could hardly snap the camera button. Nonetheless, we loved finding these places where these painters painted, and a flood of emotions overcame us that we actually stood in the same locations as these artists did generations ago. Another three-hour walk, and we returned home; Em's knee was beginning to bother her once again, and I was worried about the condition of her knee. I am to blame, perhaps, as I love walking and exploring with her, and there is so much to uncover. From the L'As du Fallafel at 34 rue des Rosiers, I brought back two delicious and healthy vegetable pita falafels, and instantly her knee felt better.

After a full day of rest and relaxation, we were greeted the next morning by a hint of sunshine. The first sunlight in eight days! We exited early to the 6th arrondissement and the old Latin Quarter on the Left Bank. A 45-minute, slow meandering to observe the beautiful Romanesque church of Saint Germain-des-Prés, past the famous cafés, through its narrow medieval streets, passing several bookshops, antique shops, and back to the church of Saint Germain-des-Prés, the oldest church in Paris. This 11th-century Romanesque church has seen many altered appearances over the past 1,000 years. I found 17th-century French philosopher Rene Descartes' tomb, which lies in this Benedictine church.

I have always admired Descartes for inventing analytic geometry linking geometry and algebra. He also was the first to have made the connection between geometry and algebra, which allowed for the solving of geometrical problems by way of algebraic equations, which was never my strong point.

This particular quarter was celebrated for its cafés:

- Café de Flore, renowned for some of its literary regulars including Andre Breton, Jean-Paul Sartre, Albert Camus and Simone de Beavoir.
- Les Deux Magots, which was frequented by the same intellectual elite from the end of the 19th century onwards, and Julia Child spent her days at Les Deux Magots. Furthermore, in 1933, a literary prize was named after it and awarded every year in January. We particularly enjoy Magots as it is the first café in the Latin Quarter to see the morning sunshine, and its elegant Art Deco interior makes for a lovely sit-down for a café creme, but pricey.
- The Brasserie Lipp was always a meeting place for men and women of letters/politics such as Valentin Louis Georges, Eugene Marcel Proust, Georges Andre Malraux, and Ernest Hemingway.

- La Closerie des Lilas at Boulevard des Lilas, where Alice B. Toklas, Man Ray and Hemingway hung out.

We left the Latin Quarter on the Left Bank and returned to the Right Bank to locate the St. Merri Quarter, near the Marais. We were looking for the Church of Saint-Merri in the Beaubourg neighborhood where the Centre Pompidou is also located. We were mesmerized by the architecture of the Pompidou. We learned that the futuristic style of the Pompidou Center was completed in 1977 by Richard Rogers and Renzo Piano. This building houses the Musée National d'Art Moderne and has a collection of 50,000 works and objects. The galleries' collection represents Fauvism, Cubism, Dada, and artists ranging from Klee, Dali, Miro, de Chirico, Matisse, to contemporary arts. We will definitely return to take the time to observe, orient and reflect on these art history attractions.

After lunch Em and I took our first walk from our book called *Frommer's 24 Great Walks in Paris* (2008) and visited the beautiful Île-St-Louis, home of the famous ice-cream maker Berthillon. It might be a historic ice-cream legend, but it was the area that really impressed us. Neatly tucked boutiques, galleries, ateliers, and a host of unique specialty shops. A great slow travel day with the help of the sun and warming temperatures.

A nice day for a morning walk, not too cold. I decided to continue with *Guide to Impressionist Paris: Nine Walking Tours to the Impressionist Painting Sites in Paris* by Patty Lurie, to guide my site visits, while Em stayed in and continued with her watercolors and embroidering her Paris street map—Cool! I found the exact location and angle from where Maurice Prendergast painted the Cathedral Notre Dame. At the left back of the church I took a photo of Notre Dame at the same angle as Maurice Prendergast did in 1907. Also, from the Quai of the Tournelle, Prendergast painted Notre Dame from the north side position. Later while researching I learned that Impressionist and Post-Impressionist Albert Lebourg painted the cathedral at this Pont de la Tournelle location in 1910. The guidebook was excellent in reproducing the locations for these Impressionist paintings; my job was to find the locations.

After Em rested her knee all day, we took our usual after-dinner walk to visit the Louvre. With fewer people on rue des Rivoli, it took us exactly 28 minutes from our flat to the inside of the museum. We showed our Louvre pass, checked our bag through the scanner, went down the escalator to the main floor of the museum. Em decided to see a new Turkish exhibit in a large hall in the Richelieu Wing (she is much more inquisitive than I), while I went straight on the Richelieu Wing to focus on the Northern European painters (mainly Albrecht Durer, Peter Brueghel, Peter Paul Rubens, Frans Hals, Rembrandt and Johnnes Vermeer). In reading *The Judgment of Paris*, Ross King talks about how the young French Impressionists were influenced by the painters from the 1400–1900s. I went to the Denon Wing and tried to see how 17th–18th-century painters such as Jean Louis David, Jean Watteau and Eugene Delacroix influenced the French Impressionists. I realized that I would need several more observations, and more reading, before I could see their significant influences. Next visit, I'll be better prepared to explore these valuable interconnections.

A rainy and cold day. I did an hour walk around the neighborhood and found out that the Picasso Museum, which is just around the corner, is under refurbishing and will not be open until March of 2012. So the next best thing is to go home and pick up Em, provided she feels like walking. Em indicated that she was ready to go to the Centre Pompidou, especially to observe some Picassos and other modern artworks. The entrance fee was 24 euro or $35 (not covered by our Louvre pass). The artwork was extremely

Pyramide du Louvre might be a symbol of the humble class gaining access to the wealth of the world in a museum.

varied and organized in historical periods, with plenty of space to observe and reflect. The museum was open-plan, airy, and had only a couple of people in each room, with plenty of space and distance to view each piece. Pablo Picasso, Georges Braque, Henri Matisse, and Paul Klee were our favorites, but Em loved the paintings by 19th-century painters Giacomo Balla and Gino Severini, leading members of the unique and dynamic vision of the future and artists, that being the Futurist movement.

I'll share what I learned about the inspiring history of the Centre Georges Pompidou.

The center opened in 1977 designed by Renzo Piano (he won the Pritzker Architecture Prize in 1998) and Richard Rogers (Italian-British architect) and is devoted to today's creative arts in all forms: plastic architecture, design, live performances and cinema. The Pompidou is set in the heart of Paris and only a ten-minute walk from our flat at #3 rue Rosiers.

The technical systems of the interior are associated with the exterior (large pipes, color coded) of the building in different colors: blue for air, green for water, yellow for electricity, red for the elevators.

A huge building of five floors has a marvelous panoramic view of the heart of Paris from the top porch.

We stopped at Korcarz's Boulangerie, 29 rue des Rosier, for our dinner of lasagnes au Saumon, mixed salad and a glass of Sancerre.

A bright and sunny day today, what joy, the second sunny day in 12 days. Up for a slow travel to the Bastille open market, a mere ten-minute walk from rue Rosiers. This market is three blocks long, and the selections are amazing. I was particularly drawn to the Italian section for its variety of cheeses, olives, and fish. Em did not go with me today, but she will experience this open market next Wednesday, as the market is there both on Sundays and Wednesdays. A Skype call, and, as usual, happy talk, everyone's well, and it appears that more school homework is being required. I didn't say anything, but I wondered what the purpose of the homework really was.

After chatting with the family and grandchildren, Em worked on her drawings and map embroidering of Paris. I walked along the Seine towards Notre Dame and to Shakespeare and Company bookstore. I had just reread Hemingway's *A Moveable Feast* and knew that he spent much time here when Silvia Beach owned the Shakespeare and Company bookstore. For a period of his life in Paris he lived just down the street on #6 rue Ferou, which I found south of the church of St. Surplice, on the Left Bank, in the 6th arrondissement. Incidentally, rue Ferou was mentioned in Dumas's novel, *The Three Musketeers*, as Athos, one of the main characters, lived on rue Ferou. I'm extremely happy for Sundays, as we have Skype time with our family and grandchildren, and we never miss that time with them.

A rather dark French gray day is in store for us today. The weather doesn't seem to be too much of a factor in deciding what to do for the day. I spent most of the morning finishing reading Ross King's *The Judgment of Paris*, a truly interesting book about the early Impressionists Edouard Manet, Pierre Auguste Renoir and Claude Monet, French history and the revolution of the Impressionists' history. I found the book very enlightening in the quest to study more about the Impressionists.

Em indicated that she could use a slow, short walk to the Place des Vosges, a five-minute walk from our flat. As we walked towards the Vosges, we passed the Hotel de Sully, a Louis XIII, 17th-century-style private mansion, and we immediately became aware of the building's distinctive yellow shades of limestone and the two pavilions that frame it, emitting an air of class and pedigree. The suburb courtyard had archways, sculpted figures and allegorical carvings representing spring and winter. The splendid manicured garden facing the courtyard presented a pleasant and harmonizing feel. At the far end, the dedicated orangery consisted of a central building resting on five archways, two pavilions and pointed roofs. It was the door on the far right that led us into the Place des Vosges.

The harmonious and peaceful Place des Vosges, the oldest planned square in Paris, 1612, is planned in the style of the reign of King Louis XIII. Constructed around two pavilions, the Queen at the north end and the King at the south part, and surrounding the square are 36 identical red brick homes. In the square's center is an equestrian statue of Louis XIII, tilia trees (in Britain they are called lime trees) and a fountain. We spent a relaxing hour chatting and gazing at the proportions, symmetry and harmony of the complex. We would return many times to this very special park in the middle of the Marais.

Em said she wanted some "fun time in the apartment." I inquired, "What is your fun time?" "I'm doing to draw a map of the Marais and embroider the streets and places we visited; also, it is very mindful and relaxing practice."

I left early to start my morning walk to the Left Bank, which is becoming my favorite area. I stopped at the Quai St. Michel and lingered at the marvelous view of Notre Dame across the river. From Quai St. Michel I moved rather quickly to the Boulevard Saint Michel toward St. Severin, perhaps the oldest quarters in Paris. Oh, yes! An observant visit to the Eglise Saint-Severin, which was built in the 13th century in the Flamboyant Gothic style. The interior had well-articulated ribbed vaulting, pointed arches and large stained glass, a typical transition from Romanesque to Gothic architectural style. I pondered its beauty. I sat on the nearest bench and asked myself the age-old riddle: Is beauty universal, how do we know it, and does beauty have to bring pleasure? Of course, I couldn't answer my thoughts entirely but came away with an understanding that beauty is solely about individual perception. I decide what is beauty, and Eglise Saint-Severin is beautiful. After that interplay of philosophical thought, I continued my walk along rue des Écoles where the main entrances to the College of France and the Sorbonne are found. The Sorbonne was founded in 1257 and was the center of theological studies. I learned that the building was restored under Richelieu in the 17th century and has been continuously rebuilt and expanded to accommodate 22 lecture halls, two museums, 16 examination halls, 22 seminar rooms, 37 tutorial rooms for teaching staff, 240 laboratories, a library, a physics tower, an astronomy tower, administration offices, and the chancellor's lodge. Only authorized personnel were allowed into the buildings. I decided I will just become a student to gain entrance.

Further on to rue St. Jacques to rue Soufflot, where the weighty and imposing Panthéon dominates the street. The Panthéon was completed in 1789 under Louis XV and was dedicated to the patroness Saint Geneviève. I'll bring Em back so she can observe the interior of this harmonious structure. Next to the left of the Panthéon was the Église St.-Étienne-du-Mont, built in 1494, with its original façade. Interestingly, despite its date the structure was built in French Gothic traditions: tall aisle walls allow for airy large windows, towering pillars and the stunning stained glasses. Saint-Étienne-du-Mont was mentioned in Hemingway's *A Moveable Feast*.

After a couple of hours, I retraced my route and strolled down the Seine and back to rue des Rosiers where I picked up Em for an inexpensive but tasty lunch at Café Dorée. On the way back to the flat we popped into Monoprix to purchase some groceries and were home by 3 p.m. An interesting day in the very lively Left Bank of Paris.

Église Saint-Severin, built in Flamboyant Gothic style in the 13th century and one of the oldest churches standing on the Left Bank.

The Panthéon and the Église Saint Étienne du Mont contains the shrine of St. Geneviève, patroness Saint of Paris.

Our 15th day in Paris was raining and foggy. Em was ready to walk with me in the light rain to get a different look at Paris during the rain and fog. We did prepare for this winter weather in Paris by bringing rain pants, raincoats, L.L. Bean hats, along with water-proof boots by Rockport. Honestly, the light rain and fog were exhilarating as we slowly walked west along rue Rivoli. We passed the Louvre and stopped at W.H. Smith Bookshop. This British bookshop had vast and varied selections along with the current most popular books, also a large section of current American and British magazines. We know where to purchase books if and when we need them. As Em was in a discovery mode, which she is all the time, we visited the Place de la Concorde, one of Paris' most attractive squares. The Place de la Concorde also happened to be where the guillotine once stood; was that her wish? The obelisk in the middle of the square is from Egypt and is 3,300 years old. If you look to the northeast you can see the Eiffel Tower and across the river the Assemblée Nationale, where government policies are debated. We crossed the street to walk back through the Jardin des Tuileries to the Louvre. I had to use the toilet, and the Louvre was the best stop. The toilets are located on the ground floor behind the coat and baggage claim area opposite the information booth—in case anyone cares to know. Once inside we focused on a few sculptures: Specifically, Antonio Canova's "Cupid and Psyche," Michelangelo's "Dying Slave" and "Rebellious Slave," Gian Lorenzo Bernini's bust of Cardinal de Richelieu, and Venus de Milo (100 BCE), that most famous Ancient Greek world statue. We are finding that if we have a special focus or a particular painter or period in mind before we go to the Louvre, it is much easier to navigate to the locations, and it becomes less overwhelming and confusing. Slow travel embellishes—slow time—to observe and reflect. We exited the Louvre, and across the street was the church of Saint-Germain l'Auxerrois; like many churches in Paris, it was rebuilt several times over the centuries, which gives the church the Romanesque, Gothic and Renaissance features. The interior is Gothic, with stained glasses and pointed arches and ribbed vaulting. Among the many treasures preserved inside was a 15th-century wooden statue of Saint Germain. The question for me: Who was buried here? I found out that painters François Boucher and Jean-Baptiste Simeon Chardin were interred here. An art history note: Claude Monet did paint Saint-Germain l'Auxerrois in 1867.

A morning full of anticipation: The open market at the Place de la Bastille! This huge market has everything from cheeses, honey, vegetables/fruits, meats, seafood, clothes, furniture to antiques. It was interested to observe how the market's customers work with the vendors to obtain just the right product. Em's knee was still a bit sour, and I left her to enjoy her coffee creme et Aux Désirs de Manon at 129 rue Saint-Antoine across the street from the market. I purchased some fruit, raisin and nut bread, olives, spinach and cashews. A great market for food selections and an enjoyable atmosphere to watch people in their open-market culture.

This morning was a typical French gray morning, overcast and gray.

After yesterday's long rest, Em was keen on visiting the former railway station–cum–Musée d'Orsay. We catch bus #69 from our Saint Paul stop to the Musée d'Orsay. Twenty minutes later we're there; it actually would have been a shorter time if we had walked, but Em wanted to save the knees for the museum. The cost is 19 euros or $27, or we can purchase a yearly pass that would pay off after ten visits, which we did. Em went straight to the Decorative and Applied Arts that included French Art Nouveau and International Art Nouveau exhibits. I directed myself to the paintings and sculptures (Auguste Rodin) and specifically to the Realism painters, including Ernest Meissonier, Honore Daumier, Jean-François Millet, Gustavo Courbet and Henry Fantin-Latour. Nearby were the Impressionists: Edgar Degas, Edouard Manet, Paul Cezanne, Berthe Morisot, Camille Pissarro, Pierre-Auguste Renoir, and Claude Monet. After reading *The Judgment of Paris* by Ross King, I actually viewed many of the paintings and artists thoroughly portrayed in his book. Em's absolute favorite was Berthe Morisot's *The Cradle*. For me, today was a fulfilling and exciting firsthand experience. "If you are a dreamer, come in," Shel Silverstein's "Invitation," from *Where the Sidewalk Ends*. And we did!

As a novice art history enthusiast, I was able to observe the contrast in size, content, colors and prevailing tradition that were used within the Realism and Impressionism 19th-century periods. I learned that France's most celebrated painter of the 19th century was the Realist Ernest Meissonier. He was a cult figure, with his small, and meticulous detailed canvases of Napoleon I battle scenes. When the artists exhibited their paintings at the 1865 Salon Exhibition, Manet's large painting "Olympia" was seen as not acceptable "art," not in the orthodoxy of the times. Was this a disappointment for Manet and for the future Impressionists such as Mary Cassatt, Edgar Degas, and Camille Pissarro. Just wait!

Em did a great job with her extended walking, and the knees held up well, but tomorrow she will have a day of rest. Em says the best treatment for her knees is rest for a day or two, and she is ready to go; such a huge inspiration to me, strong and determined.

A rainy, cold and French gray day. Em is delighted to rest, paint and work on her Paris street map embroidering. I'm off to catch the St. Paul Metro to the Place de

Concorde and walk to the Musée de L'Orangerie. I could have simply walked from our flat to the Orangerie, a 30-minute walk, but I decided to be lazy and take the Metro. The smart purchase of the d'Orsay Museum yearly pass included free admission to the Musée de L'Orangerie.

The Musée de L'Orangerie reopened in 2006 after extensive renovations; the two oval rooms on the ground floor hung with panels from the water lily series painted by Claude Monet of his garden at Giverny, known as the Nympheas. The lower floor is home to the paintings of the 20th-century European art collection. Included in these famous collections are the works of artists Chaim Soutine, Pablo Picasso, Amedeo Modigliani, Paul Cezanne, Henri Matisse, Andre Derain, Henri Rousseau, and my favorite, Pierre Auguste Renoir. The absolute highlight was a special exhibit, "Les Enfants Modeles," that featured painters Renoir, Manet, Monet, and Picasso using their children as models. A wonderful special exhibit. It definitely put a smile on my face, and I'm excited to bring Em back to experience this exhibit.

A little rain keeps on dripping all day. Em decided not to test her knee today and let it rest. Hopefully, the rest, with ice, will help decrease the soreness. She has had trouble with the right knee since her misstep on the cobblestones while living in Rome. I cannot sit still, so I went off to the Left Bank, my favorite side, to fetch some coffee capsules for our coffee maker. The Nespresso store is on rue du Bac, not far from the Musée du Louvre but on the left side. The line in the little store was out of the door. I waited my turn and purchased three cartons of ten coffee capsules for ten euros or $14. The coffees in Paris cafés are expensive if you sit at a table, much like Rome, but if you sit at the counter or stand at the counter, the price is half. We are paying about eight euro for two café cremes, or $12. This is, of course, a dear price to pay, and we would rather put that money into lunch or museum tickets. On the other hand, sitting in a café for hours for $12 is well worth the expense, I think. Along the way to the flat I ventured to 72 rue Bonaparte to purchase four of what are regarded as the "best macarons" in all of Paris at the Pierre Hermès Bonaparte. Besides, I wouldn't know the difference, as these tasty delights were not my favorite.

Nevertheless, we had coffee at the apartment, and Em was really pleased with her watercolors. I timed my walk from start to stop and returned after two hours and 24 minutes of fresh air and total enjoyment. The temperature was in the 40s, and to my delight people were out, even in the drizzle; this is wintertime in Paris. As often happens on these longer walks, I have to relieve myself at some point. Public bathrooms are not as easily found as they were in Rome. However, I sometimes stop into a café, purchase a coffee and relieve myself. I wouldn't use their toilet unless I purchased something. Today, I simply walked to the Louvre and used their facilities. While I was in the Louvre, I did stop and view the Turkish exhibit that Em raved about a couple of days ago. It is super to have our yearly pass, as we can merely pop in whenever. Later on in the evening I went for another shorter night walk to photo-record the City of Light with its lights on.

A wet, French gray day in our Paris. In the morning Em made chicken soup for dinner. After lunch we took a walk along rue des Rosiers to the Place des Vosges and to Victor Hugo's house, which is part of the Musée de la Ville de Paris. An interesting house, as it is here that Hugo wrote some of his major works during his time of residence (*Les Miserables* and *Les Contemplations*). He was recognized as the leader of the Romantic movement along with his contemporaries such as Auguste Rodin, A. Dumas, Theo Gautier, Maurice Denis, Simon Charles Henri Cros, etc. The house is filled with photos of Hugo and his family taken by the famous photographer Gaspar Navis. Side note: Photography, or the first workable camera, was invented by Louis Daguerre in about 1838; flash powder was not used until decades later. The technology and scientific advances pushed the media of photography to clearer and more detailed heights. An excellent museum, with much history to learn and an up close and personal view of his lifestyle during his residence during 1850–1885, which was interspersed with periods of his exile and after his exile.

Once again the organic pleasure when staring at the absolute brilliance of the Place des Vosges: 36 townhouses, in perfect symmetry from the day they were built in 1605. I'm thinking how fortunate to be living in Paris with my love, Emily.

A possible sunny day, maybe! Rather cool day in Paris at 42 degrees Fahrenheit. That means I am off to the Louvre. I wanted to slowly explore the 18th–19th-century French and Italian paintings again. I especially wanted to see the only Caravaggio painting presently at the Louvre, "The Fortune Teller," and also the true Romanticism-era painter, Eugene Delacroix and his rather large history painting, "Liberty Leading the People," commemorating the July Revolution of 1830, which dethroned King Charles of France, the Bourbon king. Two fantastic slow travel observations and reflections. Our de rigueur Skype chat, and thankfully, all is well. Our oldest daughter, Hattie, welcomed my daily emails, which briefly summarized our previous day's adventures. She even shares the emails and photos by Em with her workmates and traveler friends. I'm not sure our other two children actually read my brief updates, but I know our daughter-in-law, Katrina, reads and comments on every one of my messages. I don't pay any mind to who reads them; I'm just happy to keep them in close contact with us each day.

It seems that every time I'm at the Louvre on Mondays, the only museum open on Mondays, I observe that professional and amateur painters have an opportunity to set up their easels and paint directly in front of the painting they wish to copy. These artists were extremely well trained and talented as their artwork was exceptional. The paintings were almost identical to the real paintings, it seemed from my amateur point of view. Could I be observing the next potential art forger, I thought. More likely, another Artemisia Gentileschi or Berthe Morisot or Monet. While here, I must have viewed six to eight artists during the late morning and afternoon painting and finishing up their paintings. I could have watched for hours. I really wanted to ask if their paintings were for sale but thought better of it. I left to revisit the Oriental Arts section with a special exhibit of Syrian and Iranian sculptures. The most impressive site was a column capital from an Iranian palace dated 510 BCE. This exhibit was not busy, but it should be, in my personal opinion. I have to admit that I enjoyed these artifacts without the crowds as I had time to read the English notations and carefully observe. I know so little about art, but I'm enthusiastic about learning more.

One final stop at the Metro station to secure my monthly Paris Navigo Pass at 70 euros. The monthly pass actually saves us money since we have been using the passes two to three times a day. To obtain the pass all I needed was a mini-photo (photo machine is next to the office) and attach the photo to the plastic pass. The pass begins on February 1 for 28 days, and then the passes need to be renewed for the next month at a slightly reduced rate of 58 euros, providing unlimited bus and metro rides all month. Em steers clear of busy subways, to mind her knee, as some stairways are narrow, very busy, people rushing by, and she walks slowly and very carefully up and down. Besides, we enjoy seeing all of Paris from the bus.

Since the 18th century, easels were free, but one can wait up to two years to be granted the limited permits.

Ninety-Nine Days Left

We have been in Paris for 21 days! We only have 99 days to go! It was very cold and a French gray day was in store for us. As I looked from our fourth-floor ceiling-to-floor window, I smiled as a little snow began to fall ever so gently. One of the fond elements of our classic Paris apartment are the four floor-length windows, which are always light and airy. Come to think of it, we have two more grand elements: the herringbone parquet floors, and two marble fireplaces (inoperable). Em is actively involved with her neighborhood sketches and watercolors. Her other project is drawing all the streets that embrace our neighborhood and embroidering the monuments and places we have visited; it is our

"Paris Map." She is so creative, and when she is in the "flow," she is focused and enjoys staying on these hands-on activities for days. After all, we still have another 99 days to explore and discover the treasures of Paris. I'm happy that she is so content with her hobbies and crafts.

I exited early to walk to the Richelieu entrance at the Louvre. This entrance, I have discovered, allows Louvre pass holders to enter where it is less crowded (exception: only large tourist groups) as opposed to the wait line at the Carrousel du Louvre (pyramid) entrance. I've also explored the other "hidden" entrance at the Porte des Lions Louvre entrance found on the south end of the museum, which runs parallel to the Seine. I use this entrance when I am coming from the Left Bank and across the Quai François Mitterrand. Interestingly, this is the closest entrance to view the Mona Lisa and the Spanish paintings. Instead of walking from our flat to the museum I can take the Metro at St. Paul, and after four stops at the Palais-Royal Metro, I simply walk across the street to the Richelieu entrance. That takes a little over 12 minutes, depending upon the time of day. After a lingering time well spent at the museum, I walked to my next site, the imposing Ministry of Culture building, which was formerly the palace of Cardinal Richelieu at 2 rue de Montpensier. Nearby, in the Palais-Royal's courtyard, I admired the controversial candy-striped remains of a Greek temple constructed in 1986 by Daniel Buren. The striped white and black columns, now beginning to look gray, are a popular destination for tourists to take photos and there's a climbing adventure on the smaller stumps for children.

It began to snow, and the wind picked up as I was strolling through the Jardin du Palais-Royal. I headed back through the rue Merri, past the Pompidou Museum, past the St. Eustache church at 2 Impasse Saint-Eustache in the 9th arrondissement of Paris. This church I have passed several times, always closed, but today it is open. It was built similarly to Notre Dame Cathedral but in the years 1532–1632.

Saint Eustache's large Gothic style exterior has large rose windows, flying buttresses, pointed arches, flamboyant ribbed vaulting, and stained glass. The interior is an example of a masterpiece of late Gothic architecture, with classical Renaissance details. Three large mural frescoes by Thomas Couture, Manet's teacher, in the Chapel of the Virgin highlighted the chapel. I learned that the best-known painting is "The Disciples of Emmaus" by Peter Paul Rubens or his school. Everything in this painting bears witness of exquisite mastery, the gripping expressions of the disciples, and the magnificent still life of the table; I didn't want to miss this one. The worldwide reputation of the church is not only the splendor of the architecture but its musical traditions. I was overwhelmed by the nearly 8,000 organ pipes that dominate the west end of the church. This church has been a Mecca for sacred music, with composers Giuseppe Verdi, Franz Liszt and Hector Berlioz choosing to play here. Anna Maria Mozart, mother of Wolfgang Amadeus Mozart, was buried in the church.

A rather large spending day of 32 euros cash + 90 euros on Mastercard. This was definitely our largest expenditure of the first 21 days.

This January morning brings bright sunlight, a happy sunshine to the day's beginning. Em is up for a slow walk to the Palais Garnier Opera in the 9th arrondissement. Palais Garnier Opera, along the Place de L'Opera avenue, stretches down to the Palais-Royal to the splendid Place Vendome. We were amazed at the short distances between the monuments, historical sites, and the Louvre. The walk from our flat to the Louvre is about a 25–30-minute slow walk, another 10–15 minutes to the Opera. The walk from the Opera to the Place Vendome was another 4–5 minutes. Paris is a flaneur's paradise. The Opera's architect Charles Garnier designed France's first home of opera and ballet in 1673, and it comfortably seats over 2,000. The exterior combines both Baroque and Neo-Renaissance styles, indeed an architectural beauty.

A short walk from the opera house down rue de la Paix, and we are at the Place Vendome, which epitomizes the full majesty of 17th-century French design. The bronze column (made of 1,200 enemy cannons) was erected in 1810 as directed by Napoleon and was decorated with numerous military scenes. The column was torn down in 1871—an incident for which the painter Gustave Coubert, the leader of the 19th-century Realism movement, was blamed and exiled.

We left Place Vendome and walked down rue de Castiglione to the Jardin des Tuileries, which stretched between the Place de la Concorde and the Musée du Louvre. I had to use the men's room and stopped at the Louvre. I wanted Em to see the Oriental sculptures, which I appreciate the more I observe. Em was enthralled by the huge alabaster carved praying statue of the Syrian Emperor Ebih-II, dated 2400 BCE. Well preserved and beautiful.

Em traveled a good distance today. The secret seems to be to stop periodically in order to rest, then be off. Perhaps the knee is stronger with the intermittent rests at the flat and slow walking and rest when necessary. She is not going to let a knee ache stop her from exploring and enjoying our chance of a lifetime living in Paris. We also decided to use the bus more often; save the knees until we reach the destination (e.g., museum or gallery). That was a great adjustment for us as I love to ride the bus, even when I have to stand.

Today began as a bleak French gray morning. I ventured out early before the crowds to observe and photograph the star in front of the Cathedral Notre Dame that represents the point from which all distances in Paris are measured. The marker is smack in front of the cathedral. Before I returned home for lunch, I stopped at Monoprix, which is becoming our supermarket of choice, to purchase fresh chicken thighs, a bag of lentils, an onion, milk (by mistake I bought goat's milk, no one's favorite), and yogurt. Em always makes some kind of delicious homemade soup (e.g., chicken, lentil, squash) that lasts for a few days.

I asked Em if she was up for a slow, long walk; she indicated that she was perfectly happy staying inside. Fine with me as I walked straight down rue Rivoli to the Louvre, through the Jardin des Tuileries, past the Place de la Concorde to the Place Charles De Gaulle and the Arc de Triomphe (started by Napoleon in 1810 but finished in 1836). The 12 avenues that run off this square were very busy, as were the many expensive shops along the rows of horse-chestnut trees lining the avenue, I spotted Renault, Mercedes-Benz, Honda, Bentley and BMW automobile dealerships. I continued my walk from the Champs-Élysées through the Tuileries down rue de Rivoli and to rue des Rosiers and our flat. Exhilarating, as I found a wealth of treasures along the way.

A wet and French gray day is in store for this Friday. Em is comfortable doing her crafts, so I am off to the Jussieu district (Left Bank), which is dominated by the University of Paris buildings, rich in cultural diversity and science. However, my interest was to spend time at the Institute of the Arab World at 1 rue des Fossés Saint-Bernard, 5th arrondissement and the Paris Mosque. The museum of 20 Arab countries is to promote Islamic culture, history and cooperation. My Michelin book told me no entry fee to visit. However, upon arrival I was told that the fee to enter the building was 12 euros. I had gone out without any cash euros (not a smart thing to do!) and, at that moment, they didn't take credit cards. We will return another day with cash euros. Not to worry, as I was searching for the Mosque of Paris, I discovered the College des Bernardins on rue De Poissy on the Left Bank. I learned that this building was completely restored in 2008 by Jean-Michel Wilmotte. The original building (1248) led to the church of Bernardins, and what I saw today was the monks building. Absolutely stunning architecture. A gorgeous restoration to its original state, including the nave, which is 770 feet long, 154 feet wide and 80 feet high, including the former monks' dormitories, the sacristy, two auditoriums and a basement. I hung around until one of the guides was able to take me around. I mentioned that I did not speak French, and she kindly said that she did not speak English. We were a match made in heaven, sort of. I really wanted to see the Gothic-style interior, and she patiently led the way. From my Michelin Guide and subsequent translating to English from the French brochure, I compiled the following historical facts: For more than four centuries, the College St. Bernard, which began in 1248, hosted students and contributed to the intellectual influence of both the city and the University of Paris; the building was destroyed in 1810 but rebuilt in 1859; during the French Revolution, the college was seized from the Cistercians and placed in the public domain; since then, it has been used as a prison, a warehouse, a school, a fire station and finally a boarding school for the Policy Academy; finally in 2004–2008 it came back to life as a finished gorgeous building, a place for meetings, training and culture, symposia, exhibitions, concerts and a biblical studies center. The rain had stopped, and I rushed back to tell Em about this discovery. She immediately dropped everything and we walked, slowly, to the College des Bernardins. She adored the perfection of the restoration, and we had a coffee in their little café bar. She is such a great companion; I am so very fortunate indeed.

Whoa! A sunny morning with temperatures in the 50s. Em was feeling terrific and she wanted to purchase some yarn and thread at a fabric shop near the Bastille, but it was closed, thus a stroll back to the flat to enjoy lunch. She will try another time. The afternoon walk down rue Rivoli was extremely crowded, the busiest we have seen it. Rue Rivoli is the main shopping street in all of Paris. We have learned to turn slightly to make your body thinner when approaching anyone coming in the opposite direction; it seems to work just fine. The Louvre was not as busy as we would have thought, probably the result of sunny skies, thus, everyone was on the streets, I cleverly deduced. My focus today was the woman who bridged Rococo and neoclassical genres, Elisabeth Louise Vigee Le Brun, and her *Self-Portrait with her daughter*. I tried to see the bridge of the two genres but could only see the classical triangular composition and the rise of the neoclassical style. Such a special treat and nobody around me.

We merely wandered, lingered and enjoyed the little things at the Louvre. For example, Luca della Robbia's sculpted terracotta, covered over with his special formula glaze, not only brought out the vivid colors but also preserved the sculpture. There are also huge things that exhilarate the mind and body such as the famous Winged Victory of Samothrace, which was erected in the pool of a sanctuary on the Greek island of Samothrace to commemorate the victories won by the Rhodians in 190 BCE. The enjoyments of living in Paris are endless. We are just fortunate to be able to experience living in Paris, especially on a fixed budget.

Sunday in Paris, with the happy bright skies and sunny outlook, made for a great day for a slow walk. Em and I strolled to rue de Fourey to rue des Deux Ponts, over the Pont Tournelle to quai de la Tournelle to Île Saint-Louis to Boulevard Saint-Germain, around the side streets and approached the Left Bank side of Cathedral Notre Dame. At this point we visited the church of Saint-Julien-le-Pauvre (St. Julien of the poor). This small Romanesque-Gothic church was built by the Cluniac monks in the 12th century and was constructed on a sixth-century foundation, purported to be the oldest religious monument in Paris. On the Quai de Montebello we observed the Rollers and Shell Club beginning their travels on a specialized route. I had heard about this idea of allowing folks with Rollerblades to travel on a prescribed route on Sundays. The police were Rollerblading with the group as well.

All of Paris is a walker's, stroller's, meanderer's and flaneur's dream; imagine an outdoor museum. On rue Pavée, adjacent to rue des Rosiers, there was the Pavée synagogue at number 10. We learned that there are two more synagogues in the Marais; this one on rue Pavée was designed in 1913 by the famous architect Hector Guimard. Hector also did those Art Deco Metro lights in Paris.

Back just in time for our weekly Skype call. We are very fortunate, as everyone is healthy, productive and enjoying their winter snowstorms.

I left the apartment to arrive by 10 a.m., the opening time for tourists to climb the 431 steps on the bell tower of the Cathedral Notre Dame. The morning started off rather sunny, so I thought this would be a good time to view Paris from 226 feet. I passed the Great Bell Emmanuel weighing in at a hefty 13 tons and his clapper at over 1,000 pounds. The most exciting sight was the statues adorning the corners of the balustrade. These creatures, designed by Viollet-le-Duc in the 19th century, consisted of fantastic birds, hybrid beasts, and chimera (mythical monsters) perching on the towers. These statues are called "stryga," a Greek term meaning "bird of the night." Some of these ornamented sculptures are gargoyles, which are protruding features designed to drain rainwater, and some are grotesque to ward off evil spirits away from the church.

When I reached the top of the tower, the sun was out, and I began to take in the sights; however, by the time I returned to the north side of the tower, the sun had disappeared, and two minutes later the snow came down. It got extremely cold and windy; I returned to the street level. I was exceedingly pleased to be able to climb and return those 862 steps and to view Paris from a completely different perspective.

After lunch, Em wanted to go out to the American Consulate at the Place de Concorde to inquire about visiting some French nurseries and preschools. I was told that all visits inside the Consulate were by appointment only, and the guard provided us with a telephone number and email address to make an appointment. While we were so close to la Madeleine church, we spent a great deal of time looking at the exterior and interior of this remarkable 19th-century Greek-revival temple. We decided not to return via Metro stop at the Palais-Royal-Musée-du-Louvre because the sun reappeared. We did take the time to admire Hector Guimard's Art Deco Metro entrance.

Once back to the apartment Em mentioned that tomorrow we will go see the Rembrandt and Vermeer exhibit at the Pinacothèque at the Place de la Madeleine.

A super day to spend all day at the Pinacothèque de Paris because it was raining, foggy and cold. The exhibit was a joint venture with the Rijksmuseum in Amsterdam and demonstrated the history of the Dutch Golden Age of painting spanning the 17th century in the Netherlands. The highlights were the paintings by Johannes Vermeer: "Girl with the Pearl Earring," and "Art of Painting," our favorites. The museum included many paintings by Frans Hals, Jan Mijtens, Jan Steen, and other Dutch painters. The mediums used in the exhibit ranged from watercolors, sketches, drawings, and tile work to wooden miniatures. A very small exhibit hall, and the entrance was restricted by numbers in and out. No photos!

The Impressionists were taken by the realism of these Dutch paintings as they portrayed real people working, drinking, playing, and the scenes of nature and domestic life as it was. Another art history learning opportunity that I shall file away in my hippocampus, or is it the amygdala?

An enjoyable day in the City of Light.

This day is definitely for the Louvre Museum as the wet, damp and windy weather continues this morning. The Louvre was extremely busy, as usual, but Em and I visited separate sections of the three wings: Richelieu, Denon and Sully.

Em to the French sculptures and Egyptian Antiquities and I to the pre-Classical Greece and Italian sculptures. We did our first of only two Starbucks visits, as we agreed to meet there at our arranged time. Starbucks are fantastically popular in Paris. We passed some Starbucks that were in 16th-century buildings, others in ultra-modern buildings. We'd rather support the new and up-and-coming Australian coffeehouses that are making roasted coffee to Paris coffee drinkers' selective tastes.

We rode the Louvre Metro, located inside the museum, to our St. Paul Metro station—four stops, or about ten minutes, and a three-minute walk to our flat.

Today is somewhat brighter than the previous five days with a little bit of sunshine peeking through the ever-present French gray clouds. We do not complain about the weather; it was our choice to spend the winter in Paris and for no other reason than because it is less crowded and we really don't care about the weather anyhow.

This month of February is our museum month before the commencement of the full-blown tourist season. We are off to the Arts Decoratifs, located in the Palais du Louvre's western wing at 107 rue de Rivoli. The Musée des Arts Decoratifs houses 150,000 works from medieval furniture to contemporary design, including Art Nouveau and Art Deco styles, large collections of objets d'art, jewelry, toys, wallpaper, ceramics, glass and an Islamic and Oriental collection.

What made this museum so relevant for us was the story it told about the art of living from the Middle Ages to the present day, all major styles and movements from Gothic to Louis XVI. This type of "narrative" museum requires a huge amount of time to study to try to comprehend the time frame and cultural influence on style and their subsequent impact on today's trends and fashion. This was one of our favorite museums that we have been privileged to partake in. We are so very fortunate to be able to slow travel in Paris.

Hold on! It is totally sunny this morning, the first time that we actually woke up with total sunlight. We knew that we were in paradise but with sunshine as well!

We are off to visit for the second time the Panthéon in the Left Bank in the Latin Quarter. Its history is dramatic. In 507 CE there was a basilica on the present site of the Panthéon. A new basilica was built in 1755 by architect Louis Soufflot. In 1791, the monument was turned into the national Panthéon and home of Christian workshops until 1885. Today it is a monument to some of France's greatest citizens: François-Marie Arouet (Voltaire), Jean-Jacques Rousseau, Jean Jaurès, Victor Hugo, Emile Zola, Marie Curie. This huge building is a combination of different styles: Greek architecture, Corinthian and Tuscan orders, the Gothic system of pointed arches, flying buttresses and airy light sources from the 45 large windows and domes. A brilliant and exhilarating architectural experience.

Next day was our stay-at-home day. The cleaning, including vacuuming the accumulation of dust in the grooves of the wooden floors and attacking the hard calcium buildup in the toilet and shower took most of the day. Since I have chronic allergies to dust and mold, the apartment requires sweeping or vacuuming every day. It had been raining on and off, and this gave Em a chance to rest her knee and continue with her arts and crafts. We had a simple dinner of roasted chicken and a salad. We are finding staying inside relaxing and are catching up on all the stuff we have tended to leave behind because we have been out almost every day.

This is Sunday; rain or shine, everyone is outside. The shops are open in the Marais on Sundays, which is very rare, as most shops are closed on Sundays, thus bringing everyone outside mostly for lèche-vitrine (window shopping). We spent the day inside relaxing and reading. We are trying to rest Em's knee for the long periods of walking later on. An afternoon walk around the Jewish quarter topped off our leisurely day in Paris. I did take another short walk in the neighborhood in the evening. This is what is so wonderful about slow travel; we know we have time to do everything we want without having to rush or overplan, with the possible outcome of being disappointed. We Skyped everyone, and, thank goodness, all is well. The Nor'easter that dumped two feet of snow in New England has passed, and school will resume tomorrow.

This time at home also gave me a chance to reflect on our living in Paris. I was thinking about why we love living in Paris. I say I love Paris because it is the only city in the world where you can step out of a Metro station (d'Orsay) and simultaneously see the six or seven major enchantments of Paris: The Seine with its bridges and bouquinistes; the Louvre Museum; the Cathedral of Notre Dame; the Tuileries Gardens; the Place de la Concorde; the Eiffel Tower and the beginning of the Champs-Élysées. That is such a stunning and enriching environment to love; we are so fortunate.

The French gray universe awaits us this dark and gloomy morning. Never mind, we are off to the Louvre, as all other museums are closed on Mondays. We spent a lot of our leisure time at the Louvre; besides, it is almost free! I observe that there must be half of Japan in Paris, and the other half are in the Louvre. Good for them. I cannot think of too many places, perhaps Rome and Florence, where you can spend a few hours completely overwhelmed and inspired by the art, culture and history. I'm finding out that when I want to stay away from the 15,000 average Louvre visitors per day, I go directly to the Denon Wing to view the 17th–19th-century French painters and to the Richelieu Wing for the Dutch and Flemish paintings; both sections usually have very few observers. I'm not sure exactly why; perhaps the more "famous" painters and paintings are what non-slow travelers have the time to see while they are in Paris. Have the experiences but miss the meanings.

A cold and intermittently snowy day. We stayed indoors today to rest Em's knee, which is slowly getting better, and I was not feeling my best either. We spoke to our families, and the grandchildren were enjoying their respective schools, and we shared our love. So we just hung around the apartment, drinking tea, reading and writing. I am trying to make more sense of my daily notes and records from our previous slow travel experiences in Rome and Tuscany. Is there a book somewhere? I would certainly want to share our experiences in some sort of travelogue or guidebook for seniors. We found the best assortments of teas at the Mariage Frères at 30 rue du Bourgeois Tiboug, five minutes from our apartment. We also saved some money by not going out today.

A glorious day—Em's knee is feeling much better, and we are raring to go. Although it is snowing rather heavily, we are to sublimely indulge ourselves in the swanky 16th arrondissement. This is the neighborhood of foreign embassies, famous museums, and

Passy, home to many of the city's wealthiest residents. For us it is two metro trains, 14 stops away from arrondissement #4, to the Musée Marmotte Monet. We decided to try first traveling to the museum via Metro and then later on by bus. The neighborhood is a bit different from arrondissement #4 in that it is much more residential and has two huge, green parks (i.e., Bois De Boulogne and Jardin d'Acclimatation). This Paris—chic and elegant—is the location for the French Open tennis matches. The Musée Marmottan Monet at 2 rue Louis Bolly was once the former hunting lodge turned into a museum to house many of Monet's paintings. There were over 100 Impressionist paintings from Manet, Berthe Morisot, Gauguin to Renoir. A special exhibit this month also included the Fauve (wild), those 20th-century and French artists who used vivid colors and juxtaposing contrasting colors to define areas—think of Henri Matisse and Expressionist painters such as Ernst Ludwig Kirchner, Edvard Munch, Braque and Wassily Kandinsky. This wonderful, large house-lodge was not too crowded, but it was not empty either. This turned out to be one of our very favorite museums. We enjoyed a tasty lunch: grilled chicken, fries and salad + spinach quiche + two café au lait and one lemon tart at Alba Ristorante at 12 Avenue Mozart. A wonderful meal that was well worth the 34 euros. And yes, the service was outstanding.

Our journey took four hours and 45 minutes, and Em's knee is beginning to talk to her; that means rest it.

The coldest day since we have been in Paris. A bone-chilling 28 degrees Fahrenheit but feels like 13 degrees Fahrenheit, with intermittent snow. Weather isn't important in our daily activities, as we always can make alternative plans depending upon the weather conditions. Today, we plan to stay close to home to visit two important sites that are merely seven stops via Metro from St. Paul: The Galeries Nationales du Grand Palais and Petit Palais Musée des Beaux-Arts de la Ville de Paris.

First, the Grand Palais. The building was built for the 1900 Universal Exhibition. This majestic stone Baroque-style building, flora carved decoration, and crowned with a splendid metallic framed glass roof—architecturally daring in its time but softened a bit by the fact that the Eiffel Tower had just been completed in 1899, and that was controversial as well. This huge hall showcases exhibits of all kinds. The exhibit we saw today was a leading international contemporary artist named Christian Boltanski and his "Personnes." He demonstrated a powerful physical and psychological experience by spreading on the ground a grouping of 69 rectangles of coats from which arise 69 heartbeats. Personnes literally means both "people" and "nobodies." A really clever and daring artist. There was a huge mound of clothes in the center of this massive hall where a crane with a claw moves slowly down to pick up a shovel full of coats, and, when it reaches the top, it drops the coats from over 100 feet. I had the experience but did not comprehend the meaning, I'm sorry to report. Since this hall was not heated, it was very, very cold. Interesting!

We moved across the street to Avenue Winston Churchill to the Musée du Petit Palais, which was completely restored and reopened in 2006 and, like the Grand Palais, maintained its eclectic splendor of the Exposition of 1900. This was one of our most satisfying and inspiring visits so far in Paris, and the museum was free. The building alternates white and colored marble, molding and garlands, painted ceilings, mosaic flooring and opal stained-glass windows around a gorgeous interior garden. The gallery begins with the first stage of the most modern collections (1900), containing decorative murals, painters such as Édouard Vuillard, Gustave Moreau, sculptures by Louis Robert Carrier-Belleuse, Charles Christofle and the super great Emile Galle and his amazing pottery, blown-glass work, and the history of the Petit Palais.

Boltanski's "People Project," with 50 ton of clothes and 15,000 heartbeats he archived.

The second stage, my favorite, the 19th century: painters Mary Cassatt, Johan Jongkind, Gustave Courbet, Claude Monet, Paul Cézanne, Eugène Delacroix, Jean Auguste Dominique Ingres, sculptures, and Realist portraits. The third stage exhibited 18th century portraits from the reigns of Louis XIV, XV and XVI. Fourth stage, the 17th century: portraits, landscapes, still life and other historical paintings. The fifth stage, the Renaissance with jewelry, glass and metal works representing Italy, France and Northern Europe. The last stage, the classical world of Rome and Greece, Eastern Christian world and graphic arts. This was an absolutely awesome gallery that we shall return to many times. The art was so compelling, and the museum is free.

Sunny and cold but invitingly bright skies. We are off to explore a museum within our immediate neighborhood: the Musée Carnavalet, one of the historical museums of Paris which is located in two separate mansions: the Hotel Carnavalet and the Hotel le Peletier Saint-Fargeau. The Carnavalet is proclaimed to be one of Paris' most attractive museums; we absolutely agreed. The museum takes Paris from the tribal origins to the end of the Middle Ages with archaeological finds, some dating back to 4400 BCE. The museum brings back the capital's history (e.g., the French Revolutions). Another aspect that made this museum particularly impressive was its rich collection of decorative arts: paintings, carved-wood paneling, and ceilings. The literacy history was illustrated by many portraits, pieces of furniture and souvenirs evoking famous writers, including Marcel Proust's bedroom. An inspiring museum, close to us and with no entrance fee. As slow travelers, we always welcomed a detour or an unplanned find as a surprising opportunity to learn something new and exciting.

I have a curiosity about the concept of time, especially here in Paris. Time, it appears, is the independent variable; that is, it stands alone and isn't changed by other variables. Here are a couple of recent examples of my construct of time:

- Aujourd'hui (today) I had to send a copy of an insurance form to the states and needed to find a copier. In Rome, there were copier stores on almost every block, not so in Paris. OK, so I walked all around for an hour at the university area on the Left Bank to find one. I inquired twice for a location. The two plus hours to find a copier was a great use of my time since I was able to get really oriented and adjusted to this area.
- Also today, there are several fine bakeries and pastry shops in our immediate area. Our favorite is Aux Désirs de Manon–Boulangerie because it sells wonderful multigrain bread. There is always a long single line into this very small shop. Because this is a great bakery with selections of in-shop, made-fresh pastries and breads, it is obviously a favorite of the locals as well. As before, there was one single attendant who carefully wrapped each parcel, even if it was a single éclair, put a ribbon on it and placed it into a sack for the customer, then accepted their euros, hoping for the correct change. This procedure was carried on for each and every customer while everyone else waited patiently in line. The attendant did not rush nor make any extra moves to expedite the transactions; everyone was treated equally. For me, this demonstration was one of the more lasting memories of Paris. Not the time, per se, but the pride and patience demonstrated by the attendant in order to treat everyone equally and with respect and kindness. Kindness is the greatest virtue! Indeed the process today took me 35 minutes, but what I observed and learned about patience and respect I shall remember forever. Perhaps this is more about a set of cultural mores, probably the strongest of the social norms, but I was moved by this experience. Incidentally, the grain bread was worth the wait. Slow travel fosters patience, and I really need to work on being more patient and kind. Em always reminds me that we are never too important not to be kind to everyone. She is always right.

Em went out to visit Broderies at 12 rue Jacob, a fabric store on the Left Bank, while I finished up my notes on the week's events and happenings. Later on in the afternoon I attended a Spanish guitar concert at the Eglise St. Ephren on the Left Bank at 17 rue des Carmes. It is about a 25-minute walk, and Em wanted to stay home and work on her knitting or the embroidered street map of Paris. The concert was at 5:30, but I went at 4:30 to secure a ticket. I paid 20 euro for the ticket, free seating ten minutes before the start of the concert. The interior of Eglise St. Ephrem, next to the Panthéon, was small, approximately 18 × 30, and held compactly 60 seats attached together with 12 empty seats. I counted 32 American students—all with their university logo scarves wrapped neatly around their necks, of whom 19 were Japanese-American students. The remaining folks were senior citizens. The guitarist was Damien Lancelle, a Frenchman, who played Bach, Ponce, Tarrega and variations of Spanish tunes from Cadiz, Córdoba and Toledo. A wonderful late afternoon of classic guitar music, so reminiscent of our time teaching in Morón de la Frontera in Andalusia, Spain, the center of classical Spanish guitar. A very cold 30-minute walk home; it almost permanently froze my continuous smile.

A sunny but non–Valentine's Day in Paris. The French hardly celebrate such a day, as chocolates and flowers are available all the time every day and even on Sundays. I was off this morning to the market to purchase ingredients for chicken soup, our favorite cold weather food of choice. Em made a rather large supply, so we shall have Emily's special treat for a couple of days.

By late morning, the sun welcomed us to take a walk. Although it was still cold, we walked to the iconic Paris department store, the Bazar de L'Hotel de Ville, merely several blocks from our flat, on rue de Rivoli. It's a super deluxe department store with a large floor exclusively for art and craft supplies at a relatively inexpensive price. Em needed to purchase some painting supplies; plus this will be an incentive for her to continue with her watercolor paintings of Paris. When we got near the BHV, it was closed; this attraction is supposed to be open seven days a week. Across the street was the Chinese New Year of the Tiger parade and celebration, as colorful as it was crowded. We walked around the neighborhood on Sundays; everybody walked, many eating while walking, and families having a good time outside. We found a patisserie, "Pralus," at 35 rue Rambuteau and purchased one of their special treat cakes called Le Praluline: a coffee cake-like texture with almonds, almond paste, pralines and very tasty. We enjoyed a couple of slices after our chicken soup dinner. A nice slow travel walking day with plenty to see and do. Home in time for our Skype call to our families and grandchildren. We are ever so happy when we hear that all is fine, and the grandchildren are happy and enjoying their schools.

A bright and sunny day today but still cold enough to wear the winter attire. I exit early to be at the Louvre by 9:15 a.m., expecting fewer people in the museum. Whoa, such a large crowd of visitors I have not seen in my twenty previous visits. I think the Louvre allowed several large Japanese tour groups and school groups to enter before the museum was open at 9 a.m. Since all the other museums are closed on Mondays, this would be the one to visit, which explained the crowds. When the French sculpture rooms on the first floor are congested, you know it is big-time visitors. Nonetheless, I went in and out of my three favorite wings, the Denon, Richelieu and Sully, to study the French and Northern European artists. Although they were a bit more crowded than ever before, I still had the rooms almost to myself. I am so fortunate to be able to visit the Louvre any time!

Em is resting her knee today, as she wants to be out tomorrow. On the way back from the Louvre, I stopped at BHV department store, went to the second floor that is devoted to art supplies and purchased some watercolor paints, paper, sharpener, eraser and drawing pencils for Em. She was thankful and motivated.

A beautiful day: sunny and very bright. With a head full of purpose and good intent, we are off to the Rodin Museum and a special exhibit of Matisse's sculptures as well. The museum is in Arr. #7 on rue de Varenne. A couple of train rides and we were there in 20 minutes; the garden, museum and special Matisse exhibit cost 20 euros, or $28. The museum is actually in Rodin's house. Auguste Rodin took up residence here in 1908, surrounded by a park and trimmed cone-shaped evergreens. Sculptures in marble, bronze and terracotta alternate with drawings by the master, works by Camille Claudel (his student) and paintings by his friends Monet, Vincent Van Gogh, Edgar Degas and others. Of course, Rodin's "The Thinker" is perhaps his best known of all of his sculptures, although his two sculptures of Victor Hugo were impressive. We have seen many of Rodin's sculptures at the Musée d'Orsay such as a monument to "Balzac," "Gates of Hell," and "Ugolino," a magnificent master sculptor who worked in bronze, marble, plaster and clay. We were so happy to see his other works, and in his own home. We learned from the Matisse exhibit that Rodin and Matisse were separated by a generation: Rodin (1840–1917) and Matisse (1869–1952). Rodin dominated the sculpture of his time. Matisse admired the work of Rodin. Like Rodin, Matisse preferred modeling clay directly to hewing wood or stone. The sculptures of both Rodin and Matisse are tributes to the human figure in all its refined aspects.

The two artists shared the same admiration of the female nude in the intimate setting of the studio. Rodin stated, "I can work only with a model. The sight of human forms nourishes me and comforts me." Matisse declared, "I depend absolutely on my models, observing them moving about freely and afterwards I make up my mind and choose the pose that comes most naturally to them."

Just another exceptionally ordinary day in Paris.

A damp, French gray day but it's supposed to warm up later in the day. We are off to arrondissement #16, again, the chic address, to the Musée d'Art Moderne de Paris at 12–14 Avenue de New-York. In 1937, this was the site for the International Art Exhibition. This area is one of the most luxurious quarters of Paris. But it is the museum that is our focus. The museum is dedicated to modern and contemporary art from the 20th and 21st centuries. The century methods and styles illustrated the trends and evolution of artists. Some of the century's major artists' work were exhibited, including: Fernand Léger, Sonia Delaunay, Matisse, Picasso, Braque, André Derain, Juan Gris, Max Ernst, Victor Brauner, Amedeo Modigliani, Pierre Bonnard, Pierre Soulages, and Marc Chagall. It also contains Raoul Dufy's biggest picture, comprising over 250 panels over 600 square meters. This was a magnificent exhibition environment and a sublime view from the courtyard of the Eiffel Tower. A very impressive museum … and free.

Interestingly, a huge painting called "La Danes," by Henri Matisse, painted in 1910, is commonly recognized as a key point in the development of modern painting.

We agreed that there is nothing educative in an activity that does not lead the mind out into new fields of endeavors.

We stopped at a shop that specializes in frozen foods. Not your ordinary frozen foods. All nationalities of food and inexpensive as well. "Picards" is known all over the university area on the Left Bank, and it is popular due to the quality of the food and the price. We had cod in a lemon sauce on fresh grain bread and a salad of carrots-spinach-cucumbers-orange slices. An excellent meal that would have cost us three times what we paid for the package for six euros, and we still have three fish flanks left for another meal. Such a deal, great food and a great find.

A cold and gray day today. That is fine as we are to clean-polish-dust-scrub the apartment's four and a half rooms. This is our tidy-up day, and we'll save a few euros as well. Em's Paris map is coming along very well. She has drawn in all the streets that we have walked around in our neighborhood. She then embroiders all the major sites within these areas. Really creative and skillfully done.

Today, I cannot believe it, but it's another glorious bright and sunny day for everyone to enjoy. Em is staying in again today to continue with her drawings and watercolor paintings. She is getting into the groove and is quite good at representing "our" Paris. Off this morning to purchase groceries for lunch/dinner, some cleaning supplies, water, fruit/veggies and multigrain bread. Returned and out again to procure more art supplies for Em—small to large brushes and black paint. Give me an excuse to walk around Paris, and I am off.

In the afternoon I headed out alone from St. Paul metro station to Concorde metro station, changed from the yellow line to the green line to Abbesses metro station arrondissement #18 and then to Quartier Pigalle-Montmartre. Before I chugged up the steep hill, I stopped for a while at the Musée de la Romantique, a relaxing and very romantic museum. The museum, built in the 1850s as a private house, is replete with portraits, jewelry and furniture belonging to Amantine Lucile Aurore Dupin (George Sand) on the ground floor. During the mid-1800s, wealthy artists, writers and musicians were frequent guests. Some of these guests included Frederic Chopin, Eugene Delacroix, G. Sand and Jean Cocteau. An absolute must-see, and I'll bring Em back very soon to see and feel for herself the romance that is exhibited at the Musée de la Romantique.

I climbed the Butte "Little Hill," which was a rather steep incline, with quaint narrow streets and a village-like feeling. I chugged up the steep hill until I reached the crowds by the La Basilique du Sacré-Coeur. The Romano-Byzantine Basilica was completed in 1914, and it is the second-most visited area in all of Paris. In the interior space above the apse are the star attractions: the gilded architecture of the mosaics. The mosaics are stunning hues of gold and dark blues. The 475-square meter "Mosaic of Christ" is one of the largest mosaics in the world. From the church steps there was a wonderful view over the capital. After a few hours, I boarded the two metros back to the Place de la Concorde and took a slow walk through the Tuilerie Gardens, past the Musée du Louvre, along the River Seine to Pont Neuf, my favorite bridge, to Notre Dame, down rue St. Louis and to rue des Rosiers. As the day was growing short, I reflected on the recurring theme of how very fortunate we are to slow travel in Paris.

Today started out very bleak and gray, but by 9:30 it was sunny. That has been the weather pattern in Paris, much like its parallel neighbor, London. Em is resting up in order to see the new Edvard Munch exhibit on Monday. I went to the Louvre to view the Italian sculptures of Bernini, Michelangelo, Antonio Canova, and other famous sculptures, including Venus de Milo and Nike of Samothrace. Also, the largest collection of French sculptures in the world is on the ground floor, Cour Carree in the Richelieu Wing. The rooms were absolutely packed. It is an emotional and intellectual pleasure to see so many visitors observing, enjoying and appreciating these collections. The United Kingdom and France have a two-week school vacation, and along with the Japanese tour groups, naturally the Louvre was going to be busy. Just a tad too busy, so I escaped to the Palais-Royal across from the Louvre, opposite the Seine. There are charming boutiques around the Royal Park. In the main courtyard, I again had a chance to linger to observe the 280 black-and-white columns of unequal height by D. Buren, a sort of allegorical set of statues. I continued my walk through the Chinese neighborhood and back to rue des Rosiers.

A dark, overcast day welcomed our Sunday morning, starting with a two-hour walk around the neighborhood as far as the Place de Republic. Skype call to connect with everyone. All is wonderful, according to the adults. The grandchildren were busy with their homework for the next day. These weekly conversations with our children are why Sundays are our favorite days of the week. After lunch, another short walk to the Left Bank and the Sorbonne. Sundays are generally slow with only a few cars. A number of folks were walking their dogs, and a few tourists were taking pictures. The day is still hazy as the sun never showed itself today. I cannot wait for Tuesday when we are off to see the E. Munch Exhibit at the Pinacothèque de Paris at 28 Place de la Madeleine, at 1 p.m.

The day turns out sunny and warmer than three days ago. We have tickets for the new Edvard Munch exhibit at the la Pinacothèque de Paris, near the Place de la Madeleine. This exhibit in Paris took over 20 years to collect and showcase Edvard Munch's collection of work. Most of his work had to be gathered from private collections throughout the world. There has never been a major exhibition by this artist in France. The "Scream," undoubtedly emblematically famous, was only one of the 150 works. We marveled at Munch's dramatic transitions from the late 1880s to the 1930s. This distinction was made possible by the clever organization of the display, which was from his earlier to later work.

His progressive use of color, especially pinks, greens and blues, was very fashionable and sophisticated. This was a wonderful collection from someone whom I did not know other than his renowned "Scream." His biography acknowledged that he did suffer from a mental illness, and it was evident within his family. I mentioned before that most museums and special exhibits charge around 12–16 euros or $16–22 for two people. The costs for these exceptional exhibits are very inexpensive when you consider what we were fortunate to be able to observe and reflect upon.

Em's knee held up nicely as the three-day rest helped. She did not experience any swelling once we returned. This is a good sign, as we have many miles to travel.

After dinner, the fading sun left an interesting sort of multicolored orange and purple sky, so I took a walk to the Latin Quarter to take some sunset photos of Notre Dame from the quai Tournelle, Panthéon, Sorbonne, College de France, and back via St. Jacques over quay Pont Sully to rue St. Paul to rue Rivoli to rue Pavée to rue des Rosiers. I shared our treasure trove of sunset photos with our families.

Another sunny day and possibly a great day for slow travel. The temperatures are going to be in the low 50s Fahrenheit. We are planning to purchase tickets for the William Turner 1775–1851 exhibit at the Grand Palais, a huge 19th-century architectural jewel that symbolized the "Glory of Paris." The beautiful edifice is set between the Seine and the Champs-Élysées. Unfortunately, the public viewing date was for tomorrow (should have cross-checked first), so we decided to return tomorrow. Impressively, Joseph Mallord William Turner was an English Romantic landscape painter, watercolorist and printmaker. Although renowned for his oil paintings, Turner was also one of the greatest masters of British watercolor landscape painting. I learned that he was commonly known as the "painter of light," and his work is regarded as a Romantic preface to the Impressionists, an important evolutionary or transitional notion to keep in mind. These transitional references, like a good play or poem, defy summary and are best experienced directly, that being side by side. Like clever teachers who help students find relevant sources for them to continue studying their interests, we are finding such relevance with each exhibit we visit and study.

The Petit Palais is across the street from the Grand Palais, spacious and very airy. Adding the floor-to-ceiling windows makes for an extremely inviting building in which to linger and reflect. The Petit Palais was never busy, and we immensely enjoyed the museum's collection and the "hidden away" outdoor café in the courtyard.

Later, I walked to the imposing Saint-Gervais-Saint-Protais Church. St. Gervais is the only church in Paris that has a façade to include three classical orders of columns (Doric on the first level, Ionic second, and Corinthian on the third level). Its existence at this place is mentioned as early as the fourth century. The harmonic view from the nave is pleasing for its sense of balance and proportions. The church sponsored one of the most famous dynasties of France musicians, the Couperin family, and composer, organist and harpsichordist François Couperin for more than 300 years. On the other side of the church are two of the oldest medieval houses of Paris, at numbers 11 and 13. They date from the 14th century. Just another outdoor museum opportunity that exists everywhere in Paris.

Well, another fine day is promised. Cloudy, gray and dark, but the sun might come up later today. Also, it is also getting warmer as we are experiencing less intermittent raining weather. Em is resting her knee and mindfully embroidering her Paris map in order for us to visit the Turner exhibit on Friday. Also, she is more active doing her watercolors and sketching now that she has more supplies, time and innate talent. She has done some really fine work. Good for her. I am off to the extreme west of an axis along the Champs-Élysées, which starts at the Louvre and passes through the Arc de Triomphe. My destination is the business district of La Defense, juxtaposing traditional office space with highly experimental developments it's a truly exceptional environment. The quarter gets its name from a monument commemorating the defense of Paris of 1871, which once occupied the main roundabout before major development got underway. This development began in 1964, and since then 48 towers have been completed and provide office space for over 900 companies. The entire complex houses government and international offices within its 222 acres. There are parks, a botanical garden and zoo.

The first image I saw after exiting the metro station was the La Grande Arche. This gigantic open cube is 362 feet wide and weighs 300,000 tons, carried on 12 piles sunk below ground. To give you an idea of how large this arch is, the Cathedral of Notre Dame, including its spire, could fit into the arch. One immediate attraction at the opposite end of the Grande Arche was a massive sculpture by Alexander Calder, his last work, a bright red stable (his word instead of mobile) 49 feet high. The tallest building, Elf Tower, is 45 stories. There are statues by Joan Miro, fountains, shops, galleries, restaurants, and benches to sit and relax. The Moretti Tower is covered in 672 different colored tubes. This was an absolute marvel. Em will be so excited to see this attraction, and we shall visit soon. Another great slow travel day in Paris.

I might have spoken too soon about the warmer weather. It is a bit colder, wetter and grayer than yesterday. Not to worry, we are off to the farthest southeastern border of Paris, to the Château de Vincennes. First occupied by Philippe Auguste in the 12th century, it has been used as a castle, residence of kings, state prison, an arsenal (Napoleon) and a military establishment. Louis XIII grew up here, and Louis XIV stayed here. This is a half-fortified castle, half-classic palace, and a wonderful complete ensemble. The most interesting building was the keep, a real architectural feat to erect. The huge square tower was divided into six floors and flanked by corner turrets. Each floor has the same layout—a central hall and rooms in each turret. The tower is 200 feet and the tallest medieval keep in all of France. A thick wall and a deep moat, originally filled with water, protected it. The footbridge was the only way into the keep in the Middle Ages. Other rooms when used as a palace were the council room-king's reception room, bedchamber, oratory, treasure rooms, the Holy Chapel, and, of course, the prison. This was a very special structure, but it takes time to observe all of its hidden parts, as we learned a bit more about the history of France.

If there was just one thing that we took away from our roles in promoting progressive education in the past, it was that if students are to be successful or fail, it is due to motivation. We interpreted this to mean providing choice and purpose to entice intrinsic inspiration. Every time we see something that motivates us to learn more about it, we cannot feel successful until we seek out to find the rest of the story. Thankfully, Em and I are very much alike regarding wonderful ideas and our quest to learn. Wonderful ideas do not spring out of nothing; they build on a foundation of other ideas; these are our motivations that promote us to learn while we have the time and opportunity. Perhaps we are reinventing ourselves during retirement.

After lunch, we walked over to the Memorial de la Shoah on 17 rue Geoffroy-l'Asnier, a few blocks from rue des Rosiers. The memorial opened in 2005 on the site of Memorial du Martyr. The Holocaust memorial houses permanent exhibitions, a documentation

Château de Vincenne, a symbol of the power of the monarch built between 1361 and 1369, and the preferred residency of French kings in the 14th century.

library, and the names of the 76,000 Jews who were deported from France. This was quite a sad, sobering and reflective change from the morning sites. We renewed our bus passes for March at a cost of 112 euros or $137 for the entire month. We tend to save about $50–65 per month by purchasing the pass. Furthermore, the monthly pass makes it easier than purchasing individual tickets, as we just scan the pass to gain entrance. Also, sometimes the Metro box offices at the stations are closed, and you must have coins with you to purchase tickets at the machine. Moreover, it was a safe and smart bit of security to have the passes with us, as we could always take a bus or metro wherever we were instead of looking for ticket offices that may or not be open. In addition, sometimes metro ticket machines are not in working order. Intriguing economics and valid security come into play by being vigilant.

Another day beginning with French dark gray overcast skies. At least it is not snowing as it has been in New England and New York. The interesting happenstance about the weather is that by 10–11 a.m., the sun might be peeking out of the clouds, the rain will dissipate and we go out. We cleaned the apartment, talked to the grandchildren, completed the grocery shopping, and purchased our crusty baguette at Florence Kahn on 24 rue des Écouffes.

We are joyfully on our way to the special William Turner painting exhibit at the Grand Palais. Em secured tickets online, so the wait in line was minimal. The paintings by this 19th-century landscape-cum-colorist were magnificent. We learned that one of his stylistic techniques was to delicately feather in the colors toward the center of his paintings. He loved to paint the sea, boats and ships. He also enjoyed the Italian classic style in his paintings. The exhibit hall was too dark and very crowded. Visitors who were waiting to purchase tickets were allowed in at the same time that folks like us had a reserved time to enter. Consequently, the beginnings of exhibits generally are more crowded, especially in small rooms. Groups of people linger around each picture with their "audio guides," with at least three- to five-minute commentaries on each painting. That works well to gain relevant information about the artists and the paintings. We certainly understand these circumstances, as everyone wants to slowly observe the master's art. We generally move directly, if there is two-way traffic, towards the middle and end where the crowds are less and we can have the time to really enjoy the paintings, then move towards the front and exit out, when possible. I was a little disappointed with the setting—the dark maroon walls, lights on some of the paintings but not all, and just too many people in a very confined space. No complaints, just saying I think Joseph Mallord William Turner deserves better.

Em's knee was better, and we moved across the street to the Petit Palais, one of our favorites, and had a relaxing time and viewed a special jewelry exhibit sponsored by the DeBeers diamond industry, featuring contest winning jewelry pieces in each category, for example, necklaces, rings, collars, bracelets, etc. Em's knee was holding, and we did not wish to push it any further. We immediately found our bus stop and were home in 30 minutes. A nice Paris treat in two extravagantly beautiful buildings.

Wow! Such a happy, light, morning sunshine always brings smiles and excitation to our slow travels. We left early for the unique La Defense, the new business district that I had visited last week. Em was excited to see the many 19th–20th-century buildings adjacent to the highly experimental ones (e.g., the Apollonia building). The Grande Arche stood huge at one end of the district. Em was walking around snapping all sorts of interesting photos, perfect for sketching, she indicated to me. She observed and reflected while at Miro's "Fantastic Characters" sculpture and was delighted viewing from all angles Calder's "Red Spider" and Raymond Moretti's "Chimney" made up of hundreds of colored tubes. I was happy that she was enjoying the outdoor museum. With the fortunate afternoon sunshine, we were able to appreciate other high-rise buildings that provided a mirror effect or reflections onto other nearby buildings, especially on the silvered mirrored Messeturm tower. We walked around the largest shopping malls in Paris that included 220 stores, 48 restaurants and 24 movie theaters.

Em loved these experimental buildings, those buildings not built in a traditional style or materials, and often embracing convex and concave design features into their structures. We were very happy to experience this unique part of Paris.

Last day of the month. Purim, the Jewish celebration, started last night and continued throughout the day and ends tonight. Fireworks, flares, singing, firecrackers, painted faces, masks, costumes, and it's supposed to be the most happy holiday for the Jewish faith; it certainly sounded joyful! In chatting with the grandchildren, they say they are enjoying school. When asked what the best part of their day was, all three said, "recess, it's too short!" and they didn't fancy the school lunches; they will bring their own.

Today is our stay-at-home day as Em has some exciting projects to work on and some to complete. We had an after-dinner walk around our fantastic neighborhood; it looks, smells, and feels so different at night.

Today is our 60th day slow traveling and living in Paris. We are so fortunate, and we are grateful every single day.

A brilliantly sunny and warm day to start our first of the scheduled *Frommer's Great 24 Walks in Paris* by Peter Caine. We saved these 24 walks until the weather was more friendly. Before I scampered out to the Nespresso shop on rue du Bac, Em reminded me to bring along the used pods, as they recycled them. I purchased a month's supply of Nespresso coffee pods.

On the way back I detoured to rue de Furstenburg and the beautified square where the Musée National Eugene Delacroix is located. Delacroix's house and studio were open, free with my Louvre pass, and I observed the master's drawings and sketches. Delacroix is absolutely one of my favorite 19th-century Romantic Period painters.

The Monument Arch is dedicated to humanitarian ideals.

Moreover, his influence extended to the Impressionists—another important element in the Impressionist movement. I learned from the literature available in the museum that he was very much influenced by the Flemish painter Peter Paul Rubens and Verona-born painter Paolo Veronese (a favorite). Of course, I have had the pleasure many times of observing Delacroix's overly romantic and influential painting "Liberty Leading the People" at the Denon Wing in the Louvre Museum.

Interestingly, Pablo Veronese's history painting of "The Wedding at Cana" is the largest painting in the Louvre and is directly across from the Mona Lisa. I have been many times in the Salle des Etats (Mona Lisa room) on the first floor in the Denon Wing, where both these evocative and transforming paintings reside; however, few observers take the time to view "The Wedding at Cana." Veronese's Wedding in Cana painting is my favorite painting in the entire Louvre collection. I was very fortunate to view this painting at least a dozen or so times.

This is what I see each time I enter the Salle de Etats to view the painting, standing opposite the huge and anxious crowds of people attempting to catch a peek and a photo of the Mona Lisa: I see Greco-Roman architecture with Doric and Corinthian columns that surround the courtyard; I see dozens and dozens of figures coming, going, moving and dashing, but not chaos; I see contemporary Renaissance-era clothing and beautiful objects. If I look beyond the courtyard, I see a tower designed by Andrea Palladio; I see the pleasures of eating, drinking, dancing and music; I see a group of musicians playing various instruments. The elaborately detailed and colorful customs are all an apparition of realism. I see the symbolism of meat slaughter, representing the "Lamb of God," the dogs and fidelity, and the surprised looks when the jugs of water are turned into wine. I see the Virgin Mary making a cup with her hands that will be filled with wine. If I observe very carefully, I see the small hourglass, a symbol of spiritual thoughts moving to change us and reminding us that our existence is fleeting, at best. This huge (22 feet, three inches by 32 feet) painting personifies the material wealth, extravagance and upscale life of Venice. Add the prosperous-looking, gilded gold frame that surrounds the picture, and you see and feel opulence. Veronese's contemporaries often referred to him as the painter of beautiful things.

The first couple of times I looked at this Mannerist painting, it perceptually seduced me because I didn't have enough eyes and didn't exactly know where to look first. After a while I realized that this painting was meant to be viewed upwards from below. The fabrics, drapery, colors and actions flash before my eyes. The painting invites many narrative interpretations, from biblical to contemporary Venice. However, after the fifth or sixth time observing this painting, it became transformative for me, just as the jugs of water were turned into wine in two distinct ways. First, I evolved from a "looker" of paintings, to a keener observer of the ensembles of compositions, symbolic details, and the beauty of colors. Every element of Veronese's arrangement, especially the colors, the embroidered shiny silks that play on the light, and the festive mood, was challenging for me to describe for there were more perceptions than I could ever explain in words. Second, patience, as Marcus Porcius Cato, a Roman soldier, senator and the first historian to write history in Latin, implied in his writings, is the most valued of all human virtues, and I try to utilize patience, a critical observational skill, in viewing all works of art as a direct result of studying this painting.

After a light lunch, we took the metro from St. Paul to Chatelet station, and crossed over to Pont Neuf to commence the first of the *Frommer's 24 Walks in Paris*. We strolled

Named after the Prince of Furstenberg, the Musée National Eugène Delacroix is located in the square.

through the Île de la Cité, one of the two small islands in Paris (Île St. Louis being the other). The Pont Neuf is actually the oldest bridge in Paris. The walk took us past statues, squares where the Grand Master of the Templars was burned at the stake, and to the Conciergerie and Sainte-Chapelle—built in the 1240s, with its fifteen 13th-century stained-glass windows and very Gothic. The last half of the walk took us to the front of Cathédral Notre Dame; from there to the back of the church in the square de L'Île-de-France were the steps leading down to the Le Memorial des Martyrs de la Déportation. This underground memorial is dedicated to the 200,000 people deported from France by the Nazis during World War II, who later died in concentration camps. From here we took the metro back to the Chatelet and changed trains to St. Paul. Em's knee is holding out—a good sign, as this walk tested her endurance and returned enjoyment.

Walk number 2—We exited early this morning before we began our second walk to one of the most beautiful and oldest squares in Paris, Place des Vosges. When I first described the Vosges, I neglected to observe carefully and didn't mention the unified rooflines or the original symmetrical appearance: two stories with alternate white stone and red brick facings. The more time we spend at the Vosges, the more I see and feel about this harmonious square. It is our favorite place to relax, observe and reflect on how fortunate we are to live in Paris, as seniors, on a fixed income.

From the Palace des Vosges we rode the bus to the Jardin du Palais-Royal and the Palais-Royal, which now accommodates the Ministry of Culture and the Council of State. We have visited the palace a few times, but Em wanted to take another view of the courtyard of the Royal Palace; she immediately began to sketch some of the 280 black-and-white columns. The Jardin du Palais-Royal is a quiet garden surrounded by the elegant facades designed by the architect Victor Louis. We had a nice sit in the sun and watched the many nannies attentively minding their precious babies and toddlers in the

The "Colonnes de Buren," designed by French artist D. Buren, using white Carrara marble and black Pyrenean marble.

park. We had a light lunch at Doree's and walked home. Very encouraging, Em's knee is getting better each day as she walked for almost three hours today. The treatment seems to be the magic of Paris!

Another splendid morning: bright sunlight and not a cloud, so far, in the sky. I am off to gather up some groceries and milk at the Marché G20. Before the shopping, however, I continued my customary long walk to the Latin Quarter, in arrondissement #6, which formed the historical heart of Paris. Three sights in one area to celebrate: The Jardin des Plantes, the Natural History Museum, the Botanical Gardens. Nearby, the Menagerie, a little zoo with Seychelles turtles and almost 1,000 mammals, stood modestly and lonely without any children nearby.

The oldest tree, a cedar of Lebanon, was planted in 1734. There were little in the way of florae, as it is still too early. By next month the gardens should be quite stunning, and I would love to take Em there next month. A leisurely walk back, and time for lunch.

A sunny morning with bright Provence blue skies and a cold wind accompanied my morning walk. To the Left Bank I head straight to the university district: Institute of Paris–Sorbonne and to the Musée du Cluny—a national museum of the Middle Ages founded on a site first inhabited by monks in the 1200s. The museum, which is on our list of "must-sees," houses two outstanding monuments: the thermal baths of Lutetia (a name used to indicate the island in the middle of the Seine, today's Île de la Cité—hence the modern Paris originated in the fifth century), the only Gallo-Roman (culture of Gaul under the rule of the Roman Empire) monument surviving in Paris built in the first century; the first Parisian example of a private mansion between a courtyard and a garden, featuring a U-shape closed to the outside world by a tall wall from its original 15th-century structure.

Em and I will actually visit inside the museum, as I merely wanted to observe and get oriented around the outside and to locate their bookshop. I continued on rue Saint-Severin to St. Severin church. This imposing Gothic church exterior included some interesting gargoyles and flying buttresses. The ancient seven stained-glass windows beautifully depicted the seven sacraments. I'm selfishly disappointed that there aren't paintings to adorn the nave, but this is not Rome, I quietly reminded myself. Refreshed and stimulated to explore more in this neighborhood, I walked behind another of my favorite Gothic churches, St. Gervais, and discovered a lovely, peaceful, hilly lane which ran along St. Gervais from the River Seine; it was a typical Paris postcard setting.

After lunch Em and I headed to the American Library on rue du General Camou, arrondissement #7. On the way to the library we, as we do often, stumbled upon St. Clotilde Basilica, of a neo-Gothic design, completed in 1857. On rue Rapp, we discovered a wonderful asymmetrical and elegantly graceful Art Nouveau building by architect Jules Lavirotte (1901). We reached the American Library and found everything a library should have, including reference, resource centers, Internet, volumes of books, computers, and magazines. We spent a couple of hours catching up on newspaper and magazine articles that we have not seen since last December. There was a membership fee for Americans that helps to bring in new books and magazines for its members. We were delighted to pay the membership fee, as we knew that we would return often to do our continuous research agenda.

Em was yearning to stop at the famous Angelina's on our way home. Angelina's pastry shop was on 226 rue Rivoli, near the Concorde, which was on our way home. Em commented, "If you are concerned about the price, don't go in." "Why do you ask?"

"Because the price is steep as it has been famous for the past 120 years." Their claim to pastry fame ran from the "L'Africain" thick hot chocolate to the "Mont Fuji," a green tea mousse with shortbread pastry and fruit. The Mont Fuji was my special treat for my love. Em's knee was beginning to bother her, so we took the Metro straight to St. Paul station, home and put a pack of ice on her knee. A big walking day—perhaps too much? I need to be more attentive!

We welcomed a couple of days' rest and rehabilitation, which worked best for Em's knees and my continuing research. The days are becoming a standard of expectations: sunny, bright and cold, with temperatures from 37–41 degrees Fahrenheit.

"Today," Em declared, "would be great for walking," so walking we did. Our new book, *Unexplored Paris*, by Rodolphe Trouilleux, was an insightful companion to our existing *24 Great Walks* book. The point of interest to explore was the face-bust of Mary Louis Fuller, an American dancer in Paris during the 20s. She was friends with painter Toulouse-Lautrec, sculptor Auguste Rodin and Hector Guimard (architect of synagogue). Artist Pierre Roche in 1910 placed her on the Art Nouveau building at 39 rue Reaumur in the 3rd arrondissement; it was fanciful and a remarkable limestone carving.

Near rue Saint-Martin, in the 3rd arrondissement, was the Conservatory of Arts and Crafts, the location of the earliest abbey structure left in Paris. This higher education establishment is dedicated to providing research for the promotion of science and industry. We loved their motto: "It teaches everyone, everywhere!" How is that for progressive higher education at its best?

In the same neighborhood, but a distance to walk, we found the "Lady with the Bag." The large caryatid sculpture graces an Art Nouveau building on rue Turbigo. Art Nouveau style was popular between 1890 and 1910; Paris has many Art Nouveau structures. A. Emile Delange designed the sculpture of a lady holding in her left hand a sprig of myrrh and in her right holds a small handbag. These adornments were typical in this Art Nouveau cultural period. Our final discovery site was on rue Rambuteau where the 2nd–4th floors of the Troubadour-style (somewhat exuberant French equal to Gothic Revival) 19th-century building adorned with rhythm and creative stone carved heads with flower stalks and buds, a few incongruous grotesques. Just fun to discover and admire the outdoor museums of Paris.

Feeling terrific, we broke for a light lunch and café creme at our favorite café, Le Loir dans La Théière (the dormouse in the teapot), which was minutes from rue Rosiers. Em's knee is holding up, and excitement is always in the air.

The first exploration from *Unexplored Paris* was to the home of 18th-century poet and a precursor of surrealism, Guillaume Apollinaire, who enjoyed staying at the Golden Eagle Inn. Now, it is the Café de la Gare, which houses dance and theater studios. The courtyard looks surprisingly majestic, given the age and lack of upkeep. We, the unrepentant strollers on both banks, are off to find the verified "oldest house" in Paris. We found it and the verified marker above the door frame. The house was built in 1407 by Nicolas Flamel, a scribe at the University of Paris, who financed free lodgings for farmworkers and fruit and vegetable growers for nearby areas. The engraved string of works along the front wall reads: "We men and women, living under the roof of this house built in the year fourteen hundred and seven, are honorably bound to recite on Paternoster and one Hail Mary every day, and to ask God, in His grace, to forgive the sins of the poor departed. Amen."

A slow walk back to have lunch. Skyped family members and had a brief chat with the grandchildren. Everybody was healthy and presumed happy. After a couple hours of rest, we're off again to rue Geoffroy-l'Asnier and stop once again at the Memorial de la Shoah, a few blocks from rue des Rosiers. This Holocaust memorial is a tribute to understanding the past to illuminate the future. The Wall of Names is a stone wall that is engraved with the 76,000 names of the Jews deported from France between 1942 and 1944. Their names are engraved, preserving and transmitting the horrors of such a human tragedy and crime.

With due respect, we decided that we needed a change and found bus #29 that traveled around arrondissements 1–4. We stopped to peek into the Galleria Lafayette for a look at midtown Paris from atop of their 43 meters, or 140 feet, building. The store was mobbed with shoppers as a 10 percent sale drove many into the store. Because we could not find a bus going in our direction, we took the nearest metro at Opera Metro to St. Paul's in 20 minutes. This alternative bus scheduling often happens depending on the day of the week and time of day; we still prefer the bus as our mode of transport.

The early morning started out French gray and gloomy, but by 09:00 the sun broke through the clouds, and another fine day was waiting for us. First things first. Off to the boulangerie, Saveurs de Pains at 32 rue Vieille du Temple, because I love their multigrain baguettes, and it's located just a few blocks from our flat. Their baguettes are always flaky, crusty, delicious, and if I arrive early enough, still warm straight from their bread oven. For Emily's birthday I bought her a chocolate croissant, only her second, as she is very good at watching her weight as extra weight doesn't help the knees. This will be our cleaning, washing, ironing and rest day. However, as is customary or de rigueur, we did a short walk in the neighborhood, viewed some neat abstract artwork in a gallery on rue de Temple, sat for a while in the Place des Vosges; upon returning Em continued with her map embroidering, so it's back to work. Wait, we are retired.

I have been thinking about love: Is it just an emotion, or is love really about the actions (i.e., showing and doing) that make love more meaningful and deeper than simply saying, "I love you!" Reading about the renowned Zen Buddhist monk Thich Nhat Hanh teaches that to love is a learned "dynamic interaction," as we form early our patterns of understanding to love ourselves before we can truly love and understand our partner. I learned that there are four components of truthful love: loving kindness, compassion, joy and mental composure. I am still very conscious of the fact that I need to place more effort on the kindness and composure aspects, but I am making steady progress. What this year abroad has taught me is that there are no boundaries to love—Em's happiness/sadness is my happiness/sadness, and my happiness/sadness is hers. Slow travel, with our individually and mutually designed purposes and goals, brought out this capacity in me to truly love her through those actions of love often taken for granted, such as respect, kindness, attention, affection and listening.

Today was a rest and research day, as Em wants to play and work with her paints and to sketch. Moreover, the cleaning of the apartment required completion. There is a lot of dust from the old herringbone floors that have deep-aged crevices that collect dust and food, paint is peeling from some of the walls onto the floors, and the floor-to-ceiling windows are where dust comes in from the street below. Because of my allergies, I must make sure that dust and mold are reduced in the apartment, and that requires my constant cleaning attention.

I remarked how well Em's watercolors are coming along. She sketches and paints almost every place we have visited; I wish I had her discipline … and talent.

A banner day! The sun is up early, and the day is warm. The temperature is forecasted to be in the 40s and will increase another ten degrees, hopefully. We escape early to continue with Walk #6 of our "24 Great Walks in Paris." This walk took us to the beautiful southern Marais area, about 20–30 blocks from our rue des Rosiers. We stopped at the most imposing Hotel de Ville, the seat of the city's mayor and city hall. The Revolutionaries burned down the original building in 1871, and the present building was rebuilt in the late 19th century. By following our guidebook, and observing carefully, we found 22 colossal copper statues on the roofline symbolizing the regions of France. There are no visitors allowed in the mayor's quarters, but there was a free exhibition of old-time Paris through the medium of photography. An interesting and inspiring look at Paris of 200 and 300 years ago. A special treat was nine photos of Marc Chagall painting in his studio.

As we followed our guidebook to rue du Temple, onto rue des Archives, at numbers 22–24 we found the entrance to Eglise des Billettes. This cloister, built in 1427, is now used for exhibitions of arts and crafts. Today's exhibits demonstrated antiquated Oriental rugs and carpets. This remarkable cloister is the only complete one to have survived in Paris. We proceeded to rue de Lobau and found the beautiful church of Eglise Saint-Gervais-Saint-Protais, dedicated to the brothers Gervase and Protase. We have passed this imposing church endlessly as it is on our return bus route to our flat.

Flash Fact: Supposedly, Emperor Nero stood on this very site in 66 A.D. The most inspiring and interesting part of the interior of this church was the modern stained-glass windows, especially the one window depicting a sunburst that commemorates the lives of 90 local people who were killed during World War I. At the rear of the church are some wonderful modern stained-glass windows by the artist Sylvie Gaudin; it's unusual to find a woman's work in stained glass and in a church. There were a few superb sculpted stone counters with symbolic and meaningful scenes (e.g., the medieval butcher roasting meat on a spit, a cobbler with a row of clogs hanging in his shop, and a couple bathing). This was only the second time we have explored the interior of this astonishing edifice. We walked back down towards St. Paul, purchased a fresh sandwich of curried chicken and sun-dried tomatoes, and sat in the local park and had our lunch. A mellow day, and we did not overwork Em's knee. Em tells me that tomorrow we have some interesting attractions on her agenda; I cannot wait for tomorrow, as I do every day.

Such a day! The sun was bright and the temperature warm. It was forecast to reach the mid–50s. Em reserved our museum tickets for the Musée Jacquemart-André, on Blvd. Haussmann in arrondissement #16. The museum was formerly owned by the avid art collectors Édouard André and Nélie Jacquemart and contains outstanding works by artists such as Botticelli, Paolo Uccello, François Boucher, Canaletto, and marvelous frescoes by Giovanni Battista Tiepolo, the Venetian painter (1727–1804). The special exhibit for which she reserved tickets was the Greco-Dali and Goya Exhibit. These, along with a host of other famous Spanish painters (e.g., Jusepe de Ribera and Bartolommé Esteban Murillo), drew a large crowd, and everyone used the free audio guides. We adroitly sneaked past the viewers-cum-listeners to see the paintings. There was only one Greco, "The Nobleman with His Hand on His Chest," certainly one of his most famous. A well-exhibited and viewer-friendly layout for sure. A refreshingly open and airy exhibit in a marvelous 19th-century mansion; what could a better setting be? There was also a remarkable collection from the Florentine Quattrocento 14th century and Venetian Renaissance, another exhilarating display and joyful reminiscence of our time in Florence. We sprang for lunch at the famous Michelin two-star rated Musée Café, another "special" birthday gift for Em. The food was the best we'd had so far. Em had a large salad with Reggiano cheese, chicken, bits of ham, a soft boiled egg, and stewed tomatoes. I indulged in a quiche with spinach & ham bits and mixed salad on the side. We finished off with a raspberry tart we shared, and Em had an espresso. The total tariff was 34 euros or about $47. Value for the money, absolutely. We left the restaurant with sheer delight and contentment displayed all over our faces, and Em said, "You have a bit of raspberry tart on your chin," and we laughed, and she gave me a warm hug.

My allergies were getting worse to the point where I couldn't stop coughing, and the phlegm was disruptive and gross. I made an appointment to see Dr. Patricia Abello, a French allergist and asthma doctor who spoke English and worked at the American Hospital in Paris. I made the appointment and saw her at her office on 147 Avenue Malakoff, in arrondissement #16. I signed in and waited for five minutes as my appointment was for 2:30, in by 2:45. After hearing me speak, she immediately diagnosed me with asthma. Incredible, she heard my voice and immediately said that I had asthma. I brought along my previous sinus infection treatments, which she was glad to know, but indicated that the previous treatment was "scratching the wrong itch." Dr. Patricia Abello examined me for ten minutes, eyes and throat-breath force, and sat down to prescribe drugs that will help the coughing, wheezing and mucus buildup. Since she did not accept credit cards, I paid her a fee of 100 euros, or about $135, for a visit that lasted 45 minutes. We went directly to the pharmacy and received the eight prescription drugs she prescribed. Those drugs included allergy medication for my eyes and nose, acid-reflux medication contributing to the mucus, and two inhalers. The cost was 120 euros. She asked me to come back in two weeks for a review of my progress. I was feeling terrific, knowing what I am suffering from, and this treatment protocol just might work on me.

Another fabulously sunny and warm day. We must be having a bit of spring, but it was forecast to be colder this weekend. Nonetheless, we would enjoy the sunny weather. Em was resting her knee today as she has some reading and painting to finish. She is out of coffee, so I am off this morning to the Nespresso stop on rue du Bac on the Left Bank near the Musée d'Orsay. I actually love walking to the arrondissement #6 because of the beautiful plethora of men's and women's clothing shops, antique art galleries, classical sculptures, and designer household furniture. I walked through the Jardin des Tuileries in the rear of the Musée du Louvre and across the Pont Royal to rue du Bac. Since I have a Nespresso card, it was a simple task of replacing previous coffee selections. For 11 euros, Em is set for a couple of weeks. I followed my "Unexplored Paris" book selection for this area and found the delightful and peaceful School of Fine Arts. This place had a fascinating history: first a convent in the 15th century, a church, a museum of Paris monuments, and finally in the 19th century, the renowned École des Beaux-Arts. Many of America's leading architects, such as Richard Morris Hunt, Henry Hobson, Richard and Louis Sullivan, had studied at the École des Beaux-Arts. Since I was so close to the Louvre, I popped in to find more paintings and frescoes by G.B. Tiepolo because I saw one of his paintings at the Musée Jacquemart-André a day or so ago. I did not find any Tiepolos, but I found a new Caravaggio, "Death of the Virgin," in the Denon Wing in Hall #12, and two new Leonardo da Vincis, "A Portrait of an Unknown Woman" and "St. John the Baptist." Absolutely overwhelming, for I had time to linger and pause for many minutes before anyone came close.

Near the Caravaggio painting was the brilliant "Portrait of Baldassare Castiglione" by Raphael that I have stared at so many times. Baldassare (1478–1529) was a poet, diplomat, soldier, humanist and a friend of Raphael. More study indicated that Raphael demonstrated in this portrait an ideal of effortless elegance of a true gentleman of the era. Within European art history, portraits were one of the genres within the hierarchy genres as representations of people from real life. This painting fostered subsequent artists, such as Henri Matisse and Paul Cezanne, to use similarities of color and illusions in their portraits. I was fascinated with this painting because all portraits tell us about the subject and how the subject wanted to be depicted. Observing, for example, what the subject is next to or in front of, what he or she is carrying, clothing the subject wears, and, if we look carefully, the body language or facial expressions of the subject. I am feeling great to be able to observe these famous paintings, but in real time and on my time. I head straight back to have a late lunch with Em. She waited patiently in order for us to enjoy lunch together. She is like that: always patient, kind and considerate. A great day for viewing Paris, both indoors and outdoors.

Skype Time! "Today was cloudy with a chance of meatballs," I explained to our grandchildren, who, in turn, reminded me "that book is for babies." The sun is trying to come out but is having a difficult time, I'm afraid. I was hoping to take Em for a picnic lunch this afternoon. Nonetheless, Em continued with her drawing and painting. I need to continually dust our place, as my allergy-related asthma, according to Dr. Abello, is triggered by dust balls, mold and mites. The sun did appear in the sky, and we enjoyed a slow-time lunch in the park around the corner. I am aware that the seasonal pollens will contribute to my conditions, but so far I haven't experienced those allergens.

A rather cloudy day, but the sun always shines in Southern California, I mean in the Marais. A quiet day was planned. Em wants to rest her knee for one more day so we can resume our "24 Great Walks of Paris" on Saturday. I finished an insightful book called *Lunch in Paris* by Elizabeth Bard, a brilliant cross-cultural analysis between an American woman and her soon-to-become husband, a Frenchman with his new PhD. It involves the life of an American living in France and all that goes on before and during their marriage. The last chapters were the most engaging, as she juxtaposes American values and lifestyles with France's. The book's other story line is at the end of each chapter where she provides recipes for the food discussed or mentioned in the chapter. Most of her recommendations are French recipes and a few of the author's family recipes as well. We might try a couple to see what they taste like, as Em, a wonderful chef, was enthralled by the recipes.

I phoned the doctor and indicated to her there was no appreciable change, only that my wheezing is not waking Em up anymore. Dr. Abello asked me to come in for a follow-up, no charge this time. I waited in her large, airy waiting room for about ten minutes. She tested my breath force through a whistle-like instrument and indicated that my lungs must be OK. She listened to my lungs, OK. Then she insisted that it's my acid-reflux that has a lot to do with a persistent cough, the mucus that is produced and wheezing. She added another two prescriptions, presumably to help manage the acid-reflux issue. We shall see what happens in the next few days, as she wants me to ring her on Monday with an update on my status. I am very fortunate to have such a conscientious and caring physician treating me.

You know the weather had to change sometime. It did, dramatically, as it rained all night and into the midmorning. By the time I left for my morning walk, the rain had stopped, sun out, and the streets were slippery clean. While I was walking near the Place de Vosges, I noticed several mothers or caregivers with their toddlers, with boots and carrying in their strollers buckets and shovels as if they were on the way to the beach. I stealthily followed them to the Place de Vosges. Surprisingly, there is no beach in the park! Of course not, but it did rain all night and into the morning, leaving huge puddles of water from the rain in the sandy ground. The toddlers simply had a ball playing in the shallow water puddles with their buckets and shovels.

These moments are flashbacks from long ago to the recommendations of the British Educational (Plowden) Report stating that sand, water, wood and clay were absolutely necessary and relevant materials in the intellectual and social development of young children. These experiential, hands-on activities promote children's knowledge of their surroundings and form a foundation that can be built upon in order to understand their world.

Water is a compelling source of learning pleasure for children. Research has validated convincingly why water play is a key science and mathematics medium that enhances children's learning through discovery and unstructured play. Playing with water provides great opportunities for children to have unstructured play time.

The literature is replete with encouraging data that supports the use of sand to help children develop social skills like problem-solving, sharing and communicating. Sand also is particularly beneficial for developing a sense of texture, and comparing sand to grass, wood, etc., does emphasize the sensations of each surface.

Because clay comes from the earth, it's a natural material. Natural materials such as clay, sand, water, wood, mud, pine cones and chestnuts are organic springboards (scaffolding, if you like) to creative thinking and a connection to nature and the arts and crafts.

In Reggio Emilia, founder of the Reggio Emilia schools Loris Malaguzzi emphasized that the environment plays a central role in the process of making learning meaningful and relevant. He explained that a flexible environment is the third teacher, responsive to the need for teachers and children to create learning together. I was so happy and pleased, I wanted to just go up to the parents or caretakers and thank them for fostering such development; I thought better of it since I don't speak French.

Once again, Loris Malaguzzi said, "What children learn does not follow as an automatic result from what is taught, rather, it is in large part due to the children's own doing, as a consequence of their activities and our resources."

When I returned, Em was busy as ever, and I cleaned the apartment as the dust is always present, coming up from the 200-year-old herringbone-patterned parquet floors. This phenomenon of consistency was similar to the persistent tapping pattern on our windowsills by the rock pigeons. They nest on our window ledges and leave their poop. I am constantly washing their droppings away while I place my fiddle leaf fig and rosemary plants out on the ledge so they can enjoy the sunshine when it appears. Paris and slow travel invite us to find the time to take a walk, even if it is later in the evening.

A dark and dreary day after an all-night rain. The sun might appear sometime today. I took a slow walk around the neighborhood to pick up a whole wheat baguette, or "French stick." This is what I learned about "a stick." The standard baguette weighs 250 grams and comes in three slightly different varieties: ordinary—crispy and golden brown crust; molded—thinner crust with a lattice pattern on the underside; and floured—lighter in color as the crust is covered with flour before cooking. However, our two favorite breads are pain complet or pain aux céréales, multigrain, and the pain au levain, or sourdough. I found, with joy, many boulangeries having baguette aux céréales and au levain.

The side streets are empty of automobiles on Sundays, making walking an even more pleasant pleasure. Em was resting her knee to make sure that it is ache-free to do the walks next week. However, we did have a slow walk around our neighborhood as the sun finally made its way out, such an exciting neighborhood to explore. Skyped home, and all is well; we are happy. I was unable to schedule a school visit to the United Nations pre-school in arrondissement #16; for some reason they would not take visitors, not sure why; no worries, we have much to explore. My condition is basically the same—less coughing and mucus, but the wheezing is still present, especially when I exhale. I am supposed to call Dr. Abello tomorrow and report my status.

A marvelous morning indeed! A bright sun peeked between the two 18th-century buildings looking out of our kitchen window. Moreover, according to the forecast, it should be a bit warmer than usual today. I am off on my Monday morning trek to the Louvre to view the France paintings from the 1600s–1800s. After rereading "Judgment of Paris," I had a renewed interest in Jean-Auguste-Dominique Ingres, Jacques-Louis David and Jean-Baptiste-Camille Corot—all pre–Impressionists but valuable influences for what was to come in a few years. There were no lookers in the French paintings at Denon Hall, but the place was packed everywhere else by 10 a.m. I had the entire 20 rooms of French paintings pretty much to myself. I find this to be true every time I'm in the 18th–19th-century French painting wing.

Returned home for lunch with Em. After lunch we resumed our Walk Number 7 to the Bastille region. This was a walk which actually borders arrondissements #4 and #11 and Opera-Bastille. The focus of our walk was to explore the 42 artisans, ateliers and galleries that line the Ave. Daumesnil, a mere three blocks past the Place de Bastille and the column with Juliet at the top. These workshops are filled with artisans representing their craft, ranging from art restoration to furniture to textiles to ceramics to printing to paper making to needlepoint to book bonding to weaving. We stopped into the painting restoration atelier #5, where an American student, Louisa, was completing her first-year internship in art restoration. She was enjoying her year and indicated she was learning a great deal. She asked us to return anytime as she works in the atelier five days per week. The first-year students were learning the basics of repairing canvas and restoring canvases that have holes and issues of decay. By their third year, students who earn a diploma are repairing and restoring paintings that we shall see in operation on Friday.

The 45 brick archways were transformed into the 42 ateliers, galleries and showrooms and expanded for at least 10–12 blocks. At the end of the final block the stairs lead to a Promenade Plantée, an elevated (10 meters above street level) urban park above the shops and galleries from Avenue Daumesnil. Taking the Promenade Plantée for three miles you come out before the Bois de Vincennes. We stopped during our promenade walk to relish the refreshing warmth of the sun. We finished up at the Metro Bastille and returned to rue des Rosiers. A terrific day, as Em's knee held up nicely.

A delightfully sunny and warm day is in store. We are fortunate to have these marvelous bright days. I am back to arrondissement #12, where we were yesterday, for my daily morning walk. There was one feature (Cour Damoye) that we did not see yesterday, a courtyard passage that originated in the early 1700s, with most of those buildings still remaining in the passage. In the 1700s, I'm told there were businesses and workshops with lodgings above. This passage is the granddaddy of Parisian covered passageways, for it was built in one go, whereas most similar courtyards in this area were added onto through the centuries. Because of a diversion from my initial route, I discovered a brand-new church in the area, called "The Cross of Hope." What inspired my interest about this new church was its fortress-like concrete construction. The interior was made of sculpted stone and oak wood, including 18th-century oak wood for the cross. Just two red and yellow stained-glass windows on the south side, but the ceiling had strategically placed skylights to allow the sunlight to bathe the entire seating area. Sometimes modern churches use different materials and design formats to stylize their churches as direct opposites of the hundreds of century-old churches in Paris. Very impressive indeed.

After lunch we decided to go and sit in the Jardin des Tuileries, as the temperatures were in the high 50s and the sun was blasting out of the sky. The Tuileries stretches between the Louvre and the Place de la Concorde. The garden is replete with elegant statues and fountains (not yet operable) and places to sit or lie on the grassy slopes. Such people as queens, kings and emperors who took up residence around the gardens included Catherine de' Medici, Henry IV, Louis XIV and XV, Napoleon. That is quite an "A" list of actors! The gardens were inspired by Catherine de' Medici, who wished for an Italian-style park. Within the garden there were works of art by Aristide Maillol, Auguste Rodin, Alexander Calder, Alberto Giacometti, and Picasso. After a couple of hours chatting and mapping many options for our next adventures, we stopped for two lemon and honey crepes and café crèmes at Breizh Café at 109 rue Vieille du Temple, our neighborhood café. A relaxing day, with Em resting her knee for tomorrow's Walk Number 9. I spoke with Dr. Abello, and she recommended another two weeks on the meds. She assured me that this treatment will work! Thank you, Dr. Abello, for your encouraging words.

I do not know if it is the medication I am taking or the bright sunshine each day that is making me feel better. I remember something that jazz pianist Jane Jarvis said about having everything she needs to be happy between her ears; I would add that I need Emily. Whatever the reason, another warm day is in store. My morning excursion was to arrondissement #1 to find an old restaurant that first served beef in 1796. The name, "Le Boeuf à la Mode" (pot roast), got its name from the sign that represents the fashion conscious ox. After I finally found this almost hidden sign, I looked for where Jean-Baptiste Poquelin, France's greatest 17th-century playwright, known by his stage name Molière, was born. Molière created a new kind of controversial comedy. In his plays, the comic was based on a double vision that demonstrated opposing ideas; for example, wisdom and folly, bad and good, or right and wrong. I found both the commemorative plaque that indicated his birth place (1622) and the playwright's bust appropriately placed at the entrance to the Comedie Francaise, Paris's regal theater. Stopped at the Monoprix supermarché for food stuff for lunch and dinner.

After lunch we took the bus to Hotel du Ville and changed to the Metro Pyrenees' brown line to arrondissement #20. The metro at Pyrenees used escalators, which are much better for Em. This area is where we find Cimetière du Père Lachaise. Herein, using the detailed "famous people map," we found the gravesites of Honoré de Balzac, Sarah Bernhardt, Oscar Wilde, Eugene Delacroix, Gertrude Stein, Frederic Chopin, Marcel Proust, Molière, Edith Piaf and Jim Morrison. This is Paris' largest cemetery. Not only is this a pleasant place for a stroll along with over 3,000 trees but also for the quality of its statuary. Took time to observe the funerary architecture, with secular and devotional symbols.

This area is slowly becoming a gentrified neighborhood with many cafés and bars.

Not many tourists venture here, except to visit the cemetery, but it is here where you find the real diversity of the city: Africans, Middle Easterners, Indians and southeast Asians all living in this quasi-gentrified community. A great place to see and feel the more authentic Paris, and an extra bonus: few tourists. We returned thrice more to do the entire cemetery.

After two days of further researching the history of Cimetière du Père Lachaise, I came back alone. This 110-acre cemetery, with some 70,000 residents, has been a city burial site since it opened in 1804, and the crematorium built in the 1890s is nearby. It is the final resting place for foreign soldiers, victims of concentration and extermination camps and homage to victims of June 1848, as well as many famous figures in history, literature, artists and musicians. Interestingly, the popular culture reference to Père Lachaise has been evidenced in films, literary works, songs and television shows. I planned to spend more time around three gravesites of my favorite luminaries: Honoré de Balzac's large tomb, Oscar Wilde's lipsticked monuments and Frederic Chopin's. First, Honore de Balzac's large tomb, on Division #48, I observed the bronze book with a quill pen placed at the base of his stone pillar monument, which stands on one of the highest points of the cemetery. A commanding, splendid view of the City of Light. "Death unites as well as separates; it silences paltry feelings," said Balzac. Second, Oscar Wilde's quote, "Death must be so beautiful—to have no yesterday, and no tomorrows, to forget time, to forgive life, to be at peace," resonated with me as I observed the intimate lipstick kisses all over his tomb. But please, no more kisses, as the chemicals used to remove the stains are promoting the deterioration of his monument. Finally, I love Frederic Chopin's monument! Elegantly sitting on top is an angelic being playing a stringed instrument. The Romantic Period painter Eugene Delacroix mentions that his music could nourish the soul. Chopin's music lets music transport romance and love.

I'll revisit Jim Morrison, Edith Piaf, Gertrude Stein and Modigliani with Em next time. The rain began to fall rather steadily, and a downpour was waiting to happen. I know that because I had no rain gear with me. As it happened, what started out promising gave way to one drenched tourist. Dripping wet, with an appearance of a disguised water rat, I took bus #69 from arrondissement #20 to arrondissement #6, switched buses to arrondissement #4, St. Paul; by then, the rain had almost stopped. Apart from the dampness of the rain, I actually enjoyed this rather strange but artistic, dream-like experience. Here is what I learned from the many visits to Père Lachaise: Take the time to observe the symbols in cemeteries; this is especially true in Père Lachaise. Symbols are a universal language. I sought out cemeteries as they are an inventory of symbolism. Grave markers, epitaphs on tombs and headstones, some with angels, lions, eagles and acanthus leaves, are all devotional and secular symbols, for they meet the definition of a symbol— something that stands for and represents something else. I found in Père Lachaise, in addition to names, dates, and memories and thoughts of afterlife, funerary architecture that demonstrated a collection of an impressive range of architectural periods and styles. For example, periods I found included Egyptian, Neoclassical, Art Nouveau, High Gothic revival, modernist, postmodern and contemporary.

A dull and overcast morning was in store for us today. I am off this morning to fetch more coffee from the Nespresso shop at 126 rue de Bac. I sauntered merrily for about 45 minutes to the Latin Quartier to find one of the most important ancient Gallo-Roman remains from that era in Paris. The Arènes de Lutèce at 49 rue Monge, constructed in the first century CE, could once seat 15,000 spectators for circus and theatrical performances.

The only visible remains were the stone seats and the stage. While sitting on the hard concrete terraced stone steps, I watched some older men playing their favorite sport, boules or bocce in Italy. On the other side of the dirt floor of the arena were boys playing soccer, probably not knowing that performers some 2,000 years ago played in their exact same spot. Returned back for lunch with Em.

After lunch we traveled to the base of the Eiffel Tower at arrondissement #7 and walked the remaining kilometer to the Musée du Quai Branly–Jacques Chirac at 37 Quai Branly. The museum's permanent exhibits are primitive art and artifacts from the people and cultures representing four geographic regions: Oceania, Asia, Africa and America. The building was completed in 2006 and designed by architect Jean Nouvel at a cost of $256 million. There are ample videos and multimedia galleries throughout the museum, and the interior was undulated with leather-clad low walls within the glass and metal structure. However, the exterior of the building is rather odd: in fact, it was plain and drab. However, there was a wonderful garden surrounding the building and an upscale restaurant within the garden itself.

Overall, a rather unique experience, and I walk away with the feeling of just how much more we have to learn about the human race, about their art and culture.

Although it rained most of the night, the morning seemed refreshingly clean and bright. I am off to the La Grande Mosquée de Paris at the 5th arrondissement. This mosque has been used for numerous films and is strikingly beautiful. The Moorish buildings were built in the early 1920s. The fascinating and brilliant interior decorations were fashioned by Muslim craftsmen using materials from Persia-Iran (carpets), North Africa (copper and brass) and Lebanon (cedar). The courtyard encloses the garden, a symbol of Muslim Paradise. The patio was modeled upon the Alhambra in Granada. The prayer chamber was very stimulating to the senses: the sight of the colorful, geometric, proportioned decorations, the smell of the incense burning ever so lightly, and the fragrance of fruity perfumes seemed to follow me from place to place. There was also a tearoom that served Middle Eastern pastries and mint tea. The mosque borders the Jardin des Plantes and the Natural History Museum in the Latin Quarter. This was a marvelous walk that took me over the Seine to the Left Bank and back home in time for lunch with Em. I'll bring Em to see the mosque and have mint tea and an almond paste M'hanncha.

Our daylight savings time just increased our daylight one hour more in the evenings. This will make our days longer and nights lighter. We are to remain close to our apartment today as heavy rain is forecast. I have been insisting that Em have her knee checked while in Paris, but she indicated that will definitely happen once she arrives back to the states. We seem to always take a short walk on Sundays as everyone in Paris is out and about. Most of the streets are closed to vehicles, and pedestrians have the full right of way. Moreover, it is interesting to watch how our fellow travelers and "native" Parisians spend their Sundays, even in the rainy climate. We constantly ask ourselves, "Why do we love our neighborhood?" One of the most interesting streets is the famous rue des Francs-Bourgeois, one of the rare streets of Paris completely open on Sunday. The Marais, particularly towards the North near République, is also famed for a strong Chinese community, with clothing shops, grocery stores and restaurants. This particular neighborhood has joyfully experienced a growing gay presence since the 1980s, as evidenced by the existence of many gay cafés, nightclubs, cabarets and shops. These establishments are mainly concentrated in the southwestern portion of the Marais, many on or near the streets Sainte-Croix de la Bretonnerie and Vieille du Temple. Other features of the neighborhoods include the Musée Picasso (which is unfortunately closed until 2012), the Musée Cognacq-Jay (18th-century European art), and the Musée Carnavalet, marvelous and a complete history of Paris. We Skyped our families, and they indicated that they are reading my daily email briefings. Annika, Cole and Ty asked "When are you coming home?" Impulsively, we replied "soon!" That makes my efforts in the evenings more fulfilling to know that they are "with us."

We never forget to tell ourselves how very fortunate to slow travel, to live in the Marais and explore Paris every day.

A bright and sunny day, a few clouds but no rain. I am off to the Louvre. It's Monday. My infatuation with the 17th–18th-century French painters continues to take me to the Louvre. I especially enjoy these influencer painters, particularly Nicolas Regnier, Georges de La Tour, Louis-Leopoldo Boilly, Théodore Géricault and the academic movement grand master, Ernest Meissonier. Once again I had the entire floor virtually to myself, seemingly for at least for a couple of hours. The place was packed elsewhere with school groups, spring break groups, Japanese and Americans throughout this huge edifice. After many, many visits to the Louvre, the crowds and tourists are invisible to me.

I was back at the flat for lunch with Em. Later we walked to the Centre Pompidou for a read and research in their outstanding bookshop and a spot of tea in the cafeteria. There is spring in the air in Paris.

We were invited by our next-door neighbor, Claudette, for dinner tomorrow. We know that Claudette is teaching classes, researching, translating books and documents and spends most days and evenings at the university. We felt privileged, as she was so busy, that she wanted to spend time with us. We agreed on a time that works for her and thanked her for the dinner invitation. Interestingly, we have only chatted with Claudette three times after our first night upon our arrival at the apartment. It appeared that she was not home during the day, and she teaches in the evenings.

Such a dark and dreary morning, it was almost as if dawn never left. Finally, after the rain, the sun appeared for a brief moment and left again for the rest of the day, merely the winter weather rhythms of living in Paris. Nonetheless, we have only two days left on our bus-train passes, so we are going to visit faraway places; not that we could not walk to them, but given the rain and Em's sensitive knee, we bused to the Place de la République and the nearby Canal of St. Martin. This is a Right Bank region and not too far from the Marais but tricky to get there without using the Metro. Em always navigates us to our correct destination, the Place de la République. In 1854 Baron Haussmann incorporated this small square into his grand urban scheme. The bronze low-relief sculptures (1883) represent great historical events. A few blocks from the République lies the Canal Saint-Martin. This peaceful, old-fashioned canal is still navigated by numerous barges. Iron footbridges, nine locks, and rows of chestnut trees make for a serene Paris landscape. One of the oldest Parisian hospitals, St. Louis (1607), pioneered the science of dermatology. The brick and stone buildings of the central courtyard are reminiscent of the Place des Vosges, minutes from our flat on rue des Rosiers. For us, the most interesting fact about this intriguing area was the many Impressionists (e.g., Albert Sisley, Paul Signac and American Frank Boggs) who all painted the canal and barges of St. Martin. A fine exploratory morning and still back in time for lunch.

Dinner at 8:30 next door was a delight. Claudette was so kind and wanted to know more about us, where we live, and if we're loving Paris. We chatted for a bit as she finished preparing the meal. The meal consisted of roasted chicken thighs and legs, with lemon and garlic, brown rice with barley, and haricots verts with almonds, and our bottle of

Sancerre. After we continued our conversation, she presented us with a chocolate creme torte. She told us that unfortunately she did not have time to make the torte herself; it was delicious, as was the entire meal. We asked her many questions about non-tourist sites to visit, churches with distinctive architecture, new exhibits, where to find out what is happening in Paris, and what is the best jazz station to listen to. I asked if I could take notes so as to not forget, and she said, "of course." She was well versed in everything we mentioned. We learned that Claudette has been teaching at the Sorbonne, in the linguistic department, for over 35 years. She speaks fluent English, Arabic, Hebrew, Armenian and Russian. We could not help opening our months in an "O" shape as she indicated that she had studied languages for over 50 years and very quietly indicated "that she had a pretty good ear for languages." What a delightful night with Claudette. We knew that she either had some work to do that evening or an early class the next day, so we thanked her for such a marvelous evening and left before it got too late. We were so fortunate to have Claudette as a neighbor and as an across-the-apartment friend.

After our splendid time with Claudette, we wondered why she had so many complaints about the weather, food prices and the present government. Em's response was "It is a kind of sarcastic realism." I was intrigued by her projection, so I found a quote by Oscar Wilde in which he defined sarcasm "as the lowest form of wit but the highest form of intelligence." Perhaps Claudette accepts a situation as it is and just deals with it. What an inspiration to live by. We love Claudette.

Another rainy on-and-off type day—typical spring, I'm told. Em is resting her knee and continues with her excellent drawings and colorful watercolor paintings. She is becoming quite the artist, I dare say. I am off this morning to Parc Monceau in arrondissement #17, which is located just north of the Champs-Élysées district. The park was inspired by the English and German romantic style of the day. A century later (1878) elegant Haussmann-designed mansions were built around its perimeter; now it's mostly museums. The park's features included an oval Roman-style basin used to simulate naval battles, and many whimsical statues and monuments were nestled among the greenery and freshly planted flowers. I followed walk #24 from the book of "Great Walks" to a visit to the Musée Cernuschi at 7 Avenue Vélasquez. Henri Cernushi bequeathed his house and extensive collection of Oriental art to the City of Paris in 1896. Art objects range from the fifth-century stone Bodhisattva to the Tang and Ming Dynasty. I'll definitely bring Em to see this unbelievable collection.

The walk continued to Jean-Antoine Brutus Menier's mansion at #5 Avenue Van-Dyck. This chap was a chemist who was looking for a tasty coating for pills and blended refined sugar and cocoa solids. Behold! The small bars of chocolate as we know them today.

Along the walk was an excellent pagoda belonging to C.T. Loo, the preeminent dealer of Chinese antiquities, where he started his shop in the 1900s.

In keeping with the various cultured sites, I stopped at the Russian Orthodox Cathedral on rue de Courcelles, which had a very interesting aesthetic. The cathedral was designed by the Academy of Fine Arts in St. Petersburg and included five gilded onion domes symbolizing candles, each small spire symbolically burning heavenward represents a flame. Picasso married his first wife, Olga Khokhlova, here in this church. The interior is ornately decorated with paintings, icons and gold-backed mosaics.

I finished off this rather long day with another visit to Saint-Paul-Saint-Louis church, minutes from our flat, to view Delacroix's 1826 oil painting of the "Olive Jardin" once more. Just another day of enjoyment in Paris.

Another sunny and bright day as we begin our 85th day in Paris. Thus, we still have 35 days to enjoy the pleasures and treasures of Paris. As Em is working on her drawings, watercolors and Paris map, I set off to a gem of a museum called Cognacq-Jay Museum, not more than eight blocks from our flat. Ernest Cognacq, founder of the Samaritaine department store, bequeathed this collection of 18th-century European art to the City of Paris. Moreover, as this is another City of Paris Musée, it's free, and such a deal since there are many great paintings to be viewed. I found out that there are over 16 free museums that are operated by the City of Paris. The Hotel Donon, the 16th-century house-museum, was replete with 18th-century French paintings by Jean-Antoine Watteau, Jean-Baptiste-Simeon Chardin, La Tour, Boilly, Jean-Honoré Fragonard, Boucher, and Italian painters Canaletto and Tiepolo. To my utter surprise were English painters including Francis Cotes, Daniel Gardner and Thomas Lawrence, about whom I knew very little. Oh, even a Rembrandt portrait. The objets d'art section had furniture of the 1700s and a major collection of porcelain figurines by Meissen, as well as quality 16th-century tapestries. This was indeed a special art history and architectural learning experience, as one can never underestimate the treasures that are everywhere in Paris.

One of our major influencers as teachers was Eleanor Duckworth, and her intellectual and sensitive brilliance was still with us today. As we are "growing" into our new and different learning experiences, Eleanor immediately came to mind with her quote in *The Having of Wonderful Ideas*: "You don't want to cover a subject; you want to uncover it," was so right regarding her thinking about how children learn. As adults we are learning that it is more valuable to uncover (i.e., take the time to observe, orient, reflect, and study the aspects of our explorations and discoveries and not just blow by to have the experiences). Needless to say, just seeing, admiring and moving on is not quite as intrinsically motivating, nor does it promote heuristic application and results.

After lunch Em and I walked to the Isle of St. Louis to a clothing store, bookstore, and cookie shop to purchase a few birthday gifts for our youngest grandson's fifth birthday. We boxed up the gifts and went to the post office to send the gift box. Wish we were with him to celebrate his fifth. We reasoned that there would be many more birthdays to celebrate with our grandchildren once we returned.

Behold! A rather dark and rainy day is upon us, and I reckoned that Em would continue with her embroidering of the Paris streets and rest her knee. I dashed off to the Louvre to find a few of the 80–90 paintings listed in a marvelous book called *Paintings That Changed the World: From Lascaux to Picasso* by Krause Reichold and Bernhardt Graf. Their contention was that those paintings changed the world either by making history visible or creating history themselves. A rather ambitious book but certainly relevant in my quest to learn more about those areas of which I know little. The book's juxtaposition was looking at world-famous and less famous works of art and their relationship in the way we look at our world. The book also brilliantly overviews the great art from a cultural aspect: their lifestyles, milieu, and historical importance of the events depicted. Of course, not all the paintings in the book are in the Louvre, but several are, and I was off to seek and spy. I am rather obsessed with this quest to find out things and why.

However, the logistics in the Louvre on a Friday morning in April was something of a surprise. Fortunately, when I arrived early in the morning, I had the French painting rooms basically to myself. At 11 a.m. I moved to the Italian paintings, which were so packed that it was even difficult going up and down the stairs due to the volume of human traffic.

Notwithstanding the crowding, I did manage to view some marvelous works including the following:

- Viewed the recently unveiled Cy Twombly muraled ceiling in the Sully Wing of the Salle des Bronzes. Twombly was a huge hit in Rome when we were there, and we visited his special exhibits several times. The Virginia-born "pop artist" made history as he was only the third contemporary artist who had ever designed a permanent room for the Louvre; Braque was one, and I do not know the third. Twombly's ceiling covers 3,700 square feet in the Salle des Bronzes. His classical coloring scheme was blue sky along with simple yellow and dark blue spheres and dark blue Hellenic rings. He cleverly weaved names of Ancient Greek sculptures, for example, Lysippos, Myron, Phidias, Polyclitus and Praxiteles, written in Greek letters. To say that the effects were tranquil, graceful and elegant at the same time is an understatement indeed.
- Found François Boucher's portrait of Madame Pompadour. What was the reason this painting changed the historical context of the time? Madame la Marquise de Pompadour was the mistress to King Louis XV, but she became the power behind the throne at Versailles. Furthermore, F. Boucher, who was the Court Painter to the king, painted this portrait probably as a symbol and hint about her political ambitions (e.g., seal, pen and letter). Of course, she did become a power to reckon with when it came time for the king to appoint ministers and make major decisions.
- An easy find, as I have viewed the painting before: Claude Lorrain's oil painting of the "Seaport with the Embarkation of the Queen of Sheba," another French 17th-century painter. It was in this painting that Lorrain became famous in art history for being the first painter to exploit overtly the power of the play of light and atmospheric effects on paintings. This seaport painting showed sun reflecting off the surface of the water, which was a brand-new composition technique, and this method revolutionizes the use of beams of light to describe haze, fog and, coupled with the harmony of the sky-sea-land, a seascape-landscape dynamo.
- My fourth find was a painting by 18th-century painter Antoine-Jean Gros and his painting of "Napoleon at the Bridge of Arcole" in 1796. The significance of this painting in changing the world, according to authors Reichold and Graf, was that Gros' painting captured this action of a small-of-stature commander with long unkempt hair at the Battle of Arcola, which was an important victory for Bonaparte over the advancing Austrian troops. This land-taking battle painting eventually gave rise to Napoleon's prominence in the French Empire.
- For my final pilgrimage discovery, I was to find Rococo artist Jean-Antoine Watteau's "Gilles," or "Pierrot" and four other characters from the Commedia dell' Arte. This one painting was the easiest as I passed this painting many times in my exploration in the Louvre. The significance of this painting was that nobility liked to dress up, mostly to amuse themselves—not much to do anyway, I guessed—and Watteau liked to dress up as well. He was particularly taken with the character in Italian improvised comedy, "Gilles." This sad sack of a clown appears several times in Watteau's work. The work demonstrates the ethos of

Painting by Twombly located in the Sully Wing of the Louvre, in Salle des Bronzes Antiques. The blue sky and floating spheres are scripted with Greek sculptures. Twombly was influenced by his fascination with Greek and Roman antiquity and mythology, and was the first American to create a permanent artwork for the Louvre Museum.

theater during those times of the 1700s where, before this painting, nobody knew of this type of entertainment existing in a painting. This, the authors contend, changed the world leading up to the discovery of photography in the early 1800s.

Well, these were my discoveries for today. I hope to visit several more times to exploit my amateur capacities to find out.

Ode to spring: brings more rain, but the warmth of the sun shall no doubt arrive sometime today. A couple of neighborhood walks were planned for today. The resident artist is still creating and resting her knee. I take my usual walk around, as there is always something new to be discovered or revisited. For instance, the lovely and peaceful Parisian lane on rue des Barras next to St. Gervais Church, lined with quaint shops and red and blue painted facades, which are on the back side of the church. A very enjoyable and mindful experience.

As you might suspect, the Easter holiday is huge for tourists in Paris. As Sunday and Monday are public holidays and everything will be closed, Em mentioned that I ought to purchase groceries for at least three days, which I did.

Skyped home; eggs and chocolate were the focus of discussion.

Almost everything was open in our neighborhood on this Easter Sunday. This might be explained one of two ways: business is booming today as the tourists are out in force; Easter is not an engaging religious holiday in Paris. The weather is rainy and rather cold for an April in Paris. The lineup to attend Easter Mass at the Cathedral of Notre Dame was a mile long. However, we shall simply take our obligatory walk around the neighborhood, even if the weather is not very appealing. The sun shall RISE!

A brilliant sunny morning is upon us. This is the morning after Easter Sunday; everyone is out, but for some reason many shops from our neighborhood remain closed. Perhaps this is their day off after working on a holiday. We sauntered over to Place de Vosges to relax, think and reflect on how fortunate we were to be able to live in Paris for four months on a fixed income.

What a morning! The sky is dark blue with not a cloud visible. Hopefully the sun will be with us for the entire day. This day marks the three months of slow travel living in Paris. Sitting in one of our favorite outdoor cafés, Foundations, we spent a long time formulating our last month living in Paris. What to revisit? Where have we not experienced but wish to? How to proceed these next 30 days, as Em's knee is "talking" to her again, literally meaning to rest, use ice and then walk when she is ready. We gave this last month's itinerary much thought and decided to go and do whatever our minds, hearts and bodies directed us. In other words, all discovery and exploration will yield surprises and learning opportunities.

For today, we enjoyed our slow strolling through our immediate Marais environment. There are many beautiful examples of 15th–19th-century architecture, narrow medieval streets and small parks all around us, and we believed that we certainly missed many discoveries within Marais's 3rd and 4th arrondissements. The morning walk took us to the St. Paul area and off rue Rivoli, along rue Charlemagne, the medieval street that hugs the longest surviving remains of the Philippe Auguste Wall, the oldest city wall, dating to the late 12th century.

Of special interest to us was the Lycee Charlemagne, founded by Napoleon in 1804. The Lycee offers two-year courses in mathematics, physics, chemistry and engineering science to prepare students for entry to the Grandes Écoles, which are French university institutes. It was inspiring and gratifying to observe the number of female students attending this school. We have been on rue Charlemagne a number of times and have seen a good number of female students eating and, unfortunately, smoking before and after classes. This was a very quiet area, as tourists do not generally hang in this part of the Marais, although those tourists "in the know" will not want to miss the architecture and history associated with this area. Em and I walked back to the BHV department store on rue Rivoli to stock up on her art supplies. We enjoyed and appreciated our explorations.

The weather is acting as if it will eventually rain sometime this afternoon. After cleaning up the apartment and dashing to the Monoprix for laundry soap and toilet paper, I returned but exited to the Left Bank. I had no particular site in mind, just a walk until lunchtime. I arrived at the Jardin des Plantes where there were numerous attractions to delight my curiosity, for example, the Museum of Natural History, the menagerie, zoo, the Museum of Geology and the botanical gardens, whose florae will be blooming in two weeks. I did locate a rock that was recorded to be 35,000,000 years old! This large park-like setting manages to combine culture and science with pleasure, and makes science available to all. Em and I will come back in a couple of weeks to take in the Museum of Natural History and view the gardens as well.

After lunch we walked to the Musée Cognacq-Jay and appreciated the marvelous 18th-century art collection. Afterwards, we stopped at Café Hugo at 22 Place des Vosges and ordered our café creams and began to contemplate our very fortunate situation here in Paris and how pleased we were with how we have managed so far with our language and budget limitations. We give absolute credit for our confidence and happiness to the French people, who have been ever so kind and patient with us. We contemplate that we do not eat out very often, but to balance the budget and to foster exploration, we do not regret that situation. In fact, we have talked about returning sometime to Paris with perhaps more opportunities to eat in restaurants and, in those original Parisian incarnations, the bistros.

Another spring-like day awaits us as we accept the fact that this is our 92nd morning in Paris. My new plants, daffodils and crocuses are flourishing on our windowsills. It really seems not that long ago that we left the USA, our children and three grandchildren, whom we miss terribly, but with Skype, postcards and emails, we are rather well connected.

We had nothing on our agenda, so I went on a walk to find more 16th-century mansions designed by François Mansart, the architect that designed many buildings around our neighborhood. First, on rue de L'Abbé Migne I find the Baroque-style Église Notre-Dame-des-Blancs-Manteaux, or "Our Lady of the White Cloaks," original sanctuary site in 1258, and the present church from the 1600s. The interior features of this church were attractive, with magnificent Flemish carved-wood pulpit with inlaid ivory and pewter all framed in gilded and fretted woodwork, typical of the Rococo style (1700s).

From my approach from rue de Rivoli, along rue de Bretagne, I'm confronted with the 900-meter-long, almost ten U.S. football fields, Archives de Paris. The Archives make more than 5,000,000 digitized archives available to the public and stores all of France's most significant historical documents for the educational benefit of the French public.

I admired the facades of the sumptuous 17th–18th-century mansions. Accordingly, at number 58 the Hotel de Soubise—which is the oldest of the mansions, dating to the 14th century—I observed a sturdy pair of turrets and a lovely horseshoe-shaped courtyard.

The mansion at #60, built in 1650 by none other than the architect man, François Mansart—wow! The beautiful small formal garden, simple harmonious lines of the mansion, and of course the Mansart roof with the dormers at the lower section, which brought the roof lines all together in a congenial pattern. François Marsart also gave the present appearance to the Hotel Carnavalet, which is the location of the Museum of the History of Paris.

After lunch we decided to see an exhibit at the Grand Palais, that great exhibition hall near the Champs-Élysées. Unfortunately, the free exhibit was not free, and the hefty entrance fee was not attractive to us today. Our alternative was to cross the street to the marvelous Petit Palais, one of our favorite free museums, but the line was so long due to increased security measures; as it's the tourist season, we decided to have a slow, meandering walk along the overcrowded and very bourgeois Champs-Élysées. After the slow stroll, we found our bus and headed back to rue des Rosiers.

Today, for me, was an anticipated visit to the Palais de Justice de Paris. I was hoping to have a look inside this pillar-of-justice building. I must have looked somewhat "official" wearing a blue blazer and gray slacks, since nobody stopped me from looking around. I actually found this to be more social-culturally interesting than the adjacent, lovely Gothic-style Ste. Chapelle. I witnessed a court proceeding where the two female lawyers each had a go at stating their arguments in front of two female judges; obviously, I had no idea what they were presenting, but it didn't matter to me. Furthermore, I was also able to view the enormous Sainte-Chapelle interior from an altogether different perspective, that was, from high up in the law-court building. It was unbelievable and very fortunate that I was not stopped or questioned about my intrusion.

Home in time for lunch. Em and I went for a stroll in the arrondissement #5 so she could procure some fabric, yarn and Liberty border tape. We had a sit-down in a park near the St. Eustache church and gazed at one of Paris' most beautiful Gothic structures with its Renaissance decorations lit up in the brilliant sunshine.

What a really pleasant day it will be today. The sun is bright, and the clouds are nonexistent. The apartment needed cleaning and polishing, which we completed by late morning. Em and I walked to the antique fair at the St. Paul Village several blocks along rue Rivoli. The antiques were similar to all "flea market" antiques: nothing special, not even an old painting by one of the masters. We had our lunch in the park as the temperatures were in the high 50s. We had spent many days in the small parks around our neighborhood, and they have always been very peaceful and everyone cleans up after themselves, which continually makes the parks so pleasant to sit or eat or reflect in.

We are certainly getting spoiled with the spring sunshine. As in Rome and Florence, the closer to spring and the nicer the weather, the busier and more hectic the city becomes. The Paris tourist season is well ahead of that in Rome at this time of the year. Of course, Paris has more people concentrated in such a small geographic area than Rome, but still it appears to "grow" more people each passing day. We knew from our Rome experience to visit the museums and historical sites early on in the winter before the "people–bloat" commenced. Therefore, our remaining days feature more leisure time, reading, talking and walking to and from the park. We have visited most of the major museums and exhibits in Paris, so we can relax and enjoy watching the visitors rush about, most trying to find where the museums are located and looking for the historical markers, which are of course all over each arrondissement and neighborhood. Today was such a day, as we enjoyed the bright skies and sunshine and avoided contact with the masses. We never forget how fortunate we are to experience this slow travel in Paris.

We are off this early morning to the Champs de Mars and the Eiffel Tower. The lines were lengthy and the rain clouds began to form. A change of direction led us to visit both the permanent and temporary exhibits at the Cité de L'architecture at 1 place du Tro-cadéro in arrondissement #7. This museum's permanent collections illustrated an insight-ful history from the Middle Ages to present day. The three galleries that made up the Musée des Monuments Français were: the gallery of casts, which offers a chronological journey through France's heritage from the 12th to 18th centuries, with ancient models to show the connections; the gallery of wall paintings, a collection of copies of wall paint-ings from the 12th–16th centuries, mostly representing works of French mural art; and a gallery of stained-glass copies which included the methods to make stained glass, various forms and colors of the glasses.

There was also a temporary exhibit of Claude Parent's drawings and building designs from 1960 to 2000. We learned that he designed everything: power plants, supermarkets, private houses, and commercial buildings. His designs were very modern, using con-crete, aluminum, curves and unique windows. We read from the plethora of available books, articles and documents that Claude Parent was one of France's most revered mod-ernist architects and an elected member of the Académie des Beaux-Arts. What I partic-ularly fancied about Claude was his "La fonction oblique" theory (1965) for which he is most famous. He declared that buildings should be all about ramps, slopes and angles, wall-free when possible, and most importantly, that space should predominate over the surface. We studied his detailed and fanciful drawings. Just a fabulous discovery of such an avant-garde legend. Well done, Em.

A charming day is in store for us today. All the atmospheric conditions we love in Paris would certainly highlight the brilliance of the architecture: a bit of fog, a bit of sunshine, a bit of clouds and a bit of drizzle. Off for a delightful walk to the Bastille neighborhood next to the Marais in arrondissement #7. We found, near the Cologne de Juillet, where the Canal Saint-Martin enters into the River Seine. Our purpose today, as always, was to seek new sites, statues and plaques that are everywhere if you carefully observe. Along our walk we found an interesting statue commemorating the famous French poet Arthur Rimbaud (1854–1891), and the Hotel Fieubet (1519), the home of the first President of the Math Society of France; very impressive finds, I might add! A slow walk home in time for lunch. An inspiring and successful treasure hunt in the arrondissement #7.

A splendid sunshiny day greeted us. It seems that almost every morning we man-age to walk down rue des Rosiers to Francs-Bourgeois into the Place des Vosges. We have been watching as Paris slowly has been colored by the spring, especially in the Vosges, as the chestnut trees are displaying their pink and white blossoms and are almost in full bloom. We noticed the magnolias springing to life, apple blossoms fronting the Hotel de Ville, and the lovely cherry blossoms around the Cathedral of Notre Dame. Springtime in Paris is something very special.

After lunch we walked to the Musee National du Moyen Âge Thermes et Hôtel de Cluny (aka the Musée Cluny) at 28 rue du Sommerard, 5th arrondissement. This museum encompassed two architectural marvels: The Gallo-Roman baths, dating from the second century BCE, and the Hotel des Abbes de Cluny, built in the 1400s. The exterior was exuberantly detailed with interlacing curves on the façade—it is so Middle Ages! Behold! Inside we find sculptures, ceramics, tapestries, and medieval art. However, the highlight, "The Lady with the Unicorn" tapestries, are world famous, and we were to observe them in their glory. These tapestries were the finest examples of floral designs that were woven in the Netherlands during the 15th century. Incidentally, we were able to get up close and personal to the artifacts, whereas in most medieval buildings it had always been difficult to see the details on the capitals, stonework, carvings or columns. The museum had devoted 24 galleries to the Middle Ages, including stained glass, ironworks and illuminated manuscripts. Em's knee held up fine. We stopped to rest and have a couple of café cremes at Jodi Café near the Panthéon. We are so lucky to be able to live in Paris and observe, study and learn amongst these historical opportunities. We sat outside watching the people, mostly energetic students, seemingly from every part of the world, as the Sorbonne is a couple of blocks away.

Whoa, such a grand day for everyone. It will not get past the mid–50s but with the glorious sunshine for everyone to enjoy. Our morning walk took us to the Palais-Royal to see the magnolia trees and horse chestnut trees faithfully blooming. The last time we were here there were no fountains operating nor were the trees or flowers in bloom. How rapidly spring weather changes the florae and somehow turns on the fountains. A short walk and we are at the Louvre's Richelieu gate; the line at the pyramid was always long and slow moving, but we used the Richelieu entrance because of the yearly membership pass, and we moved straight through. I had convinced Em to join me as I was studying the German, Dutch and Flemish Renaissance painters. First, I wanted to know more about them, especially the 17th-century Dutch Golden Age painters, and second, there was never a crowd there. Em, having recently studied Albrecht Dürer, pointed out to me several features and techniques he used as evidenced in his masterful woodcut prints. Em knows so much more about art and architecture than I will ever know, but I'm learning. I lingered, stared and admired the compelling realism of Hans Holbein's portraits. Moreover, I was totally intrigued and fascinated with the works of Rubens, Rembrandt, van Eyck, Hals and everyone's favorite, Vermeer. Our "free" access to the Musée du Louvre encouraged us to spend slow time there and learn much during our remaining time in Paris.

This is our 100th day of slow travel in Paris. A bright, sunny, but chilly day was ready for us to explore a number of very old, decorative stone heads that have been submerged into the old stone walls around Square George Cain, a small park on rue Pavée, a few blocks from rue des Rosiers. The stone faces we reckoned were probably 250–300 years old and have faded into the existing stone walls that surround the park. We have been here many times but never to look carefully at these rather invisible old faces, quite similar to us humans when we get older. However, we believe that we have not lost one ounce of exuberance, energy, endless curiosity, or active learning in our lives, thanks to slow travel. As we are getting up in the age bracket, sort of, we like to think that we have not withered like a leaf nor feel that we are no longer needed by our family, or are losing our sense of purpose for growing our interests and uncovering wonder. The greater the repertoire of our actions, thoughts and study, the more capable we are to see and feel relationships and connections in our minds and hearts. Slow travel does this to you.

In the afternoon we slow traveled to arrondissement #6, in Montparnasse, and to the Musée Zadkine. Ossip Zadkine, a Russian-born sculptor, moved to Paris in 1910. He sensitively sculpted in wood and stone. He came through the Cubist period, taking inspiration from Greek and Roman classical art, which gave his work an abstract suppleness and movement and feel. Zadkine bequeathed all his possessions to the City of Paris when he died in 1967. The Musée Zadkine is the only public collection holding his work. This is another of the City of Paris' free museums and another example of a wonderful museum that cost nothing to enjoy in Paris. A temporary exhibit at the Musée Zadkine by Chinese sculptor Wang Keping, who moved to Paris in 1984 after he suffered from the anti-culture movement of Mae Zedong's Cultural Revolution. Over 30 sculptures in wood were presented. His work is large, bold and exotic. His use of natural wood to develop movement and grace was special. Between these two sculptors, we were fortunate to witness a very special exhibit. How thankful we are to experience such art as we slow travel in Paris.

We took a bucolic walk through the elegant Jardin du Luxembourg, created by Queen Marie de' Medici in 1612, and an oasis of greenery that is split into a French and English garden in the heart of the Latin Quarter. This is a very popular place where locals, tourists, and students can sit and absorb the airy and inspiring atmosphere of Paris' premier garden. Em's knee held up beautifully for almost five hours; found our bus and back to rue des Rosiers. Great job, Em!

Park sitting is another approach to loving Paris. Accordingly, today we are off to the far southeastern border of Paris to enjoy the wonderful weather at the huge Bois de Vincennes, a vast woodland with natural attractions such as flower gardens, a zoo and sculpture garden. Therein is a mighty time-warped medieval fortress: Le Château de Vincennes. Each area of the park specializes in a particular type of flower (e.g., tulips, azaleas, etc.). Of special interest were the outdoor sculptures created by Calder and Giacometti within the Parc Floral. Another added attraction was the four seasons garden that was growing medicinal plants and bamboo. Because the entrance fee for this park was suspended until May 1, it was absolutely packed with families and park lovers just like us.

Interestingly, we saw little evidence of birds in Paris, so we were excited to see swans, mallards, sparrows, magpies and mourning doves. Perhaps later on in the season more birds and butterflies will appear. A short walk to the metro station and in 20 minutes we are at St. Paul's station and on to rue des Rosiers. A lovely nature day at the southeastern border of Paris.

Behold! What a day! Temperatures in the 60s, beautiful dark blue skies and dry. This has to be the overall best weather day of our 102 days so far. Everyone is out and about, and all the shops, restaurants, bakeries and bars are open and busy. The streets around where we live are closed off to vehicles on Sundays, so walking is a dream. We opted to go to our favorite bakery and purchased a chicken sandwich with sun-dried tomato, a raspberry tart, and a bottle of water and went to the nearest park, Jardin Des Rosiers, around the corner from the bakery. We got lucky and found a bench, as all the other stone benches were completely full. We placed a couple of napkins over the bird crap and sat down and congratulated ourselves with the lucky seat timing. We found out very quickly why no one was sitting on that bench. Pigeons were taking dead aim from above at that bench; quickly, we moved to the edge of the park and waited five or ten minutes before someone left, and we took that bench. Skyped everyone and we laughed!

One really gets the sense of Parisian family life while sitting and watching in neighborhood parks, especially on Sunday. This particular playground, similar to most, had only a sandpit and a miniature climbing slide. Parents were very observant but basically left the children to play without much interference. The children generally played well with each other, with the occasional sand throwing, but that was quickly suspended with gentle parent intervention. Most of the families at this time of the day bring their light lunch, as we did, and eat and allow the children to have fun. An observation: the children sat with their parents; there was no running around eating. That, apparently, was a no-no, at least from our perspective. Occasionally, there were American and British families in the park, and their two- to six-year-old children merely merged effortlessly with the other children to play. Today we saw three children with plastic swords chasing each other around the playground. We have yet to see play guns or knives, just swords. Skyped home, a tad later than usual, but everyone welcomed our call and chats. For some reason the three grandchildren looked taller, appeared to be very happy, and chatted about school. We told them that we missed them; Cole asked him when we would be returning.

Just an awesome day. Fortunately, we met our neighbor in the hallway, and Claudette told us that the gold–glassy dust we will see overhead is from Iceland's volcano. We always chat with Claudette when we see her, which, unfortunately isn't enough. She had a tutor class at 9 p.m., so she had to run. She was an incredible woman, knowledgeable about art, music, theater, languages, history, and jazz. She explained that TSF Jazz 89.9 was the best. Now we listen to that station all the time.

Today is all about Em. I walked to rue de Bac to purchase her coffee. Returned to the Louvre and for the third time entered via Port of the Lions—never any lines and it takes me straight to the Spanish paintings on the first floor of the Denon Wing. I read a biography of Diego Velázquez and was interested in his work and painters of his 17th-century Baroque contemporaries, including Francisco de Zurbaran, José de Ribera, and Bartolomé Esteban Murillo. My favorite painting by Velázquez was his character portrait in brilliant naturalistic style of the young princess, called Las Meninas. Incidentally, Velázquez' naturalistic approach to his paintings later influenced the arising styles of both Impressionism and Realism. Had the experience, found the connective meaning. The Louvre was not that crowded when I arrived, but, by the time I left two hours later, it was packed. Stopped at Naturalia shop on 59 rue Saint-Antoine for Em's chai tea, the only shop that sells chai tea and almond milk. Home for lunch.

Today to the Musée National Gustave Moreau at 14 rue de la Rochefoucauld in arrondissement #9. Gustave Moreau was an 18th-century painter in the Symbolism Movement. He was influenced by the color technique of Eugène Delacroix, Italian Renaissance, and the painter, Théodore Chassériau. Moreau's paintings feature all three styles: fantastical, biblical and mythological subjects. When Moreau died, he bequeathed his house and life's collection to the French nation, including 850 paintings, 7,000 drawings, 350 watercolors, and wax sculptures. He was a particularly detailed artist, and his paintings reflect his dedication to his combined styles. Hidden behind a small door was a rare portrait painting of Moreau by his friend, E. Degas. An unusual, terrific museum to visit, linger and reflect. Nearby we found the local park and had a nice sit-down after the confines of the smallest Musée-house. Em's knee held up fine. Yay!

Another fine spring morning for us and everyone else. We exited early this morning to enjoy the marvelous Musée du Petit Palais. Although there were long lines waiting for entrance due to the special Yves Saint Laurent exhibit, Em found another entrance that saved us the long wait in line. We headed straight for the Café at the Musée. We had a simple lunch before exploring once again this huge and airy museum. This museum was completely restored in 2006 to include everything from medieval and Renaissance art to 19th-century paintings and paintings by Delacroix, Courbet, Pissarro and Mary Cassatt, our favorite. It is just a pleasure and a comfort to be inside this place as one feels completely at ease amid the leisurely flow through the collections. Afterwards, we sat for a while in the Jardin des Tuileries and reflected upon our good fortune and health.

Our hearts are singing as the deliriously marvelous weather continues. Em is resting her knee today, as she should occasionally. Plenty to do: clean the flat and plan on where to have a great lunch. We celebrated our fourth or fifth restaurant lunch out during our stay at Le Sévigné at 15 rue du Parc Royal, just a few blocks from our flat. This was a typical French bistro, and the staff and owner were very friendly and patient with us non–French-speaking Americans. A simple meal—an omelet with mushrooms, ham and cheese, spinach quiche, two green salads, a small carafe of house wine. Wonderful meal, lovely atmosphere and great staff.

Another fine day—we have been fortunate to have such a dry and sunny April, as it should rain a lot during April in Paris.

"The charm of spring" lyrics sung beautifully by Ella Fitzgerald, Doris Day, Frank Sinatra, Billie Holiday, and Sarah Vaughan and performed very tastefully by Glenn Miller, Thelonious Monk and Count Basie.

With those endorsements, we are off for an afternoon at the Musée du Louvre to view many visual languages of sculpture, tapestries and paintings. Em scampered off to view the French paintings of the 15th–17th centuries while I hightailed to view the Middle Ages tapestries and French sculptures. I am reading an unbelievable, inspiring book by Susan Groag Bell called *The Lost Tapestries of the City of Ladies*, a true legacy about a woman writer (1364–1430) named Christine de Pizan. It is an allegorical story, which is about 200 women: warriors, scientists, queens, philosophers who built cities, and the tapestries told her story. The lost tapestries developed from de Pizan's book went missing until just a few years ago. This unique story reveals the historical, cultural and linguistic aspects of this story and provides a fascinating account of medieval and early Renaissance tapestry production and of Christine de Pizan's remarkable life and legacy. I had to observe very carefully to appreciate the work of those artists. Although the original six panels of tapestry in the book are not at the Louvre, it motivated me to become more interested in the Louvre's tapestries. After three hours, we met at the Starbucks inside the museum for the second time.

Wow! Another brilliant, sunny and warm day in the "marsh" (Marais) of Paris. This probably will be the warmest day of the spring (i.e., into the high 60s). Em is resting her knee, and the apartment requires cleaning as we've been opening the windows to enjoy the fresh air. I pop into the bakery to procure lunch in the park at Square du Denon, minutes from rue des Rosiers. We brought plenty of reading materials and, of course, our daily notebook to plan for upcoming events and a projected return site list. We take our obligatory after-dinner walk in the City of Light.

Simply speaking, just another spring-like day in Paris—sunny, warm and plenty busy. These days are so rewarding as they allow us to leisurely lunch in the park. Today a return visit to Square George Cain, which is minutes from our flat. The setting is gorgeous with 10–12 benches, full blooming tulips, pansies, daffodils, and a myriad of various colored flowers. We share one baguette of chicken, sun-dried tomatoes, lettuce and a splash of lemon-basil dressing, a half pint of strawberries and a bottle of water. A simple, healthy, weight-and-calorie controlled lunch. Part of sitting in the park is watching people and children playing; for this is enjoyable low-cost entertainment and a reminder of our grandchildren.

On my afternoon walk I encountered two events: First, a French real estate woman speaking English to an American chap in front of a period building on the famous rue des Francs-Bourgeois. The overheard discussion was about the sales price, somewhere between 900,000 and 1,000,000 euros, and exactly when he could move in. It was interesting to observe because the American chap had his small computer in his one hand and was talking on his mobile, presumably with his partner or buyer.

Event number 2: at the other end of rue des Francs-Bourgeois was a professional fashion photo shoot. This event was replete with the young model, a truck for changing, various mirrors, a lighting crew, several women groomers, a makeup staff and four photographers. I have not seen anything quite like this arrangement, which happened to be smack in front of such a busy pedestrian street. Oh, yes, I forgot, we did see such excitement during the Autumn-Fall Fashion Week. Just another day in the park and happenings on rue des Francs-Bourgeois.

Another brilliant spring day is in store for all to enjoy. A typical Sunday and everyone is all about. The parks are full, and the streets are hopping. We had tentative plans today, but Em wanted to finish her book, and I have several daily reports to complete with some final details. We also had to make some simple arrangements for our departure that must be made this week. Our Skype day, looking forward to chatting with everyone.

Only ten more days; how does time slip by so quickly? A super weather morning to begin the week. Em is off to Modern Art Museum and I to the Louvre. After reading the book about Christine de Pizan's "Tapestries and the City of Ladies," I again headed straight to the Renaissance tapestries. Although the six tapestry panels are not to be found here, I did have to admire the 30 or so "woven paintings" at the Renaissance wing. I certainly have a better appreciation of and more insight for how these incredible works of art were made. I really have a new fondness for this type of visual arts. In the 14th century, rare tapestries were more valuable than paintings.

A couple of insights I learned about hanging around rooms dedicated to tapestries were they must be kept cool, cooler than other artwork, and the lights must be dim so the cloth does not fade. So we have a cool room with natural light and beautiful pieces of art to ponder and enjoy. When Em returned from her very productive day at one of her many favorite museums, we shared our impressions, thoughts, and gratitude and called our "field day" a fantastic success.

A splendid day as we begin our wind-down of museum visits before we depart. We are off early this morning to see if the Palais Galliera-Musée de la Mode de la Ville de Paris was finally open for business. The last two times we were there, a sign indicated that it was closed for security reasons. This grand edifice built in Italian Renaissance style has over 60,000 articles of clothing from the 1700s to present. Unfortunately, the same sign indicated the same results. However, after a lovely coffee and pastry at Café Valentin at 1 rue de Chaillot, we diverted straight to the two museums that were next to each other—the Palais de Tokyo, which we found out is not a museum at all but a large space for a laboratory of the visual and performing arts. We moved next to the adjoining building, the Musée d'Art Modern de la Ville de Paris, which showcased the main trends in arts of the 20th century. Paintings representing this period include Chagall, Picasso, Matisse, Dufy, Braque and Leger. The courtyard faced the Eiffel Tower, and we enjoyed this remarkable symbol of Paris, up close and personal. This was a long day, and Em's knee held up nicely. A two-bus ride back to St. Paul to rue des Rosiers completed an exceptionally fine day in arrondissement #16.

Once again, the agreeable weather welcomes us this morning. We are simply going to have a leisurely walk along the River Seine. The weather was perfect for slow walking and watching people. We stopped for coffee at Boot Café on rue du Pont aux Choux and watched a tour group of 45 mature folks walking very slowly, resembling something like a string of ants, in single file and following the zigzag contours of the streets and lanes. It was indeed delightfully comical, and we wished them well. The day was so inviting, we enjoyed a simple lunch in the park. It's the simple pleasure that will last forever.

We are getting used to the glorious spring weather and getting out much earlier than before. We are off to Cité de L'Architecture et du Patrimoine's amazing bookstore to purchase an architectural drawing book that Em has had her eyes on for weeks. The beauty of this particular setting, in addition to its grand bookstore, is that the museum's patio is situated directly in front of the Eiffel Tower. We can enjoy the inexpensive coffee at five euros versus the average cost of seven to nine euros, and we have this amazing view. Because the patio is on a hill overlooking the tower, the gentle breeze keeps everything cool. After lunch we walked over to the Galeries du Panthéon Bouddhique de la Chine et du Japon, which is housed in a superb Neoclassical mansion. In the rear of the museum is an intimate classic Japanese garden, complete with a pond with koi, a bridge, and an operating fountain. Such peace and harmony. Em's knees are holding up rather well as we have extended our daily sightseeing to four to five hours. Great job, as Em is listening to the body and taking care of her knee.

My allergies have only been a bother recently. With the flowers, grasses and trees in bloom, I'm experiencing the typical reaction to seasonal allergies. My asthma symptoms have been suspended, thanks to Dr. Abello. This is the last day of the month of April, and it has literally gone too fast. We are enjoying the spring weather as it has allowed us to enjoy the simple things that Paris has to offer such as the greenery and peacefulness of the squares and parks, the expansion everywhere of the floral colors as seen on our window boxes, and seeing happy folks that are now able to show off their tattoos. Today, Em has really taken her watercolors to a higher level, and she will be able to share these watercolor memories with the grandchildren upon our return.

I made the airport transfers and shuttle service arrangements for our return trip home.

After lunch we took a stroll to the Place des Vosges, our absolute favorite square in all of Paris, for a sit-down and people watch. As we walked on rue de Tournelles, we came across a terrific men's hat shop. I whispered to myself, "Perhaps someday I'll purchase one of those Stetson hats."

Another first for us on our walk was finding an old synagogue, no longer in use, but a beautiful building, nonetheless. Finally, we found a Moroccan restaurant and tea room at 14 rue des Tournelles. The "grandma," which she calls herself, tells us she makes all their 20 assortments of small two-bite size almond cookies and authentic mint tea. Two delightful women demonstrated how the mint leaves are wrapped around the loose tea so the loose tea leaves do not escape into our sweet mint tea. The restaurant served authentic Moroccan food such as La Marina and La Vegetarienne; we sampled and enjoyed both dishes.

It seems, as in Rome and Tuscany, that everywhere we explored we discovered not only exceptional and inspiring sites, but the people we met, even casually, were very gracious, kind and so very patient with us. These kinds of experiences during our slow traveling kept reminding me that nobody is too important not to be kind to people.

We are merely relaxing in our final few days in Paris. We purchase fresh bread, chicken, sun-dried tomatoes, seasonal strawberries, a bottle of water and a few nuts at G-20, the other market was closed, and shuffled off to Buffalo—not exactly, but to one of our many favorite parks or squares, Jardin Anne Frank at 14 Impasse Berthaud, as this bucolic garden pays tribute to Anne Frank. There are three different and unique parts to the park, and chestnut trees were in full bloom. The perfect setting to spend our day in the middle of the sublime scenery.

On the way back to the apartment we stopped at the Swedish National Cultural Institute to look at their permanent exhibit and paintings; regrettably, none of the painters we recognized. However, Em chatted with the guide about their favorite Swedish authors, such as Astrid Lindgren, Kerstin Ekman, and Stieg Larsson, while I didn't have a clue about those authors. However, there was an awesome mobile created by the Swedish painter/sculptor Curt Asker. I inquired how Asker made this incredible mobile; I was told that he merely used catgut to make the pieces almost appear to be suspended without any support. I should have observed that but did not.

After dinner, we took the bus to the Left Bank to visit three architectural wonders:

Église Saint-Sulpice, a church featuring a Renaissance façade with Florentine decorations, and in the Chapel of the Holy Angels, Delacroix's exquisite three paintings on the walls and ceiling: "Jacob wrestling with the angel," "Heliodorus Driven from the Temple," and "Saint Michael slaying the demon" were a fantastic experience.

St.-Germain-des-Prés, the 11th-century Romanesque church which is the oldest in Paris, and the Saint-Germain-l'Auxerrois, a unique confluence of Romanesque to High Gothic to Renaissance.

The significance was architecture from Romanesque 11th-12th centuries to Renaissance 16th century, displayed almost in line with the Boulevard Saint-Germain.

A slow walk back to complete a wonderful and insightful day.

A rather funky day. We started out early to the Musée d'Orsay since we had the yearly pass. However, by the time we arrived, about 10:30, the lines were ten miles long! All bags must be checked. The line would have taken an hour or so to enter the museum, and I could imagine how difficult it would have been to see the paintings with all those folks. We have visited the d'Orsay many times, so we did not think we missed much, although you never can see everything at the d'Orsay.

Because Paris is Paris, there are so many interesting buildings, shops, parks, squares and gardens to see that you can fill up the time without any problems. We walked around the Latin Quarter, just meandering and chatting for hours. We happened to find (hint: name plaques with dates are on the buildings) houses of writers Oscar Wilde, George Sands (nom de plume used by Amantine Lucile Aurore Dupin) and painter Edouard Manet, all of whom lived in this small area. We stopped for a café creme at the Café Les Deux Magots, a famous gathering place for artists, poets, writers, and Julia Child of the '40s–'60s. This café is directly placed across from Saint-Germain-des-Prés. We continued our walk on rue Bonaparte towards the Seine. "Oh, what is this," I cried! On rue Bonaparte we find the famous bakery, Ladurée of Paris! "Is this our pastry day, Em?" "Well, yes, but only a couple." We purchased a few of their famous macarons—airy, crunchy, and made of almonds, sugar and eggs.

We finished our walk by taking the Pont Neuf, which led directly to the Musée du Louvre. We looked at the Pyramid to see what appeared to be a cast of thousands waiting at the entrance. Our bus stop was near the north side of the museum, and hopped on to our flat. Em did great with the knee as we were out for four and a half hours. A funky day indeed but certainly enjoyable. Our only Skype call we have missed. We arrived at the apartment too late to call. I emailed to explain our neglect but was reassured that everything was fine, merely call tomorrow.

A dark and wet day is in store today. We have had such a long string of warm and sunny days we are bound to have an occasional cloudy and drizzly day. Skype day—All is well—Super! Em is resting her knee after her long walk yesterday, and I scamper off for my last visit to the Louvre. Monday mornings are usually not crowded when the Louvre opens, but today the entire building is full. The large groups of Japanese and French and other visitors made for slow and careful access to the tapestries and sculpture rooms. The tapestry hall was not busy at all, but expectedly the Donatello, Michelangelo and Leonardo da Vinci rooms were extremely busy. I had an enjoyable time as always just being in the Louvre. I worked out that by purchasing the Louvre pass for 90 euros, we saved 259 euros or about $390—that included 27 visits to the Louvre. Terrific value for the mind, heart and the money.

As the day was growing short, it began to drizzle, but I stopped to purchase Em's tea and something for dinner. As I took a different route to the apartment, as it happened, I looked at the lunch menu for the month of May at the local nursery school. Every school menu we have observed during our time in Paris, the children received a meat or fish choice, a variety of cheeses and salads, cooked vegetables, fruit of the season and a dessert. I am going back to school, for sure.

A rather cool, damp day, and the sun failed to make an appearance. I enjoyed a walk to Place des Vosges and a sit-down to watch a class of probably 5–7-year-old children running uninhibitedly in the park as their lone teacher sat at a bench and read. I did casually observe a couple of children urinating on a statue and seemingly as happy as the worms in the grass after the rainy morning.

The weather is back to being chilly, windy with intermittent sunshine. For my walk I took my absolutely last visit to the Louvre to observe the many French sculptures in the Richelieu, ground floor. The museum was not as busy when I arrived, but the lines were huge outside when I left at 11:30. This is Paris at its finest.

Today was a serious cleaning of the apartment as we must leave it in perfect shape in order to secure our $2,500 deposit. In the morning we took a walk to the BHV department store to search for grandchildren's gifts. No luck. Their toys are the same as in the states and much more expensive. We walked over to the Red Wheelbarrow Bookstore on 9 rue de Medicis and found six children's books about Paris, a French edition of "Where is Waldo in Paris?" and a French version of Monopoly. Em suggested that the Monopoly game might help my French.

We always prepare a pre- and post-list of essential things to do. For departure, our checklist included bringing all electronics and cords, leaving some books behind, but collecting all documents, passports, medicines, journals, and clothes. Fortunately, we were able to say our goodbyes to our loving and very kind neighbor as she was getting ready to leave for work. We gave her a Soeur scarf and an assortment of Mariage Frères teas; she was so very thankful. We hugged, and I thought I saw tears on Claudette's cheeks—they were matching ours.

As instructed, I left both sets of keys on the marble tray.

Left rue des Rosiers at 9:30 a.m., arrived at Charles De Gaulle airport at 10:35 a.m.—a bit slow due to Friday commuter traffic and two accidents along the way. A seven-and-a-half-hour flight to Boston and home by 12 our time.

Looking forward to reuniting with our own children and of course with our three grandchildren. We will have several months with them and time to decide if and when we shall continue our quest to explore, learn and wonder some more.

Paris awakened new curiosities and created a demand for more information. A truly remarkable experience in many respects. We are grateful for the privilege of being able to live and learn in another culture. We were thankful for and appreciative of the French people's kindness, attentiveness and patience. We are now more confident than ever to continue our slow traveling on our fixed income, knowing full well that we must be creative in managing what resources we have.

Reflections on our nine months of slow travel living in Rome, Florence and Paris

My fear was contaminating our memories by overthinking about them, as I know that false memories are oftentimes slippery. However, our goal when we left our families and our grandchildren for nine months was to be perpetual learners; basically, learning how to learn about the wonders of history, culture, art and architecture. From our relevant, organic and interdisciplinary experiences in Rome, Florence and Paris we perceived those active, hands-on involvements as building blocks or scaffolding for our continuing slow travel. We have already decided to return to Rome and Paris

In education, scaffolding consists of experiences (relevant, organic and interdisciplinary) used to move students progressively toward deeper understanding and greater independence in their learning process.

"The search for wisdom begins with wonder," said Socrates.

Our nine months abroad as seniors in Rome, Florence and Paris allowed us to appreciate and love each other's thoughts, feelings, idiosyncrasies, curiosities, purposes and dispositions. Accepting and respecting our enduring, individual attitudes of minds were important consequences as they relate to subsequent slow travel adventures. Such habits of mind as humor, wonder, curiosity and helpfulness were true reconciliations between our hearts and minds.

Our most persistent theme throughout this nine-month endeavor was the critical importance of linking our former educational beliefs to new learning and experiences. Our educational beliefs derived from the notion that meaning can be grasped only by first calling to mind more familiar things and then tracking out the connections between them and what we do not understand. These ideas are related to careful observation and reflection in a sustained effort to develop our own theory of life, of reason, from the beginning of learning. We developed, over this time, a dynamic change in the "concrete" acquisition of knowledge (e.g., ideas, facts, concepts, constructs and schemes of thinking about thinking (metacognition) through a combination of active, not passive, learning, observations, study, discussion, questioning and analysis).

Our ultimate purpose, I suppose, when we composed our junior year abroad as seniors, was to improve the learner's (our) understanding of the world. We understand more now than before, but the results of our nine months abroad as seniors encouraged us to continue to learn, seek the historical and cultural connections and view the world with a more inclusive and sensitive open mind and heart.

Eleanor Duckworth said, "Wonder arises not from ignorance but from consciousness of ignorance." We know that we have a lot more to learn.

For Em and Russ, slow travel was a journey into our own ignorances in order to be less ignorant in return.

Our slow travel journey ended in true romance. But then, it began with a purpose and a passion.

PART SIX

Conclusion

Emily and I have had numerous conversations, especially in cafés, about how slow travel has made us more compatible and emphatic and in many ways changed our lives. Of course, each of us has our own individual interpretations and perspectives about these questions. Accordingly, we are in total agreement with respect to the advantages that slow traveling has afforded us.

Yes! Call me egotistical, selfish and insensitive; one would think after 45 years of marriage that I could not have been so blind to what exceptional capacities Emily has as she has enlightened me so brilliantly over the past nine years of slow travel. I've learned that Emily is a decisive decision maker, especially in challenging situations, and we have had several. She has developed into a super navigator, map reader, photographer and bus and train transport mapper. Furthermore, what has been most helpful in our enjoyment of this year's slow travel together is her uncanny problem-solving abilities, which have eased a number of problematic situations that we encountered. I've learned to slow down and observe, orient before just leading off on my own—patience. I have learned to trust Emily's instincts and respect her intuition—these capacities have been instrumental to our continued enjoyment of travel, and sometimes even survival. I became more calm and thoughtful; I certainly improved on becoming a better companion and therefore a better person.

I might mention that Emily might have had a head start on me regarding her Sicilian childhood experiences, her tolerance and inclusionary acceptance. Emily came from a city-living experience, whereas I came from a small rural farming community. She took buses around her city at age eight, walked alone to the library at six years old. I walked or rode my bike to a one-room schoolhouse until fifth grade. Em went to school where her classmates came from different ethnic, religious and cultural backgrounds. I never saw a person of color until I was 15 years old. I did not know what a Jewish or a Muslim person was; she did and understood their culture and mores. I celebrate her background and accomplishments within her neighborhood, as they paid off enormously in my adjustments to people and appreciation for the differences within the many foreign cities and towns during our slow traveling.

The Benefits—And How to Achieve Them

- Find a new purpose. A purpose, passion or idea doesn't exist unless you do something about it. Having spent ten years teaching in England, Spain and Germany lit the initial fuse to learn more about antiquity, art, buildings and cultural history.

- We became active learners by informing ourselves about art/architecture, history, science and other cultures. Always trying to find the meaning of those experiences by studying, observing and reflecting upon the treasure around us. It seems that we have always been inspired by wonder and curiosity. We broadened our horizons further than just books or films might do. We deeply learned to share visual arts expressions.
- We became accountable and reliable researchers and better consumers regarding budget-conscious decisions on accommodations, sight visits, car leases, foreign exchange rates, flights, and everyday customs and living costs in a foreign country.
- We became more aware of suspending judgments or stereotyping. Being aware of the greatest virtue in life, which is kindness, we were only visitors in these countries. We must remember that we are never too important not to be kind to people and try to practice every day.
- We must always remind ourselves in our actions and in our avoidance of conversations about politics, religion or capitalism. We must be responsible American citizens as visitors to their country.
- We have become more agreeable, compromising and more empathetic. We had to be strong and respectful of each other's thoughts, creative notions and feelings so we didn't get derailed or frustrated when unforeseen events and spontaneous challenges arose when traveling overseas. Under challenges and uncomfortable situations, we began to better understand ourselves and how to make those adjustments and improvements.
- We have become more confident in meeting new people, notwithstanding the language barriers. We learned so much from the citizens who live and work in the countries we lived in. Tolerance and understanding was enhanced as a result of uncertainties and our limited knowledge of customs and language.
- An appreciation for the throngs of people who made our slow travel stays so memorable and joyful. They provided us with new knowledge, philosophies and skills. Humbleness is a continuous, slow growth disposition.
- Promoted and enhanced our creativity. Em has always possessed an artistic and creative aptitude. However, during the subsequent ten years since we have returned, she has designed and quilted many colorful and unique art-quilts. She makes most of her own clothes, has learned to draw and use watercolors as memories of our many trips. Creativity for me was to listen, observe, do and learn from her ideas and suggestions. My cognitive flexibility has sharpened, so I'm told. Perhaps even my capacity to integrate art-architecture-history-culture has made some progress. This is because we always had an agreed focus and an engaged purposefulness about where and what we actively pursued. "If not now, when?"
- We have continually improved in living a healthy lifestyle, both abroad and in the states.
- Truth be told: Em's arthritic knees have now become a chronic condition—one reason she always avoided subway stairs in Paris and was extremely careful when attempting all those steep medieval village stone stairways. I have always had seasonal allergies, but traveling in different countries at all seasons has confounded my allergies into aggravating and uncomfortable asthma symptoms. A knee that never felt uncomfortable before, recently required surgery. Travel has interesting sides.

- We have made lasting memories for ourselves and celebrated with our children and grandchildren. They joined us for some of our overseas slow travel stays.
- Happiness, oh, how do I define you? Perhaps we learn to live in the moment—a positive mindset needs to be a constant theme. You realize when traveling and afterward that life is a wonderful gift—Enjoy it to the maximum! An artist acquaintance once told me that "we are but a walnut in the dough of the universe."
- We believe we have enhanced our longevity by living, sharing and loving our joyful life together.
- We are hopeful that we can promote slow travel to everyone that is interested: baby boomers to seniors to students.
- We have learned to value the slow travel experiences over things. Don't think by just having the experience that we also understood the meaning; you have to uncover and explore what you don't understand.
- We built stronger and happier relationships with those people we love back in the USA. The heart grows fonder when away from those you love. Love also grows deeper when we are with them.
- We have learned, over time, to accept and appreciate serendipity and meaningful coincidences that happen when we travel to unfamiliar territories. Em's intelligence, intuition and decision-making capacities made the positive differences.
- Slow travel improved and motivated us to stay healthy. It is difficult to travel when health pre-conditions or handicapping conditions might prevent one from traveling. However, Europe is working towards accommodating those situations in order to make traveling overseas more comfortable and a positive experience.
- It is true that nobody comes back from a journey the way they started it. You bring back more than you brought to a new situation.
- Coping strategies that we learned and accepted have helped us during the coronavirus epidemic. We live in a studio apartment of 575 sq. feet. For the past ten years we can relate to our European living conditions that mostly consisted of small studios, hotel rooms and one-bedroom accommodations for several months at a time while traveling. When you live so closely in small areas you learn to make adjustments in space and in your relationship. We have been married for 55 years, so I have learned how to behave. Living overseas one quickly learns that we cannot control what we cannot control—just like the present situation worldwide. We remind ourselves to purchase (as we were on and still are on a fixed budget) only what we need. No hoarding of t-paper, Clorox and sanitary wipes! Asthma requires strict precautions. Thanks to Silver Sneakers we are practicing yoga and meditating. We never did these wonderful activities before. However, we stayed active when traveling by walking miles and doing simple exercises in our hotel or studios. We can state that slow travel resulted in us being more active and eating healthy and certainly provided the impetus to want to continue to slow travel when it becomes safe to do so.
- Now that we have had first hands-on, real-life experiences as a result of hundreds of hours spent in museums, art galleries and medieval churches, we have been inspired to take online courses from various colleges and universities to continue making connections between and within art, architecture, history, science and culture. Our slow travel experiences have fostered a continuing quest to learn

more and enjoy completely what we could never have if not for our ten years of slow traveling.

There have been many health and cognitive scientists who have studied and written extensively about the benefits of travel.

Larry Alton's article "5 Scientifically Proven Health Benefits of Traveling Abroad" documents the results from a joint study from the Global Commission on Aging and Transamerica Center for Retirement Studies in partnership with the United States Travel Association, proves five benefits of traveling: travel makes you healthier, relieves stress, enhances creativity, boosts happiness and satisfaction, and lowers the risk of depression and heart attacks.

Adam Galinsky, professor and social psychologist at Columbia Business School, has authored several studies that investigate the concrete links between creativity and international travel. Galinsky's finding indicated that foreign experiences increase both cognitive flexibility and depth of thought, the ability to make deep connections between disparate forms. Furthermore, people who have international experience are better problem solvers and managers. For Galinsky, traveling alone isn't enough; therefore, travelers must purposely engage and adapt within the foreign culture.

Thomas Gilovich, professor of psychology at Cornell University, found that most people tend to be happier when they're traveling. This Cornell University study shows that people also experience a direct increase in happiness from just planning a trip, which is far greater than anticipation of acquiring a physical possession. The benefits of traveling abroad begin before the trip and last much longer.

A study published in the *Wisconsin Medical Journal* from the Marshfield Clinic in Wisconsin found that women who vacation at least twice a year are less likely to suffer from depression, chronic stress and tension than women who vacation less. In addition, they found that marital satisfaction decreases as the frequency of travel decreases.

The American Association for Retired People conducted several "Surveys Connected to Health and Wellness Benefits of Travel," from 2018 to 2020. The studies show health benefits experienced during all stages of travel: Travel promotes better emotional and physical health and improves relationships and productivity. Overall well-being is one advantage of travel which begins at the initial planning phase and extends beyond the trip. The survey shows four in five boomers experience at least one health benefit during a trip, and 73 percent notice at least one health benefit post-trip, such as better sleep, more energy, quality time with loved ones and mental clarity and intellectual curiosity. Wellness is not an underlying reason to travel but is a byproduct.

Recommended Reading:
Books That Worked for Us

Burke, Peter. *Hybrid Renaissance: Culture, Language, Architecture.* Central European Univ. Press, 2015.

Childs, Julia. *My Life in France.* Knopf Doubleday, 2006.

Erasmo, Mario. *Strolling through Florence.* 2015.

Farman, Marie. *500 Hidden Secrets of Paris.* Luster Pub., Belgium, 2015.

Freedberg, David. *The Power of Images.* Univ. of Chicago Press, 1991.

Frommer's 24 Great Walks in Paris. Wiley, 2009.

Frommer's 24 Great Walks in Rome. Wiley, 2008.

Goy, Richard. *Florence: The City and Its Architecture.* Phaidon Press, 2002.

Grigoletto, Luisa. *500 Hidden Secrets of Rome,* 2015.

Hersey, George. *Architecture and Geometry in the Age of Baroque.* Univ. of Chicago Press, 2001.

Horowitz, Helen. *A Taste for Provence.* Univ. of Chicago Press, 2016.

Jacobs, Emma. *The Little(r) Museums of Paris.* Running Press, 2018.

Kahn, Robert. *City Secrets of Paris.* Univ. of Chicago Press, 2016.

King, Ross. *Brunelleschi's Dome.* Bloomsbury Publishing, 2000.

Mayes, Frances. *See You in the Piazza.* Crown/Archetype Publisher, 2019.

Meyers, Jeffery. *Impressionist Quartet.* Harcourt Books, 2005.

Morrissey, Jake. *The Genius in Design.* HarperCollins, 2009.

Napias, Jean. *Quiet Corners of Paris.* Little BookRo, NY, 2007.

Parks, Tim. *Italian Neighbors.* Grove Press, NY, 1992.

Popmann, Fredd. *A Paris Walking Guide: Charming Strolls through the Streets, Courtyards and Gardens of Paris.* Parigramme, 2009.

Prose, Francine. *Caravaggio: Painter of Miracle.* HarperCollins, 2009.

Robertson, Jamie. *A Literary Paris.* Adams Media, MA, 2010.

Trouilleux, Rodolphe. *Unexplored Paris,* Parigramme, 1996.

Wallace, William. *Michelangelo: God's Architect.* Princeton Univ. Press, 2019.

Recommended Viewing:
Paintings We Sought Out During Our Slow Travels in Florence, Rome and Paris

A partial list of the hundreds of paintings and frescoes that brought us joy and purpose for further study. The museum locations are next to the page numbers of the paintings or frescos. There are too many significant secular and devotional architectural sites and sculptures to list.

Angelico, Fra:

Annunciations—page 134—Convent of San Marco, Florence, Italy.

Caravaggio, Michelangelo Merisi da:

Bacchus—page 121—Uffizi, Florence, Italy.

Boy Peeling Fruit—page 121—Longhi Collection, Florence, Italy.

Boy with Basket of Fruit—page 121—Galleria Borghese, Rome, Italy.

Calling of St. Matthew—page 64—Contarelli Chapel, San Luigi dei Francesci, Rome, Italy.

Conversion on the Way to Damascus—page 40—Cerasi Chapel, Santa Maria del Popolo, Rome.

Crucifixion of St. Peter—page 48—Cerasi Chapel, Santa Maria del Popolo, Rome, Italy.

Death of the Virgin—page 184—Louvre, Paris, France.

Deposition from the Cross—page 58—Pinacoteca, Vatican, Vatican City, Rome, Italy.

Entombment (Deposition)—page 91—Pinacoteca, Vatican, Vatican City, Italy.

Fortune Teller—pages 90, 182—Musée du Louvre, Paris, France.

Inspiration of Saint Matthew—page 64—Contarelli Chapel, San Luigi dei Francesi, Rome, Italy.

Judith Beheading Holofernes—page 58—Musée du Louvre, Paris, France.

Madonna and Child with St. Anne—page 58—Borghese Gallery and Museum, Rome, Italy.

Madonna of Loreto—page 64—Église Sant-Agostino, Rome, Italy.

Martyrdom of St. Matthew—page 64—Contarelli Chapel in San Luigi dei Francesi, Rome, Italy.

Mary Magdalen—pages 68, 107—Doria Pamphilj Gallery, Rome, Italy.

Medusa—page 121—Gallerie degli Uffizi, Florence, Italy.

Narcissus—page 58—Galleria Nazionale d'Arte Antica, Rome, Italy.

A Portrait of Alof de Wignacourt and His Page—page 223—Musée du Louvre, Paris.

Portrait of Fra Antonio Martell—page 134—Palazzo Pitti, Florence, Italy.

Rest During the Flight to Egypt—pages

Holbein, Hans, the Younger:

Portrait of Henry VIII—page 58—noting from the Roman numerals that Henry VIII was 49 when Holbein painted his portrait.

Le Brun, Elisabeth, Louise Vigée:

Portrait de Madame Vigée Le Brun and Daughter—page 162—Musée du Louvre, Paris, France.

Lorrain, Claude:

Seaport with the Embarkation of Queen of Sheba—page 197—Musée du Louvre. Presently in the National Gallery, London, United Kingdom.

Manet, Édouard:

Olympia—page 156—Musée d'Orsay, Paris, France.

Masaccio:

Holy Trinity—page 117—A fresco in the Dominican Church of Santa Maria Novella, Florence, Italy.

Matisse, Henri:

La Danes—page 170—Two versions, both in the Musee d'Art Moderne de la Ville, Paris, France.

Michelangelo (di Ludovica Buonarroti Simoni):

The Last Judgment—page 92—Fresco in the Sistine Chapel—Vatican City.

Monet, Claude:

Nympheas—page 147—Musée de l'Orangerie, Paris, France.

Morisot, Berthe:

The Cradle—page 156—Musee d'Orsay, Paris, France. Em's favorite painting.

Munch, Edvard:

Scream—page 198—Exhibit at the Pinacothèque de Paris, Paris, France. Presently in the National Museum, Oslo, Norway.

Peruzzi, Baldassare:

Madonna with Saints—page 49—Fresco in Ponzetti Chapel, Santa Maria della Pace—Rome, Italy.

Raphael (Raffaello Sanzio):

La Fornarina—page 58—Note the armband engraved with Raphael's signature: Raphael Vrbinas (Urbino)—Galleria Nazionale d'Arte Antica in Palazzo.
Portrait of Baldassare Castiglione—page 210—Musee du Louvre, Paris, France.
Sybils—page 61.
Transformation—page 108—Pinacoteca Vaticana, Vatican City.

Rubens, Peter Paul:

Disciples à Emmaüs—page 184—Église Saint-Eustache, Paris, France.

Tintoretto, Jacopo Robusti:

Finding the Body of Saint-Mark—page 86—Exhibit at the Scuderie del Quirinale, Rome, Italy. Presently at the Pinacoteca de Brera, Milan, Italy.
Miracle of the Slave—page 86—Exhibit at the Scuderie del Quirinale, Rome, Italy. Presently in the Gallerie dell'Accademia in Venice.
Saint-George and the Dragon—page 86—Exhibit at the Scuderie del Quirinale, Rome, Italy. Presently at the National Gallery, London, United Kingdom.

Twombly, Cy:

Hellenic Rings—ceiling painting in the Salle des Bronzes—page 194—Musée du Louvre, Paris, France.

Vermeer, Johannes:

The Art of Painting—page 163—Pinacothèque de Paris, France. Presently in the Kunsthistorisches Museum, Vienna, Austria.

Girl with the Pearl Earring—page 163—Pinacothèque de Paris, France. Presently in the Mauritius Museum in The Hague, Netherlands.

Velázquez, Diego:

Las Meninas—page 202—Musée du Louvre. Presently in the Museo Nacional del Prado, Madrid, Spain.

Veronese, Paolo:

The Wedding Feast at Cana—page 177—Musée du Louvre, Paris, France.

Warhol, Andy:

Last Supper—page 9—Seen in Reggio Emilia. Presently in the Guggenheim Museum in SoHo, New York City, United States.

Marilyn—page 9—Seen in Reggio Emilia. Presently in the Tate Gallery, London, United Kingdom.

Watteau, Jean-Antoine:

Gilles or Pierrot—page 194—Musée du Louvre, Paris, France.

Zuccari, Federico and Taddeo:

Frescos in the Pucci Chapel in Trinita dei Monti—page 50—Florence, Italy.

Bibliography

Alighieri, Dante. Musa, Mark, translator. *The Divine Comedy–Vol. 1.* London, UK: Penguin, 2002.

Angelou, Maya. *Wouldn't Take Nothing for My Journey Now.* New York: Random House, 1993.

Archambault, Reginald D. *John Dewey on Education: Selective Writings,* University of Chicago Press, 1964.

The Art Story. New York, www.theartstory.org.

Aurelius, Marcus. *Meditations,* Nashville, TN: Skylight Paths, 2007.

Bard, Elizabeth. *Lunch in Paris: A Love Story with Recipes.* New York: Back Bay Books, 2011.

Bell, Susan Groag. *The Lost Tapestries of the City of Ladies.* University of California Press, 2004.

Bentley, James. *Most Beautiful Country Towns of Tuscany.* London: Thames and Hudson, 2001.

Berlioz, Hector website: *Berlioz in Italy–Florence.* www.hberlioz.com.

Birch, Dinah. *John Ruskin: Selected Writings.* Oxford University Press, 2009.

Blackbyrds. "Walking in Rhythm," on the Fantasy Label, recorded in the Sound Factory, Los Angeles, 1979.

Blue, Anthony Dias. *Anthony Dias Blue's Pocket Guide to Wine: 2007.* New York: Fireside Press, 2007.

Boyd, William. *The Emile of Jean Jacques Rousseau.* London: Methuen, 1967.

Browning, Elizabeth Barrett. *Poetical Works of Elizabeth Barrett Browning and Robert Browning.* London: British Library Historical Print, 2011.

Cagliari, Paola, Marina Castagnetti, Carlina Rinaldi, Vea Vecchi, and Peter Moss. *Loris Malaguzzi and School of Reggio Emilia: A Selection of His Writings and Speeches 1945–1993.* London: Routledge, 2015.

Carson, Rachel. *The Sense of Wonder.* New York: HarperCollins, 1987.

Child, Julia. *My Life in Paris.* New York: Anchor Press, 2006.

Csikszentmihalyi, Mihaly. *Flow: The Psychology of Optimal Experience.* New York: Harper Perennial Modern Classics, 2008.

Darin, Bobby. "Mack the Knife." Atco (US) London Records. Written by Kurt Weill, Bertolt Brecht and Marc Blitzstein and released in 1959.

Dewey, John. *Experience and Education.* New York: Free Press, 1997.

Dewey, John. *Later Works of John Dewey: Volume 3.* Edited by Boydston, Jo Ann. Carbondale: Southern Illinois University Press, 2008.

Dewey, John. *The School and Society: The Child and the Curriculum.* Chicago University Press, 1990.

Doerr, Anthony. *Four Seasons in Rome.* New York: Scribner, 2008.

Duckworth, Eleanor. *The Having of Wonderful Ideas and Other Essays on Teaching and Learning.* New York: Teachers College Press, 2006.

Duckworth, Eleanor. *Teacher to Teacher: Learning from Each Other.* New York: Teachers College Press, 1997.

Dumas, Alexandre. *The Three Musketeers.* Hare, Hertfordshire, England: Wordsworth Editions Limited, 1993.

Dunn, Rita, and Kenneth Dunn. *Teaching Elementary Students Through their Individual Learning Styles.* Upper Saddle River: Pearson Publishing, 1992.

Dworkin, Martin S. *Dewey on Education: Selections.* New York: Teachers College Press, 1959.

Edwards, Carolyn, Lella Gandini, and George Forman. *The Hundred Languages of Children: The Reggio Emilia Approach—Advanced Reflections, Second Edition.* Greenwich, CT: Ablex, 1998.

Edwards, Carolyn, Lella Gandini, and George Forman. *The Hundred Languages of Children: The Reggio Emilia Approach to Early Childhood Education.* Santa Barbara: Praeger, 1993.

Egan, Kieran. *Getting It Wrong from the Beginning: Our Progressivist Inheritance from Herbert Spencer, John Dewey, and Jean Piaget.* New Haven, CT: Yale University Press, 2002.

Eliot, T.S. *Little Gidding,* Eastbourne East Sussex, UK: Gardners Books, 1943.

Elkind, David, and John H. Flavel, editors. *Studies in Cognitive Development: Essays in Honor of Jean Piaget.* Oxford University Press, 1969.

Elkind, David, and Irving B. Weiner. *Child Development: A Core Approach.* Hoboken, NJ: Wiley and Sons Inc., 1972.

Freedburg, David. *The Power of Images.* Chicago University Press, 1991.

Frommer's 24 Great Walks in Paris. Hoboken, NJ: Wiley, 2009.

Frommer's 24 Walks in Rome. Hoboken, NJ: Wiley, 2009.

Galilei, Galileo. *Dialogues Concerning Two New Sciences*. Overland Park, KS: Digiread.com Publishing, 2011.

Gallagher, Jeanette McCarthy, and D. Kim Reid. *Learning Theory of Piaget and Inhelder*. Austin, TX: ProEd, 1984.

Gardner, Howard. *Multiple Intelligence: New Horizons*. New York: Basic Books, 2006.

Goy, Richard. *Florence: The City and Its Architecture*. New York/London: Phaidon, 2002.

Hacker, Douglas J., John Dunlosky, and Arthur C. Graesser. *Handbook of Metacognition and Education*. Abingdon-on-Thames, Oxfordshire: Routledge, 2009.

Hanh, Thich Nhat. *Teaching on Love*. Ypsilanti, MI: Parallax, 2002.

Harvey, John. *The Master Builder: Architecture in the Middle Ages*. London: Thames and Hudson, 1971.

Heafford, Michael. *Pestalozzi*. London: Methuen, 1967.

Hemingway, Ernest. *A Farewell to Arms*. London: Arrow Books, 1994.

Hemingway, Ernest. *A Moveable Feast*. New York: Scribner, 2010.

Hersey, George. *Architecture and Geometry in the Age of Baroque*. University of Chicago Press, 2001.

Hicks, Robert Drew. *Diogenes Laertius: Lives of Eminent Philosophers, Volume I, Books 1–5*. Cambridge, MA: Harvard University Press, 1925.

Hollis, Leo. *Historic Paris Walks*. Guilford, CT: Cadogan Guides, 2006.

Hubbard, Howard, and Shirley Hubbard. *Michelangelo*. London: Routledge, 1985.

Hughes, Robert. *Rome: A Cultural, Visual, and Personal History*. New York: Knopf, 2011.

Jestaz, Bertrand. *Architecture of the Renaissance: From Brunelleschi to Palladio*. London: Thames and Hudson, 2010.

Katz, Lilian, and Sylvia C. Chard. *Engaging Children's Minds: The Project Approach*. Norwood, NJ: Ablex, 1992.

King, Ross. *Brunelleschi's Dome: How a Renaissance Genius Reinvented Architecture*. New York: Dover, 2004.

King, Ross. *The Judgment of Paris*. New York/London: Bloomsbury, 2007.

Kohn, Alfie. *The Schools Our Children Deserve*. Boston: Houghton Mifflin, 2000.

Kolb, David A., and Alice Y. Kolb. *The Kolb Learning Style Inventory: Version 3.0*. Boston: Hay Resources Direct, 1999.

Kraus, Dorothy, and Henry Kraus. *The Hidden World of Misericords*. New York: George Braziller, 1975.

Lilley, Irene, M. *Friedrich Froebel: A Selection from His Writings*. Cambridge University Press, 2010.

Longfellow, Henry Wadsworth. *A Psalm of Life: What the Heart of the Young Man Said to the Psalmist*. Chicago: Poetry Foundation Magazine.

Los Zafuros. *Bossa Cubana*. Recorded/Produced in EGREM, Havana, Cuba, 1963–1967.

Lurie, Patty. *A Guide to Impressionist Paris: Nine Walking Tours to the Impressionist Painting Sites in Paris*. Sun Lakes, AZ: Robson, 1997.

Mayes, Francis. *Under the Tuscan Sun*. New York: Crown, 1997.

McCarthy, Mary. *The Stones of Florence*. San Diego: Harcourt, 1976.

McNally, Terrence. *The Stendhal Syndrome*. New York: Dramatists Play Services, 2005.

Meyers, Jeffery. *Impressionist Quartet*. San Diego: Harcourt, 2005.

Michelin Green Guide: Paris. Paris: Michelin, 2010.

Michelin Guide: France. Paris: Michelin, 2010.

Michelin Tuscany Guide. Paris: Michelin, 2010.

Morrissey, Jake. *The Genius in the Design: Bernini, Borromini, and the Rivalry That Transformed Rome*. New York: HarperCollins, 2009.

Napias, Jean-Christophe. *Quiet Corners of Paris*. New York: Random House, 2006.

Parent, Claude, Monsan Mostafavi, and Paul Virilio. *The Function of the Oblique: The Architecture of Claude Parent and Paul Virilio*. Camden, UK: Architectural Association, 1996.

Park, Tim. *Italian Neighbors*. New York: Grove, 1992.

Prose, Francine. *Caravaggio: Painter of Miracles*. New York: HarperCollins, 2009.

Read, Herbert. *Education Through Art*. London: Faber and Faber, 1958.

Reichold, Krause, and Bernhardt Graf. *Paintings That Changed the World: From Lascaux to Picasso*. New York: Prester, 2003.

A Report of the Central Advisory Council for English Education: Volume I—The Report (Plowden Report) London: Her Majesty's Stationery Office, 1967.

Roberson, Jamie. *A Literary Paris*. Adams, MA: Adams Media, 2010.

Rose, Mary Beth. *Women in the Middle Ages and the Renaissance*. Syracuse University Press, 1986.

Ruskin, John. *The Lamp of Beauty (Arts and Letters)*. New York: Phaidon, 1995.

Russell, Bertrand. *Basic Writings of Bertrand Russell*. London: Routledge, 2009.

Russell, Bertrand. *Portraits from Memory and Other Essays*. Eastbourne, UK: Gardner Books, 1995.

Senz, Paul. *Cloisters Are a Blessing to the Church and the World*. El Cajon, CA: Catholic Answers, 2010.

Steiner, Rudolph. *The Education of the Child*. Hudson, NY: SteinerBooks, 1996.

Steiner, Rudolph. *The Essentials of Education*. New York: Anthroposophic Press, 1997.

Steves, Rick. *Florence and Tuscany: 2008*. New York: Avalon, 2007.

Stravinsky, Igor. *Poetics of Music in the Form of Six Lessons*. Cambridge: Harvard University Press, 1970.

Taylor, James S. *Poetic Knowledge: The Recovery of Education*. Albany: State University of New York Press, 1998.

Trouilleux, Rodolphe. *Unexplored Paris*. Paris: Parigramme, 2009.

Vasari, Giorgio. *The Lives of the Artist*. Oxford University Press, 2008.

Washington, Dinah. "What a Difference a Day

Makes." Mercury Label. Released in 1959. Song written by Maria Grover and Stanley Adams.

Wilde, Oscar. *Canterville Ghost*. New York: Classic Comics, 2010.

Williams, Ellen. *The Impressionist Paris: Walking Tours of the Artists' Studios, Homes, and the Sites They Painted*. Hong Kong: South China Printings, 1997.

Wittkower, Rudolf. *Alberti's Approach to Antiquity in Architecture*. New York: JSTOR–Text journal database, 1995.

Wittkower, Rudolf. *Architectural Principles in the Age of Humanism*. London: *Journal of the Warburg and Courtauld Institutes*, 1962.

Index